MARKETING

David Evans

ACIM Dip M

West Oxfordshire College

General Editors
John Eve
Birmingham Polytechnic

Allister Langlois
Guernsey College of Further Education

Oxford University Press   1991

To every student who needs this book

Oxford University Press,
Walton Street, Oxford OX2 6DP

Oxford New York Toronto
Delhi Bombay Calcutta Madras Karachi
Petaling Jaya Singapore Hong Kong Tokyo
Nairobi Dar es Salaam Cape Town
Melbourne Auckland

and associated companies in
Berlin Ibadan

Oxford is a trade mark of Oxford University Press

© David Evans 1990

ISBN 0 19 833536 9

A CIP catalogue record for this book is available
from the British Library.

Typeset by Times Graphics, Singapore
Printed and bound in Great Britain by
Butler & Tanner Ltd, Frome and London

Contents

Acknowledgements

The publishers would like to thank the following people for permission to use photographic material:

British Nuclear Fuels plc p.97;
Robin Bryant (Salvation Army) p.181 btm;
Consumers' Association p.230;
Crittall Warmlife p.121 top;
Dunlop Slazenger p.34;
Format (Melanie Friend) p.181 top, (Brenda Prince) p.239;
Harlow Gazette p.40 right;
Lloyds Bank plc p.107 btm;
Ian MacDonald p.37;
Marks and Spencer plc p.89, p.121 btm;
Adrian Meredith (for British Airways) p.151;
Midland Bank plc p.107 top;
Archie Miles p.11, 134, 135, 171, 230;
Neilsens p.50;
Parfums Chanel p.121 btm right;
J Sainsbury plc p.20 (all 3);
John Smith and Co p. 155;
Today Newspapers p.93 (both);
Tottenham Hotspur plc p.40 left;
Volunteer Link Up, Oxon p.188

Introduction

It is important to study this introduction before making use of the book.

Approach and method

This book has been written primarily for students studying for the Business and Technician Education Council (BTEC) National Level award, of which the unit *Marketing* is an option normally available only in the second year of the course. This book accordingly assumes some knowledge of the topics covered in the first year core modules.

The BTEC award does stress the need to develop skills and regards study as a very active process on the part of students. The emphasis, then, is on the *application* of the knowledge acquired. Moreover, there is emphasis on the needs of individual students, coming as they do from diverse backgrounds and with different experiences.

This book attempts to marry together both the theory and practice of Marketing. It introduces topics based closely on the *indicative content* of the *principal objectives* of the module. It then provides a series of activities based on those topics which aim to enlarge the students' knowledge and develop a wide range of the skills identified as important by BTEC. It is obvious that it would be impossible for every student to complete every activity in the book during a one-year course. The intention, therefore, is to provide sufficient choice to suit the differing requirements of students (both full- and part-time) in different parts of the country.

Activities vary from short, class-based, tasks to ones which are in effect similar to major assignments. Lecturers may wish to split or amalgamate activities; or modify them to suit local needs.

By making use of all blocks in the book, students will have covered all the principal objectives of the module. (Please note that the blocks do not always follow the precise order of the objectives as they are listed in the module specification; nor are all items of the indicative content always dealt with under the particular principal objectives that BTEC have chosen to put them. The aim has been to cover the topics in a logical, progressive, fashion. Notwithstanding this, lecturers may choose to vary the order in which the material is presented; or choose relevant sections for, say, a short course in marketing.)

The book

The book has several significant features:

1 It is clearly divided into self-contained but logically connected parts.
2 Its scope is broad enough to apply to students from diverse backgrounds, both full-time and day-release.
3 It can also be used for a wide variety of introductory courses to marketing such as those given as part of Higher Level BTEC courses in, say, computing; and other Higher Level courses.
4 It can be used by individual students for home study.
5 Examples are drawn from situations likely to be understood by the students.

How to use it

Students
1 Study each topic until you understand it.
2 You should then tackle the appropriate activities set by your lecturer, before moving on to the next topic.
3 If you do have study problems or find any part of the course difficult, do not hesitate to ask for help from your lecturer, librarian, or someone at work.

Lecturers
You will need to decide on a suitable selection of activities before covering each Block. Whilst some activities can be undertaken individually, there is a definite bias towards group work. By ensuring that each group elects a chairman, secretary, or spokesperson for any subsequent report-back sessions, both social and communication skills are also enhanced.

General Objectives and Indicative Content

BTEC courses at National Level are designed to promote
the development of skills in students that can be used in the
business world. These skills need to be developed and
applied within a course framework. This framework comes in
the form of 'General Objectives and Indicative Content' in
each unit.

This book covers all the indicative content of the Marketing
unit. The following list of general objectives is amplified by the
content used to achieve those objectives.

The Blocks where the coverage is achieved are indicated here:

A Understand the concept of marketing and its significance in commercial and non-commercial organizations

Marketing as the promotion of demand,
the regulation of demand. A channel
for information and an influence on
behaviour.   Blocks 1 and 2

B Identify, obtain and apply statistical, numerical and other information, relevant to marketing issues and activities, considering all relevant constraints

Marketing research	Blocks 3 and 4
Sources of information	Block 3
Quantitative and qualitative data	Block 3
Risk of research	Block 4
Cost of research	Block 4
Forecasting techniques	Block 4
Application of research data	Blocks 4 and 7

C Plan a range of marketing activities and calculate their financial implications

Marketing budgets and budget allocation	Block 11
Pricing and pricing strategies	Blocks 2, 5, 11
Financial objectives, profit and its implication for the marketing function	Blocks 10, 11
Marketing costs	Blocks 4, 7, 11

D Analyse and assess the importance of the factors affecting client behaviour

Patterns of behaviour – models for industrial buyers/individual consumers – influencing the buyer through various sales techniques	Block 5
Trends and behaviour	Block 5
Human motivation	Block 5

E Identify and design marketing campaigns which combine verbal, non-verbal and visual forms of communication

Visual communication: advertising, advertising agency systems	Block 6
Verbal communication: radio, spoken word	Block 7
Non-verbal communication: direct marketing, editorials	Block 7
Effectiveness of communications media	Blocks 6, 7

F Identify and evaluate a range of marketing problems and techniques applicable in non-commercial activities

Matching service to need	Block 9
Reasons for use and non-use of services	Block 9
Excess demand: rationing	Block 9
Promotion of non-commercial services	Block 9
Compulsion and choice in provision and receipt of services	Block 9
Pricing and charging for non-commercial services	Block 9

G Investigate how organizations' approaches to marketing are affected by their management styles and organization strategies

Alternative management styles	Block 10
The implications for the marketing function	Block 10
Marketing planning and control	Blocks 10, 11
The role of the marketeer	Blocks 1, 2, 10
Allocation of resources	Blocks 3, 7, 10, 11
Corporate strategies	Block 10

H Investigate the processes involved in marketing and evaluate their effectiveness

Tangible and intangible 'products'	Blocks 1, 9
Physical and other processes	Block 8
Distribution channels/dealer networks	Block 8
Choice of outlets, eg retail, mail order, party selling	Block 8
Distribution trends	Block 8
Distribution costs	Block 8

I Identify legal, social and moral constraints upon business activities which affect marketing activities

Consumerism and watchdogs	Block 12
Pressure grops	Block 12
Ethics and code of practice	Block 12
Impact of marketing techniques	Block 12
Consumer law	Block 12

J Evaluate a range of marketing strategies from an investigation of current products/services

Methods of marketing services, places, people and organizations	Blocks 1, 2, 5, 6, 7, 8, 9 12
Alternative approaches to the marketing of products	Blocks 6, 7, 9
Campaign planning	Blocks 7, 10
The marketing mix	Blocks 2, 9
Branding	Blocks 6, 7
Competition	Blocks 3, 5, 6
Sponsorship	Block 7

Many of these objectives can be linked with specific objectives in the other books in the series, and the other BTEC units. General objective C above, for example, is related to general objective H in the Finance unit.

An important feature of both teaching and learning in BTEC courses, is to attempt to see a study of business as only being possible if you are prepared to look for links between the content of separate units and learning materials.

Block 1
Introducing Marketing

Introduction

This first block is designed to help you become familiar
with what marketing is about. Through the case study which
follows, marketing is shown as a range of activities, as an
exchange process, as an attitude of mind. A series of current
definitions of marketing are examined, and related to the
development of the marketing concept.

To understand current attitudes to marketing, we shall need
to look at the development of organizations from being
mainly production orientated, to being marketing orientated
and beyond.

Finally we will look at how marketing is organized, and the
degree of emphasis that companies place on various marketing
activities.

The activities in this block are designed to help you 'get the
feel of' marketing. You will be involved in one or more of the
following: examining your own firm or college from a
marketing standpoint, analysing the behaviour of others, or
taking part in role-playing sessions or discussions.

Every subject has its own language, jargon, and technical
terms. In the rest of the book new ideas, terms, and phrases
will be introduced as you work through each block, but for
this first and most important block, a glossary of terms or
words which may be new to you is given at the end.

Disco's
Mark Crayford

Disco Records

Discuss the points raised by each activity in groups of two
or three and then report back in your groups to the course
as a whole, comparing results.

Mark Crayford is the young, go-ahead **Marketing
Manager** of Disco Records. The company engages
leading groups and singers, records their music and

produces a wide range of mainstream pop and rock singles and albums. Disco Records also works for other record companies, eg producing records for them on a contract basis. Recording facilities exist for hire, and Mark is keen to promote unknown groups if he feels they have potential. He is thinking of moving into the CD business.

Researching Disco's Market

Yesterday was a busy day for Mark, as this page from his diary shows.

AUGUST

10 Monday Week 33 222 143	**11** Tuesday Week 33 223 142	**12** Wednesday Week 33 224 141
9.00 am Letter dictation. Deal with singles meeting agents 10.00 am Jean Job Rock Review 12.00 Lunch with Gerry Glaister 2.30 pm Review figures with export department 4.00 pm Tom and Bill re Paris visit (settle agency query)	Trip to Paris 11.00 am Gaston Phillipe - agency agreement 2.15 pm Visit Expo'Hall 6.00 pm Return to London	8.15 am Claire Rowlands - Musad (14 -25 promotion campaign) 10.00 am Wayne Orlov ? Recording facilities (check with Partridge) 11.15 am Partridge 12.00 'Betackers' PR Launch 2.15 pm Sylvia Miles - re, new appointment 3.00 pm Catch up on correspondence, reports etc.

Before 9 am he was visited by Claire Rowlands, an **account executive** with Musad, the **advertising agency** used by Disco. Together they discussed a new advertising and **promotion campaign** aimed at 14 to 25 year olds. A few months ago, at Mark's request, Claire had commissioned research into the kind of people who buy Disco records i.e. the **target market**. Musad had, for example, identified what percentage of retail customers were male/female, their age range, what jobs they had, and what their incomes were. Mark was keen to learn as much as he could about his record-buying public. 'After all,' he told Claire, 'these are the people who keep us both in business'.

Before she left, Mark asked Claire to look at the CD market. 'What kind of people buy CD players, Claire? Might some of them be parents of our youngest record buyers?'

Activity 1	Using information from the case study so far discuss:

Using information from the case study so far discuss:
1 Why Mark feels he wants to find out more about the people buying Disco records in retail shops.
2 Why Mark would not have this information in the ordinary course of business.
3 Why Mark contracts out the research work to an agency, instead of using his own staff.
4 Why Mark is interested in researching the CD player market.

The points that you brought up probably included:

1 The more Mark knows about his customers, the more he can be sure what he offers is likely to be acceptable, i.e. he can find out what they really want, and will be more likely to keep track of changes in fashion.
2 Disco sells only to **retail** outlets, i.e. records shop chains and local shops. Accordingly Disco are not in contact with the final consumers – the record-buying public.
3 Conducting research about customers is a specialized and time-consuming task. Most firms use specialist outside agencies as and when they need them.
4 To see if customers in Disco's current target market own CD players or have access to them and if there is a potential market for selling CDs to them.

Disco Records 2
Dealing with customers needs

Wayne Orlov, **senior buyer** from 'Singles', a large chain of music shops in the Midlands, was Mark's next visitor. Wayne wanted to launch a series of **own label** albums, and wondered if Disco could provide recording facilities and produce the records (complete with sleeves). 'I must have some idea of what it's going to cost by next Friday,' Wayne urged. 'You'll have preliminary prices by Wednesday,' smiled Mark, 'to cover all your requirements. Shall I bring them round myself?'

Charles Partridge, Disco's **Production Manager**, met Mark at 11.15 am. 'This short run of 1000 pressings for the Savages is a bit of a nuisance. We're got quite a lot of work on at the moment, and I'd like to put it back a month.' Mark's reply was short and sharp: 'We promised them by next Wednesday. They are paying cash on the nail, and as far as I am concerned they will have them by next Wednesday.'

Activity 2 Consider Mark's interviews with Wayne Orlov and Charles Partridge and discuss:
1 Mark's attitude to customers, and their needs.
2 Whether or not Mark was right to put the customer before production schedules.

Most of you would probably agree that Mark feels that customer relations is the most important part of the working environment: the company's greatest asset. You *can* argue that customers always come first, but Charles Partridge is trying to please other customers too.

Disco Records 3
Promoting the product

Just before noon, Mark arrived at the Excelsior Hotel where Disco were hosting the launch of the first album by an up-and-coming group, the Beteckers. He met their agent, socialized with the press and the music critics. He introduced the group to the guests, who included leading retailers, presenting each one with a copy of the new album. All went well, so he returned at 2.15 pm to his office to meet Sylvia Miles, a trainee **sales representative** working in the Thames Valley.

Mark explained to Sylvia that her progress merited a transfer to the North-East Region to look for new business where there were few outlets at present. 'To develop your **territory** you should find out everything you can about customers before you get there. Check on the **legal status** of each outlet, its **credit rating** and financial standing. When you get there, look around and note the whole range of its activities and how they fit in with records and tapes. Oh, yes, and find out what kind of customers they have. Meet the manager and find out if it's he that makes the decisions. If he doesn't, try and find the person who does. Get him or her to tell you all about their buying policy and what they need and expect from suppliers, in the way of deliveries and discounts.

'All this will help you match your selling points to each customer's needs. And finally, Sylvia, remember that to the customers, *you* are Disco records. Good luck!'

| Activity 3 | 1 Discuss the reasons why an album launch could be a good way to publicize a pop group. Why did Mark invite the press, music critics, and retailers?
2 Make a list of the reasons why Sylvia's sales talk will be improved if she finds out a great deal about a retail outlet before she sees the manager. |

Your discussions may have been along these lines:

1 You can argue for and against special 'launches', but Mark wants to influence the influencers, ie the journalists and critics. A good write-up could encourage demand. Meeting the customer could promote sales! Contacts can often be turned into contracts.
2 Sylvia can stress those selling points which match the customer's known preferences, if she knows what they are.

As Mark left his office to catch the train home he carefully adjusted the notice hanging above his desk. It bears the slogan: 'The customer must have what he wants — yesterday, today, and tomorrow.'

| Activity 4 | Looking at the whole of Mark's day:
1 Make a list of all the different kinds of activity Mark engaged in during his time at work. Does he have a narrowly-based or a wide-ranging set of responsibilities?
2 Identify and list every occasion when Mark stresses the importance of the customer.
3 Do you think customers are as important as Mark seems to believe they are? |

Points to note:

1 Nearly everything that Mark does has the customer in mind, even though his job is wide ranging.
2 If businesses did not have customers, there would be no businesses!

The concept of marketing

This section of the book examines what marketing is all about. You have already seen that a marketing manager can be responsible for a wide range of activities, such as market research, advertising, sales promotion, managing the sales function, dealing with customers, and so on.

Advertisements for marketing managers

> **MARKETING MANAGER**
>
> **£30,000 + Car** City
>
> Grass roots opportunity to set up marketing function of City organisation. You are aged 30-40 with an impressive track record which will probably include selling and, more recently, marketing and new business development. Responsibilities will include marketing strategy, corporation image, PR, and developing new business at an international level. Languages an advantage. SF0503

> **MARKETING MANAGER**
>
> **To £35,000 + Bonus** City
>
> Your knowledge of L.T. and the City, together with your proven commercial flair and entrepreneurial spirit, are of considerable interest to this rapidly expanding hi-tech organisation servicing the City. Your role will be to develop and assess new products, undertake competitor research and devise a comprehensive policy to promote the corporate image, both locally and abroad. Additional requirement for sales executives with appropriate product knowledge. SF0504

These advertisements give us some other clues about the job. Marketing managers can be responsible for distribution (getting the product or service to the consumer), research and development of new products or services, pricing, and packaging.

Lists like these suggest that marketing can be described as a **range of activities**. Typical definitions based on this idea are:

1 'Marketing is all those activities involved in getting goods from producers to users, including buying, selling, storing, transporting, advertising, and promoting the goods.' (Adapted from Converse, Heugy, and Mitchell; *Elements of Marketing*, Prentice Hall, 1975)

2 'Marketing is the promotion of demand, the regulation of demand. A channel for information and an influence on behaviour.' (BTEC Option Unit Specification, *Marketing*, 1987)

A second view sees marketing as a **process** whereby goods or services get from supplier to customer. The aim of the firm is to convert potential customer purchasing power (people with money to spend) into effective demand (people who have a real desire to buy). This done, the firm aims to deliver the goods or services to the customer or user. This view is summed up by the following:

3 'Marketing is the performance of business activities that direct the flow of goods and services from producers to customers.' (K E Runyon, *The Practice of Marketing*, C E Merril, 1982)

A development of this idea is to regard marketing as an **exchange process**: the movement (one way) of goods or services from the supplier to user, and the movement (in the opposite direction) of money from user to supplier.

4 'Marketing is the set of human activities directed at facilitating and consummating (ie completing) exchanges.' (P Kotler, *Marketing Management*, 1972)

A third approach is to regard marketing as an **attitude of mind** in which the customer is central. Various versions of this notion exist too:

5 'The purpose of a business is to create and keep a customer.' (T Levitt *The Marketing Imagination*, Free Press, 1983)

6 'Marketing is selling goods that don't come back to people that do.' (Anon.)

7 'Marketing involves finding out what customers want; then planning and developing a product or service that will satisfy those wants; and then determining the best way to price, promote, and distribute the product or service.' (W. J. Stanton, *Fundamentals of Marketing*, McGraw-Hill, 1981)

Activity 5	When you have considered the seven definitions given above: 1 Decide which definition Mark Crayford would choose, bearing in mind the information you have gained about his views. 2 Choose, on the basis of what you already know about marketing, the definition you consider most appropriate. In each case justify your choice.

Of the definitions listed, the last one is closest to current marketing thinking.

The Institute of Marketing has a slightly shorter version of the last definition, which adds the need to be profitable as well:

8 '(Marketing is) the management process responsible for identifying, anticipating, and satisfying customer requirements efficiently and profitably.'

Look at the key words in this definition:
Identifying: finding out exactly what your customers' needs or wants are, even if they may *not* be immediately conscious of such needs until or unless approached. There is also an

implication here that the customers themselves have to be identified first.

Anticipating: working out in advance which of the identified needs will or might arise, and when they will arise; and then being prepared to meet them. For example, making your retailers get their Christmas stock in good time or anticipating changes in fashion.

Satisfying: providing those products or services which satisfy the needs or wants that have been identified.

Needs and wants: the difference between these is examined in Block 5. If products or services are designed to meet or satisfy known wants, then the process of persuading potential customers to buy them will be that much easier — and cost less!

Profitability: enterprises in the private sector will need to trade profitably. For non-profit making organizations (eg colleges, libraries) the stress would be on 'efficiency'.

The rest of this book looks at ways in which these key activities of Marketing can be best carried out.

The development of the marketing concept

It would be silly to believe that until recently no supplier took much notice of customers, but the development of the marketing concept, ie that the customer is central, is a recent one.

The Industrial Revolution

The Industrial Revolution which began around 1740 was a time, like our own, of great technological advances, particularly in those areas which relied on steam as an energy source. Engineers, inventors, innovators, and entrepreneurs were the central figures. Between them they funded, designed, and ran the engines, plant, and other equipment which utilized steam power. They began to employ ever-increasing numbers of workers. These new employees, though poorly paid by our standards, eventually began to purchase a wide variety of goods and services.

At this time the emphasis was on the technology, the design of the products, and their application. Because demand at first increased with little competition there was little need for marketing in our modern sense. A consequence was that the captains of industry, and their managers, were either designers, engineers, production specialists, or those very much influenced by them.

Those employees working in what we would now call 'the sales side' were mostly engaged in getting the products distributed. 'Good products sell themselves' was the general assumption. If competition *did* appear, the reaction was to make a bigger, better, faster product; or to produce more efficiently, ie at a lower cost. These factors show how organizations were **production orientated** at this time.

The age of over-production

The production-orientated stage lasted for nearly 200 years, until the introduction of mass-production methods meant that large numbers of products (household goods, bicycles, motor cars, etc.) came onto the market, manufactured by different, competing, suppliers. For the first time the supply of many products matched or even exceeded demand. The Great Depression of the 1930s left many firms having to work very hard to sell their products, as just making a better saucepan, brush, or motorbike no longer brought an assurance of success. Selling now became a very important activity, and the emphasis changed from being production orientated to being **sales orientated**.

This change saw the arrival of the 'commercial traveller' or the 'rep', both words meaning salesman (very few women were 'on the road' in the 1930s). Considerable attention was paid to choosing and training the sales force, but in the end results were what mattered. The stress was on the 'hard sell', getting the products sold by a variety of methods : discounts, free gifts, aggressive 'foot-in-the-door' salesmanship, readily available credit. Hard selling soon got a bad name, especially when sub-standard products were sold in unscrupulous ways.

But whilst the customer was now courted, it was still the producer who decided upon the product. The skill of the sales people was to get the customer to take what was offered. Sales managers became important executives, though production staff still had considerable influence.

The marketing approach

Even during the sales-oriented stage, there is evidence that some firms, eg General Motors of the US in the late 1920s, were beginning to realize that to convert their large-scale outputs to large-scale consumption required more than the efforts of armies of sales people. Customers' needs had to be taken into account.

Since the 1960s there has been a considerable shift towards the marketing approach. The result has been that the customer (or prospective customer) is the first consideration when organizations plan their designs, products or services, distribution networks, after-sales back-up, and so on. This has led some companies, particularly American ones like Pepsi-Cola, to declare that their business *is marketing* not making or producing things.

The social responsibility stage

An even more recent trend has been called the **social responsibility stage**. Customers' needs and wants are still central to the organization's profitable existence, but there is

Environmentally
friendly products

an awareness that the local community (near the place of business), the public at large, pressure groups, eg Greenpeace, political parties, or the 'anti-additive' lobby, are influential and their views, wishes, or needs must be taken into account. Firms are now conscious of the need to promote a good image of themselves, and realize that it is no good satisfying customers in Leeds, but at the same time polluting the atmosphere in the Cotswolds. For some time Friends of the Earth have attacked manufacturers using aerosol dispensers for destroying the Earth's ozone layer. Before international action was taken, most notably with the Montreal Protocol in 1988, many firms had turned to alternatives in an attempt to become ecologically sound.

| *Activity 6* | Divide into two groups. |

Group A is the management of GASE (Gravel and Sand Extractors Ltd), soon to start digging close to a pretty village. You are contracted to supply material for a government programme of major motorway network improvements, and must start producing on schedule in about 18 months. Besides excavating 200 acres of farm land (most of which will end up as a chain of lakes), you will need to build an unsightly plant in the centre of the diggings, visible across the fields. You would really like to dig within 50 metres of a listed building.

Group B represents the villagers' Action Committee. You cannot oppose planning permission, but you are worried about the noise from and the unsightliness of the proposed plant. Other concerns are the excavation work, the spoiling of an area of natural beauty, the danger to children (they might fall into the workings) and dirty lorries speeding through beauty spots. You want both to influence the appearance of the restored area at the conclusion of the work, and to have access to it and use of it.
1 While Group B meets to prepare a case to put to GASE, Group A will decide how to deal with the fears, needs, and aspirations of the villagers, so production can start on time.
2 If there is time, a joint meeting of the two groups can be held to negotiate an acceptable package.

Unfortunately, even today, many organizations have not yet become marketing orientated, never mind getting any further. For example, in the 1970s Rolls Royce provided a classic example of a production-orientated organization, and in the early 1980's British Leyland was still striving to sell a small range of ageing models with an aggressive sales-orientated approach.

The total marketing approach

Ideally, a total marketing approach should be found at every level in the firm. Production staff as well as the sales force, top management, and sales assistants should believe and act as if the central purpose of their organization is to seek out, win, and keep customers; and to win the approval of the public at large.

What business are we in?

When adopting the total marketing approach, it is necessary for every organization to identify what business it is in; establishing what *needs* are being satisfied, what *benefits* are being marketed. A typical answer to 'What business are you in?' is 'We make X', or 'We sell Y'.

As you can see from Table 1.1, the marketing-orientated view gives some guidance as to what else should be offered besides the basic provision.

Table 1.1: What business are we in ?		
Organization	*Answers*	
	Production-Orientated	*Marketing-Orientated*
1 League football club	We run a football club.	We are in the entertainment business.
2 Passenger railway	We run a railway.	We offer fast, comfortable, traffic-free travel.
3 Sports centre	We operate swimming pools, squash courts, and weight training facilities.	We market exercise, healthy competition, a chance to meet other people.
4 Bank	We borrow and lend money.	We provide opportunities for unearned income, for starting up and expanding businesses, improving homes, buying cars.

The football club in Table 1.1 will have to think of what other facilities it needs to offer, as well as football, to meet its claim to be in the entertainment business. Possibilities include dances, outdoor and indoor sports, displays before or during matches, a supporters' clubhouse and summer outings.

| *Activity 7* | 1 Full-time students in groups consider: |

1 Full-time students in groups consider:
  a What business is your college in?
  b Whether the college seems to be:
    Production/service orientated
    Sales orientated
    Marketing orientated
in respect of the courses it runs in competition with other schools and colleges or which it provides for industry.

2 Part-time students to consider individually:
  a What business are your employers in?
  b Whether the organization for which you work is:
    Production/service orientated
    Sales orientated
    Marketing orientated?

If there is time, each group or individual could prepare a written report. This should include any discoveries made about marketing during your research for this activity.

How marketing is organized

The purpose of the **marketing function** is clear: to integrate all the customer-related activities within the organization. How this is done varies widely. A **functional** marketing department, as shown in the diagram below, divides into various activities.

Marketing research and advertising could be handled by outside agencies, but a senior executive would co-ordinate this work. The work of creating new products is handled by Research and New Product Development (R&D). (In production- or sales-orientated organizations R&D usually comes under a production director/manager.)

Home Sales in split into *Key Accounts* (ie important customers who regularly re-order,) and *areas* or *regions* on a geographical basis. Field sales managers look after 5 or 6 sales representatives. Export sales managers control overseas sales people, or, more often, use agents in specific countries.

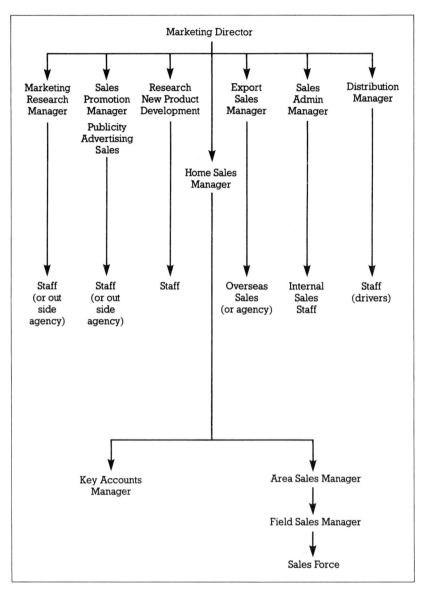

Structure of a functional marketing department

Sale Administration covers all the internal paperwork involved in executing orders, and possibly invoicing. Finally, the distribution manager oversees the despatch of goods.

This *functional* type of structure is commonly found in manufacturing organizations, but some of these have a **production-based** marketing structure. Here a firm is split into product groupings, each under a product manager. This executive is then responsible for the whole range of marketing functions relating to the product group as shown in the diagram below .

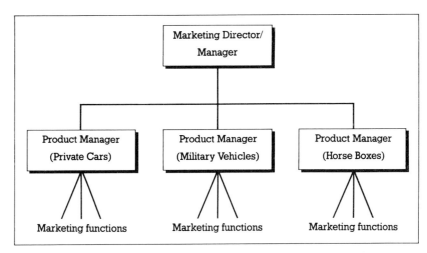

Product-based organization

A **regional-based** marketing structure is suitable for firms with many outlets capable of being grouped in areas eg the North-East, South-West, Scotland, etc. Other structures found include *customer-based,* where different categories of customers are serviced in the way best suited to them, eg mail order, wholesale, supermarket chains; and **matrix** in which **brand managers** look after each brand. These managers can be responsible for drawing up budgets, and be concerned with purchasing, production, advertising and selling. Brand managers can be in competition with each other, as well as facing outside competition.

Activity 8	Investigate individually or in groups either:

1 Your college's marketing structure (full- or part-time students); or
2 The marketing structure at your place of work.
Choose the option most appropriate to you or your group.
You will need to produce an organization chart to get some idea of the job descriptions of those engaged in any form of marketing activity, and to prepare a report. You could also interview (by appointment) members of staff involved in the marketing function.

Marketing organization: a national picture

The national picture of the way marketing is organized is interesting. In a recent article in '*Marketing*' (15 May 1986, pp 34–6) Dr Nigel Piercy (of UWIST) reports that he random-sampled 600 firms employing 100 or more people. The overall response was just over half (56 per cent). Only 45 per cent of those replying had a separate marketing department: this group was mostly made up of medium-sized firms with 500 to 1000 employees. In fact only 130 firms had some formal marketing structure with a high-ranking person in charge. The functions found were:

1 Advertising and marketing research only   51%
2 As 1, plus trade marketing and sales   21%
3 As 2, plus customer service and exporting   13%
4 As 3, plus distribution   15%

New product development was controlled by a *separate* R&D function in 55 per cent of firms replying: only in 36 per cent was it controlled by the Marketing Department. Whilst the survey was only part of a much larger study, there are still some conclusions to be drawn :

1 Whatever the 'official' definitions of *marketing* are, organizations tend to use the term to describe their own particular set of activities.
2 Considerable differences exist between one firm and the next in the way marketing is structured.
3 Considerable differences exist in the responsibilities undertaken by the marketing section in different firms.

Glossary

Account executive
Each customer (or client) of an advertising agency is called an '*account*'. An account executive acts as a go-between or link between client and agency, and interprets the clients' advertising needs to the agency.

Advertising agency
An organization which carries out, on behalf of clients, the functions of planning advertising campaigns, designing advertisements, contacting **media owners** and purchasing advertising space and time.

Benefits
Features or characteristics, of a product or service, such as price, size, quality, or reliability, which satisfy customer needs.

Brand manager
See **product manager**.

Consumer durables
Products for the home or household, which last over time, eg vacuum cleaners, washing machines, etc.

Credit rating
That level (amount) of credit which could or should be allowed by a supplier to a customer; sometimes assessed by independent bodies such as trade protection societies.

Functional (as applied to departmental structures)
A department is 'functional' if its personnel are grouped into separate functions or areas of activity, eg marketing research, sales, etc.

Industrial capital goods
Items (usually plant and machinery) used by a manufacturer in the production process or which the organization needs to meet its objectives.

Key accounts
Those customers providing the largest sales revenue (income): important customers.

Legal status (of a firm)
Whether it is a partnership, PLC, corporation, sole trader, etc.

Marketing orientated
The state of a firm attempting to identify, anticipate, and satisfy the needs and wants of actual or prospective customers.

Matrix organization
An organization where some executives, eg product managers, have responsibilities for products across normal functional boundaries. A diagrammatical representation of this structure looks like a mathematical matrix, hence **matrix organization**.

Medium (media)
As used in advertising a medium is a specific newspaper, magazine or TV channel. The term *Media* is used as a generalization for all the mass-communication channels.

Own label (of a product)
Goods (especially packaged foods) which are made by manufacturers especially for a store or supermarket chain, eg instant coffee for Tesco, Waitrose, etc.

Product manager
An executive whose function is to co-ordinate all the activities associated with the marketing of a particular product.

Production manager
A senior executive in a manufacturing or processing organization in charge of the production function.

Production orientated
The state of assuming customers will buy well-made products (provided there are enough to meet orders) without the need for sales or marketing.

Promotion campaign
Has various definitions, but here, a specific campaign to increase the sales of a particular product, which makes a precise offer to defined customers within a given time limit. For example, offering a new line at an initially reduced price to stimulate sales.

Random sample
Sampling technique used in marketing research where each member of the population has an equal or known chance of being selected.

Research and development (R&D)
A department in an organization with the task of developing new products, lines, services, or of improving existing ones.

Sales orientated
The state of assuming customers will only buy well-made products in large quantities through substantial selling and promotional effort.

Sales representative
An employee whose prime task is, through personal contact with customers, to advise, inform, influence, and persuade them to purchase goods and/or services.

Selling points
Aspects of a product or service, believed to be benefits, which are stressed in advertisements, promotions, and sales representatives' visits to customers.

Senior buyer
A senior executive in the Purchasing Department with authority to place orders with suppliers.

Social responsibility
The state of realizing that besides being marketing orientated, there is a need for organizations to take into account the views and wishes of the public at large and to behave in a socially responsible and acceptable manner.

Target market
A specific person or group of people with a unique set of characteristics, whom you wish to attract as customers (eg female high-income earners living within 25 miles of Central London, aged 30 to 45).

Territory (sales)
A specific geographical area (usually marked out on a map) within which a sales representative has sole rights to operate (for his/her organization).

Summary of skills

The intention of the study involved in this unit is not only to learn facts about marketing, but also to develop skills which will be of use in the business world. The section at the end of each block indicates the skill areas covered by each activity.

Skills

Skill	*Activities in which skill is developed*
a Learning and studying	All activities
b Communicating	All activities
c Identifying and tackling problems	6
d Information gathering	6, 7
e Working with others	All activities

Block 2
More about Marketing

Introduction

Following on from Block 1, *Introducing Marketing*, this block examines three further key ideas in the understanding of marketing.

First we will consider the **matching process,** ie the way in which a marketing-orientated organization attempts to match its products and services to the needs and wants of customers. Next, we will look at the most important part of the matching process — the **marketing mix**; four independent factors or ingredients which together add up to the organization's total offer to customers.

Each ingredient in the marketing-mix will be examined in turn, and the concept of the **product life cycle** will be introduced, that is, the process which a product or service will undergo over the period of time from its original conception, to growth, maturity, and eventual decline.
Finally, in this block you will learn to appreciate that marketing and its techniques apply to all organizations, not just to profit-making ones. The learning activities in which you will be involved will centre round these ideas, putting them in the context of organizations with which you are familiar.

Matching customers' needs

In the first block we saw a marketing-orientated organization was both sensitive to customers' needs and endeavoured to satisfy them. This area of activity is called the **matching process**. Ideally, it results in both satisfied customers and profitable business for suppliers.

The diagram below illustrates the matching process sequence.

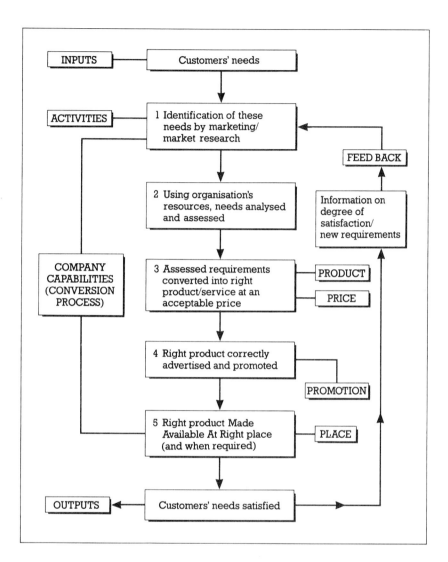

The matching process

For the matching process to occur, several conditions have to be satisfied. First, information is required about customers' needs. (This is usually obtained by research, as discussed in Block 3, *Marketing through Research*.) Once obtained, successful matching depends upon how well it is assessed and analysed and then how well it is used to develop an acceptable product or service. It also relies on customers being aware that the product is on offer, and finding it easily available at an acceptable price. These particular aspects of the matching process are often called the **4 Ps**, ie **product, price, promotion**, and **place**.

The 4 Ps are also the most important elements of the **marketing mix**.

The marketing mix

The term marketing mix was invented in the 1950s by Neil
Boden, an American businessman. It embraces the basic idea
of a recipe, made up from different ingredients — just like the
recipe for a fruit cake, for example. Ingredients can be altered
in quality, quantity, and relative proportions to suit different
tastes. The skill of the host lies in being able to anticipate
guests' preferences — even for things like the amount of sugar
in a cup of tea, or in providing the most desirable mix of
ingredients in a savoury dish.

In the same way, a supplier needs to co-ordinate the
ingredients of his total product to meet customers' needs and
preferences. Before we look at these ingredients or **'variables'**,
as they are often called, we should note that some people in
marketing suggest that the list should be a lot longer than the
4 Ps and should include marketing research, product
development, pricing, packaging, advertising, sales promotion,
selling, merchandising, and after-sales service.

| Activity 1 | Look at the longer list of variables given above. In small groups try arranging the items listed under the 4 Ps, as the key variables. Back in your course group compare the results. |

How far your lists will agree will vary, but some items do
seem to fit under more than one heading. For example,
'packaging' is a part of promotion, but some might argue
that a product is not complete without its packaging.

Product

All suppliers must have a product. The term **product** does in fact, as you have probably realized, cover items such as record players, and services such as those provided by colleges, dentists, and advertising agencies.

Every product has what we call **characteristics**, as the examples below illustrate. Each characteristic will have to be considered carefully during the product development stage, or when we come to a reappraisal of an existing product. The reason for this is simple: to ensure the final set of characteristics is aimed primarily at satisfying customers' needs.

Quality (level of)
Special features
Degree of difference from similar products/services
Size
Shape/styling
Nutritional value
Service back-up
Ease of maintenance
Taste
Rate of interest charged
Speed of response
Durability
Colour
Output
Comfort
Heaviness

Some examples of product/service characteristics

| *Activity 2* | Either in groups or individually take any product which is immediately available, eg: three pin plug, radio, tape recorder, digital watch and: |

Either in groups or individually take any product which is immediately available, eg: three pin plug, radio, tape recorder, digital watch and:
1 Make a list of the the product's characteristics in detail (e.g. Colour: blue; service back-up: one year's guarantee; Special features: cue facility).
2 Compare this list of characteristics, ie. the **product mix** with the item's use. Does the product really match the needs of the average user? Make a note of any shortcomings it may have.

Redesigning the tennis racket: a case study

By 1981 the tennis racket — the market in which Dunlop had been a leading supplier for decades — was moving away from the traditional wooden racket. The threat came from rackets made abroad in new, lightweight, materials. A further problem was that one US manufacturer had produced a metal version with a much larger head, which became popular.

Dunlop's reaction was to produce a racket with a new set of characteristics, made from a plastic composite (using plastic injection moulding to reduce labour costs). By offering this new racket in two sizes (conventional and mid-sized) they were able to regain market supremacy. The new racket was attractive to players at all levels: it was lightweight and gave easier ball control. Its composition absorbed much of the shock of striking the ball, thus causing less injury to players' arms and wrists.

Racket developed in response to foreign competition

The product life-cycle

Ever since the number of manufactured products available increased during the Industrial Revolution, it has become clear that not only do products have a 'life' with stages very similar to a human life, but that they also eventually 'die'. They become obselete, outmoded, or of no further use as new products replace them. The process and the parallel with the human life cycle. What is important is that the demand for a product (and its profitability) will vary over time, as shown in the graph below.

Just because a firm has a successful product on the market, it does not imply that it can sit back and take the profits. Over time the product will contribute less and less to the business,

Comparsion of
human
and product
life cycle.

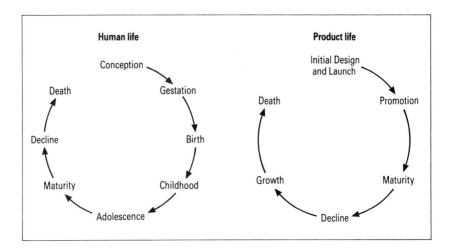

Typical product
life cycle

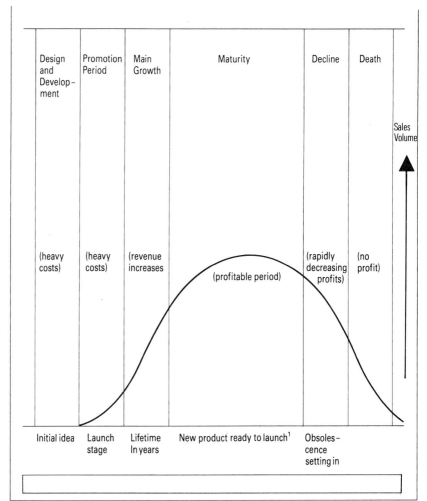

Note:
Profit margins can
start to decline even
before
obsolescence. To
maintain overall
profitability, a new
product or products
will have to be
introduced at this
stage. See also
'Product
replacement
programme', below.

and so it is important to have a continuous product replacement programme as outlined in the graph below.

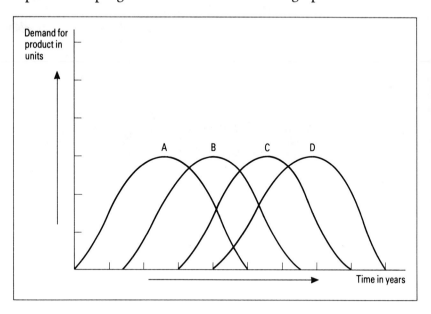

Product Replacement Programme

There are two significant trends in product development within the Western nations and Japan. First, there is a trend towards shorter and shorter life cycles. Products in fields like computers, word processors, and information technology become obsolescent only a few years after their launch. Secondly, there is a trend away from long-run, totally standardized mass-produced items and towards shorter-run, more sophisticated, products to meet specific needs or gaps in the market, ie a basic product with different versions.

As a product approaches the 'decline' stage, there are ways in which its life can be extended. These are termed **product extension strategies**. The product can be revamped, put into new packaging, changed by something being added, and then offered as a 'new, improved' version. Alternatively, a new use or a new market can be found for it. For example, transatlantic liners have gone into the cruise market now that people fly to America. Similarly, when British Rail discontinued the railway service between Kidderminster and Bridgenorth, a group of enthusiasts took over the rehabilitation and running of the line. The Severn Valley Railway is now run to provide recreation for the general public, as well as real pleasure for those running it.

However, there comes a time when a decision to discontinue a product must be made; usually when there is no prospect of

The results of success

reviving a declining market, and/or when insufficient profits are being made. Indeed the fate of some products may be decided even before the launch. A manufacturer may plan to make a model for (say) four years, then to replace it with an updated version with new features, and a re-style. Such a programme for phasing out a product is called **planned obsolesence.** Some critics however, question **planned obsolesence**, especially where the 'new' product is essentially the old one re-styled.

| *Activity 3* |

1 In groups, or individually, identify one product or service you know about, which is:
   a In the post-launch or *growth* stage of the cycle. How recent was the launch?
   b In the mature stage. How long do you think it will stay mature?
   c In the decline stage. Will the decline be permanent?
   d Now obsolete. When did it become obselete and why?
   Part-time students in employment could, instead, review their firm's product ranges, past and present, to see where selected products fitted into the life cycle.

2 The product life cycle model has its critics, especially when applied to services. Some go so far as to say it is doubtful that the model suits many services at all: The core ones, such as banking, have gone on for hundreds of years.
   Consider the following services. Discuss whether you feel the model fits them:
   a cheques
   b slimming clubs
   c cross-channel ferries
   d the Samaritans.

In those cases where you think the model does fit, try and identify what stage the service has reached; and what its future might be (either in its present or some modified form).

Price

Price and pricing policies are dealt with in greater detail in Block 10, *The Marketing Planning Process*. Here we are concerned with getting an idea of the **price mix** available when fixing the price for any good or service. Rather than use the term characteristics as we did for the product, it is more usual to refer to pricing **elements**, **policies**, or **variations**.

Examples of pricing elements

> Time allowed to pay
> Amount of outside Funding offered
> Allowances/trade-ins given
> Variation to meet Changes in demand (eg 'off-peak' electricity, gas, rail travel)
> Geographical (when transport costs are involved)
> Profit margins aimed for
> Competitors' prices
> 'Just below' pricing (eg £9.99)
> Amount of demand for product (eg goods in short supply can be priced up)

Any of these elements (usually more than one) can be found in the make up of a particular price. One firm might charge a high price for a good, but offer generous finance at a low rate of interest (as low as zero per cent). Another may offer a range of prices dependent upon the time of day/level of demand (eg British Telecom)

Activity 4

1 You run a taxi service in your locality. Would you charge more, less, or the same for journeys after midnight? Why?
2 Assuming you are a retailer, would you offer HP finance for:
   a   The purchase of a washing machine?
   b   The hire of a car for a week?
   c   A grocery bill for £100?

3 Work out a *price mix* for a car dealer, selling brand-new cars to the public, many of whom already have cars. (Don't forget methods of payment.)

Price can also be related to the product life cycle. At the *launch*, prices could be very high. For example, when Biro pens were first marketed just after the end of the Second World War, they were regarded as prestige products, and were very expensive. Alternatively prices could be very low to promote sales, eg the introductory offer.

During the *growth* period, there could be a range of prices in different markets. This would apply where a product is launched in several areas over a period of time. Once the item has reached *maturity*, the price would tend to stabilize over time, (eg, established newspapers). When *decline* sets in, there may be an equivalent fall in price to try and maintain sales in the face of competition from replacement products.

Promotion

Promotion is the term given to a collection of methods by which an organization attempts to communicate either directly or indirectly with its market (ie, its customers). The aims of such methods include:

a To create a demand for a new product or brand.
b To maintain or expand sales of an existing product or brand.
c To maintain or expand the organization's share of a particular market.
d To create a favourable image (for customers, the public at large) of the organization.

Some promotional methods

Promotional methods	
Indirect ('mass selling')	**Direct ('personal approach')**
Advertising (TV, newspapers — all media)	Selling face to face
	Telephone selling
Publicity	Direct mail
Point-of-sale material (displays, showcards)	Sales promotion — free 'tastings', free samples
Merchandising	'Personality' appearances (eg
Packaging	opening a new shop)
Competitions	Manned exhibition stands

Static (unmanned) exhibitions	Public relations (eg personal visits; press conferences)
Free gifts	
Sponsorship (eg sporting)	

Many of these methods are considered further in Block 6, *Marketing Communications*. Here we need to decide how to choose the best combinations of promotional methods, (ie the **promotional mix**), in any given situation.

We shall need to take into account:

1 *How much money* can be spent : the promotional budget.
2 *The nature of the market.* Are the customers few or concentrated in a small area? Then personal selling could dominate. If they are many or widespread then TV advertising could be more appropriate. A charity looking for funds might conclude that national advertising would be more productive than door-to-door visits.
3 *The nature of the product.* Large, so called 'white goods' (washing machines, fridges, etc.) are normally promoted by national manufacturers' advertising, through displays in retail shops, and by personal selling inside the shops. Computers for industry will be advertised by direct mail or in specialist magazines read by senior people in industry; but personal selling will be the way orders are eventually obtained.

In brief, *direct methods* or *personal selling* will dominate in a geographically concentrated market, when products have a high unit value, when they are 'made to order' (ie to customers' specific requirements), and when they are technically sophisticated. *Indirect methods* (particularly *advertising*) will dominate when the market is geographically dispersed, when the number of customers is large and when the products are widely available and relatively inexpensive.

| Activity 5 | Working singly or in small groups, decide what *promotional mix* you would recommend (assuming sufficient money is available in each case) for the marketing of the following products or services: |

a Life assurance policies for newly-married couples.
b Security cameras and intruder detectors for industry.
c A new brand of potato crisps. (This needs promoting to wholesalers and retailers, as well as to the public.)
d An exclusive unisex hairdressing salon in a town centre.

Place

Even when product characteristics, price elements, and promotional methods have all been decided, the product still needs to get to the customer, as and when he (or she) wants it. Two factors are covered here: location and availability. The ways in which products or services are made available, ie **distribution**, and the channels through which they pass are considered in Block 8 *Marketing Distribution*.

Location

Location may be dictated by the product or service: for example, most people require the GPO to deliver letters direct to their homes, say before 9.00 am and they would not take kindly to the idea of collecting mail, after 9.00 am, from town centre post offices. In comparison, some prefer their newspapers to be delivered at home: others choose to buy them at newsagents or railway stations.

A comprehensive range of products available in one place may be so desirable that shoppers will be prepared to go several miles to a shopping precinct or to a hypermarket. The selection of goods which they can now buy easily grows ever wider. For example, ASDA have recently introduced babywear in their stores.

However, choosing the best location for a shop like a supermarket is becoming increasingly difficult from both the customers' and the retailers' point of view. Choosing the 'wrong' place can be a serious error: the average cost of opening a large new store is measured in millions of pounds. Indeed some consultants are already 'location analysts', using computer models of the immediate neighbourbood. Another problem is the attitude of planning departments in local authorities to proposed developments.

The combination of different kinds of business in the same area can be an extra attraction, eg house agents next to building societies, with a firm of solicitors opposite, will be very welcome to people moving into a town.

The location of a business may in other cases be largely irrelevant, if goods or services can be delivered where they are wanted, eg for the Post Office letter sorting office, mail order firms, the AA or RAC breakdown services.

| Activity 6 | In small groups or on your own, examine the following business, and decide (from experience or by finding out) where best to locate them. Some possible choices are given. |

1 *TV repair service.* Choices: town centre; out in the countryside; in a suburb: location irrelevant.
2 *Further Education College.* Choices: town centre; on the edge of a town; a little way out of town; deep in the country; location irrelevant.
3 *Industrial cleaning service.* Choices: town centre; in the suburbs; on a trading estate; on the edge of town; location irrelevant.

Have you noticed that all the organizations in Activity 6 are services? There is a choice of location for services. Whereas for farmers, and large-scale manufacturers the final decision on location rests on outside factors, eg climate, availability of skilled workers and raw materials.

Availability

Availability of products and services, their being ready when needed, in the quantity and of the quality required, is partly the job of distribution, partly of storage, and partly a function of production planning — keeping to pre-arranged schedules. Programmes, for example, must be ready before a show's first night, and crackers should be on sale well before Christmas.

Marketing and non-commercial organizations (NCOs)

By now, you will be aware of several of the basic marketing concepts: marketing as meeting customers' needs, the product life cycle, the 4 Ps. So far we have applied these ideas in the main to commercial, or profit-making, organizations in the manufacturing and service sectors. But marketing concepts do have a use and significance in the non-commercial, non-profit-making sector too. So government departments, the National Health Service, churches, local sports clubs and leisure concerns, political parties, the Scouts, Guides, Boys' Brigade — all these can be (and increasingly are becoming) marketing-orientated. Many now use professional advice on advertising, sales promotion, influencing behaviour (eg smoking less; becoming members; giving money). The 1987 AIDS awareness campaign is one example of this trend: so were the political parties' General Election campaigns that year.

The marketing mix these organizations use may reveal some marginal differences from those of the commercial world, however. For NCOs, the 'product' is either a service (eg having your appendix out on the NHS), an idea, a change in attitude or behaviour (eg not drinking and driving), or a person (eg the promotion of a local/national political figure at elections). Charities do offer items for sale, but services predominate. The question 'What business are we in?' is still important for NCOs marketing a service and will affect the *service mix* offered. For example, a church which views its prime mission as one of saving souls will offer something different to one with a broader view of its purpose. (The latter may also see welfare provision, marriage guidance, drama groups, and its school as part of the service it provides.)

Pricing can be less important when, for example, the aim is to help those in need. One charity, Volunteer-Link-Up, exists 'to respond to individual need, and requests for help in the community, by providing volunteers to meet that need'. Even when a price *is* charged (say for part-time students at college), remissions can be made in certain cases.

Place *is* an essential ingredient in the marketing of an NCO service. Salvation Army Citadels, for example, are not found in up-market, fashionable areas, but where the Army's help is most needed. Mobile libraries go out to villages, so that those unable to visit central libraries can still borrow books.

Promotion is a more visible element in the marketing mix given by NCOs: colleges advertise courses, clubs advertise special events. Direct mail is used to solicit donations to charities; as are door-to-door collections (a form of personal selling).

| *Activity 7* | Working on your own or in small group and using the guidance notes below, critically investigate and assess the way in which your college is marketed. Write a formal |

report, addressed to your tutor, with your findings, conclusions, and recommendations for any changes that you feel would be beneficial.

In particular look at:
1 How marketing is organized (the individuals, committees etc. concerned).
2 Whether the college is product-, sales-, or marketing-orientated.
3 The composition of the college's marketing mix.
4 The product life cycle of any one course currently offered. (This can be treated as an optional extra.) Part-time students could look at their own organization instead, and choose any product or service it offers.

Guidance Notes

1 This activity is a substantial one, and will take several weeks to complete. (You will find it very rewarding if it is done well.) You may need to use some class time for part, if not all, the research involved.
2 Whilst this activity can be attempted by students individually, it is better to work in groups of three or four sharing out the tasks.
3 It is suggested that in your research you should interview key members of staff (better done by appointment), fellow-students, and the public at large. This information can be shared between groups.
4 Careful preparation of the topics to be raised, or questions to be asked during interviews should be undertaken beforehand.

Summary of skills

The intention of the study in this unit is not only to learn facts about marketing, but also to develop skills which will be of use in the business world. The section at the end of each block indicates the skill areas covered by each activity.

Skills

Skills	*Activities in which skill is developed*
a Learning and studying	All Activities
b Identifying and tackling problems	5, 6, 7
c Information gathering	2, 6, 7
d Communicating	All Activities
e Working with others	All Activities

Block 3
Marketing through Research 1

Introduction

Blocks 1 and 2 have shown that marketing is a key activity in business and non-commercial organizations, and that it is partly about getting and (keeping) customers. Without customers there would be no business. It is essential that an organization matches its products and services to the needs of its customers. So it follows that it is essential to discover exactly what those needs *are* as far as is possible.

Needs also change as time passes. This means that to keep in profitable business, an organization has to change its products to match new needs. Complex decisions then have to be taken about products, price, promotion, and place. Such decisions could be made on the basis of past experience, guesswork, or hunches. However, since considerable risks are involved, it is far wiser to make these decisions with the best information available about the market to hand, which has been obtained in a planned and disciplined manner.

Many organizations also like to have essential background knowledge about their markets, and general industrial and commercial trends. The progress of competitors and how they price and distribute goods is of considerable interest. In short, to provide this knowledge large amounts of information are needed which must be objective, systematic, unbiased, current, appropriate, and complete.

Marketing research, properly done, gives this sort of background knowledge, so that informed decisions can be taken and risks minimized. In this block you will be introduced to marketing research, its scope and organization and how data is captured and collected. You will experience some of its associated problems, especially in preparing questionnaires and interviewing members of the public.

What is marketing research?

You may be puzzled as to why we refer to **Marketing research.** It is not the term 'market research', with which most of you will probably be more familiar. There is a difference between the two, as the diagram below shows. *Market research* is a rather restricted set of activities, and forms just one aspect of the broader function of *marketing research*. Even the seven 'branches' shown do not cover every area.

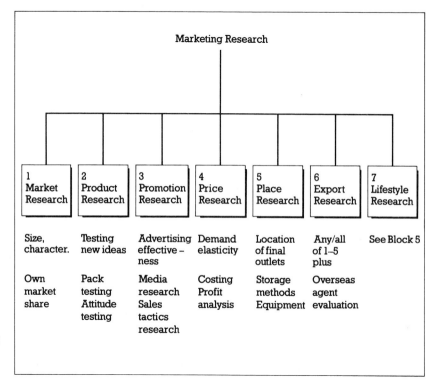

Marketing Research and some of its activities

(Social research, for example, is used to establish public opinion on topics of general interest, such as Trade Union legislation, lung cancer and smoking, town plans, and motorway routes.)

Unfortunately, the terms market research and marketing research are often used by people in marketing as if they both had the same meaning. This is probably because much more market research is done (and more time and money spent on it) than any other kind of research. The bulk of this work is concerned with consumer research surveys, involving interviewing purchasers of mass-produced, frequently purchased, household goods. So in this block we will be concentrating on this aspect of research.

Some definitions of marketing research

The following definitions are self-explanatory:

1 'The systematic gathering, recording, and analysis of data about problems relating to the marketing of goods and services.' (American Marketing Association, 1961.)

2 'It is the systematic process of gathering, analysing, and interpreting relevant information for decision-making.' (P C Murphy, 1980.)

3 'Research undertaken within any area of marketing planning, and operations.' (G Oliver 1980.)

(Note the emphasis on 'systematic': it appears in other definitions too.)

How is marketing research organized?

In very large organizations, especially where all-the-year-round research is required, it could make sense to employ permanent staff to do this work, but the normal procedure is to contract out the work to agencies. These are either advertising agencies who provide a research facility as well as their more usual services, or specialist research agencies.

By buying in research as and when it is needed, an organization need only spend money whilst the research is being done; avoiding the overheads of premises, expensive research data banks, and the problems of organizing teams of field workers. In the same way, research agencies do not employ large numbers of permanent survey workers but hire people for the duration of specific projects from a large pool of contacts (usually women) who prefer part-time work.

A typical assignment could be a survey of a range of competitive brands in a clearly defined product area, eg washing powders, breakfast cereals, or instant coffee.

Stages of a survey

The diagram of the stages in the research process shows eleven separate stages, though these they can be grouped under five main headings.

1 *Client/research executive discussions*

The **client** (in this sector of business customers are called *clients*) is the person or company who asks for the work to be

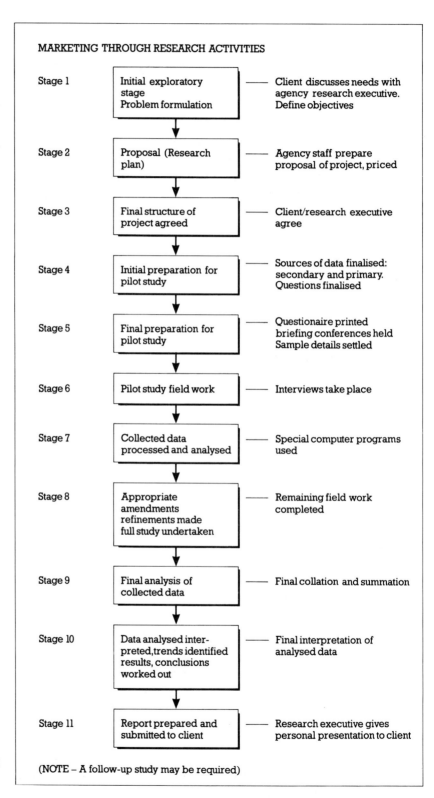

MARKETING THROUGH RESEARCH ACTIVITIES

| Stage 1 | Initial exploratory stage Problem formulation | — Client discusses needs with agency research executive. Define objectives |

| Stage 2 | Proposal (Research plan) | — Agency staff prepare proposal of project, priced |

| Stage 3 | Final structure of project agreed | — Client/research executive agree |

| Stage 4 | Initial preparation for pilot study | — Sources of data finalised: secondary and primary. Questions finalised |

| Stage 5 | Final preparation for pilot study | — Questionaire printed briefing conferences held Sample details settled |

| Stage 6 | Pilot study field work | — Interviews take place |

| Stage 7 | Collected data processed and analysed | — Special computer programs used |

| Stage 8 | Appropriate amendments refinements made full study undertaken | — Remaining field work completed |

| Stage 9 | Final analysis of collected data | — Final collation and summation |

| Stage 10 | Data analysed interpreted, trends identified results, conclusions worked out | — Final interpretation of analysed data |

| Stage 11 | Report prepared and submitted to client | — Research executive gives personal presentation to client |

(NOTE – A follow-up study may be required)

The stages of a marketing research survey

done and pays for it. Typical clients are advertising agencies (who are contracting out a part of a large project), industrial firms, food processing companies, government departments, and political parties. In short, a client is anyone who has a problem which may be solved by marketing research techniques.

Stage one of almost every survey is a meeting between the client and a **research executive** from the agency which has been selected. The research executive is similar to the **account executive** we met in Block 1, Introducing Marketing: a salesperson with knowledge of marketing research and how it can be applied to particular problems. At this meeting the client's requirements are discussed fully. The research executive will possibly then need to take some advice from specialists within the agency, and with their help prepare a written proposal.

The **proposal** will describe the problem, what kind of survey will need to be undertaken, how many people will need to be interviewed, and what type of people they would be. A draft **questionnaire**, i.e. the list of questions to be asked at interview, is included. The client will also want to know what kind of information the survey will provide, how long it will take to carry out, and naturally, how much it will cost.

Sometimes the proposal will be acceptable to the client, but often it becomes the basis for further discussions until both parties agree on the objectives of the survey, on how it is to be done, and on its price.

2 'Pilot' Study

Before any important project is put out into the field, it is usual to conduct a limited survey. Interviewers are briefed to note any problems or difficulties they meet and to report back later to a conference about their experiences.

The objectives of a pilot study are to ensure:
1 The questions are the right ones (and are properly worded).
2 The questions are in the right order.
3 The right people are being interviewed.
4 Sufficient time is available to carry out the daily interview target.

Between this pilot study and the main survey not only questions but also sampling methods can be amended. The sample interviews play a vital role in the final planning.

Market research
in action

3 Field Work

Once the final study is complete, the field work proper can
start. Obviously it would be impossible to interview everyone
in the UK: it would be too costly and time-consuming.
Accordingly a sample is identified (see 'sampling' on pages
58–60), and interviewers are told exactly what kind of people to
approach. The project is now under way. Interviews normally
take place in town centres, major shopping areas, company
offices, or peoples' homes.

3 Data Processing

Completed questionnaires are returned to the agency, checked,
and processed. These days most survey data is computerized,
but for small surveys hand tabulation is quite adequate, and
often quicker. A typical tabulation might look like this:

(Imaginary) Print-out
Details — Lipstick
Purchases (For an
explanation of the
'class' category see
below)

		AGE		CLASS		AREA	
	TOTAL	UNDER 35	36 AND OVER	ABC1	C2DE	NORTH	SOUTH
Sample size	2000	500	1500	700	1300	740	1260
No.buying lipsticks (Base=100%)	1200 (100%)	400 (100%)	740 (100%)	620 (100%)	600 (100%)	260 (100%)	960 (100%)
Brands last Purchased	%	%	%	%	%	%	%
Lipglow	39	30	50	40	44	30	45
Queen	37	40	29	44	22	40	34
Elfin	16	23	14	14	18	21	14
Others	8	7	7	2	16	9	7

SURVEY 10/88 PRODUCT MARKET–LIPSTICKS
ANALYSIS OF LAST PURCHASE BY AGE, SOCIAL CLASS, AREA
(SAMPLE–HOUSEWIVES)

Activity 1	Individually, or in small groups, consider the data given in the print-out. (An example of data interpretation is to take the figures for 'Lipglow'; it seems to be a product bought mostly by older women (35 or more), and those in social classes C2DE.)

How do you interpret the data given about:

a Queen?
b Lipsticks as a product group?
c The preferences of northern and southern housewives purchasing lipsticks? Is there a 'north–south divide'?

Note: The notion of social classes ('socio-economic groups' as they are sometimes called) is one you have perhaps already come across. It is dealt with in the next section, and you may wish to read that before tackling this Activity.

5 *The Final Report*

At the conclusion of the project all data is analysed and interpreted. A detailed report is prepared for submission to the client. If it is a complex one, it may be necessary for the research executive to explain the features personally, and answer questions. Some agencies give formal 'presentations', using graphics and slides, to groups of client executives.

You will by now be quite familiar with report writing. There are however some special points to note about research reports which are dealt with in Block 4.

Social class (social grading)

It has been clearly established that our social or economic status not only affects how much we have to spend, but also our tastes, habits, and life-style. An essential part, then, of virtually every marketing research survey involving people is to classify those interviewed (often called 'respondents') by social grade. This classification is as important as that of sex, age, or location.

The social grading used universally in marketing research is based on jobs or occupations. (When people are called on at home, their households are assessed according to the *occupation of the head of the household*, that is, the occupation of the highest-paid wage or salary earner in the household. There can be some anomalies with this usage but most agencies have a host of supplementary rules to deal with these problems, too many to deal with here.)

Table 3.1: Social grading system.

Group	Social class	Occupation type	Percentage of total UK population (approx)
A	Upper middle class	(Non-manual) Higher managerial, administrative or professional. Examples: public school head, board-level personnel, stockbroker, chief constable, university professor.	3.5%
B	Middle class	(Non-manual) Intermediate managerial, administrative, or professional. Examples: sister tutor (large hospital), university/technical college lecturer, chief bank teller, supermarket manager, area sales manager, flight lieutenant (RAF).	12–13%
C1	Lower middle class	(Non-manual) Junior managerial, administrative, professional, clerical. Examples: School teacher (Scale II), bank clerk, civil servant (clerical grade), shorthand typist, driving instructor, insurance agent (door-to-door collector), small shop keeper.	22%
C2	Skilled working class	(Manual) Skilled manual workers. Examples: foreman (up to 14 workers), craftsman/woman (bricklayer, carpenter), typesetter, long distance lorry driver, coach builder, RAF corporal, AA/RAC patrolman.	32–33%
D	Semi-skilled/unskilled working class	(Manual) Semi-skilled and unskilled manual workers. Examples: labourer, and 'mate' of C2 grades, apprentice, agricultural	19–20%

		worker, shop assistant, taxi driver.	
E	Lowest level of existence	(Existing on state pensions/grants; no other income: low paid workers) Examples: old-age pensioner, casual worker, supplementary benefit drawer; student.	10%

Note: these percentages change over time. There is a continuing shift from workers in semi-skilled manual jobs to self-employment; the population of pensioners is steadily increasing.

It is essential that any classification system used in research is based on occupation rather than income (which can often change rapidly over a short period of time), so that comparisons can be made with results from previous years. In cases where respondents refuse to indicate their occupation, or there is no similar occupation on which to base an assessment, interviewers have to make a guess on factors such as speech, appearance, property or area lived in.

Activity 2	1 As a group, examine all the jobs advertised in a local paper (weekly or evening). Attempt to allocate them to the 'ABC1C2DE' grading system. 2 Discuss a possible explanation for the fact that two major groupings are often used: ABC1 and C2DE. Do the constituents of each group have anything in common? 3 Attempt to grade the following occupations: ambulanceman; commercial airline pilot; bricklayer; watch repairer; bishop (C of E); electrician's mate.

Data in marketing

By 'data' we mean raw facts about the world. Once facts (data) have been assessed, coded, sorted, collated, interpreted, and so on into a meaningful pattern they become 'information'. In effect data is the raw material; information the finished product. But without data there is no information. Marketing research's first task, then, is data search and capture.

Kinds of data

Two kinds of data are used in marketing research: 'secondary' data (data already in existence; published or on a file somewhere, though not necessarily in the possession of the researcher); and 'primary' (new, 'original' data, gathered specially for an investigation on hand).

It makes economic sense to use secondary data if it is available (and suitable). In the UK a wide variety of secondary data is available from government agencies, such as census returns, labour market statistics, family expenditure surveys, and so on.

HMSO. or LIBRARY. ⟵

Organization's own records	Annual abstract of statistics
Government departments' statistics	Teletext JICNARS (joint industry committee
Employers' associations (CBI etc.)	Viewdata for national readership surveys)
Universities	Census of population
Reports/surveys published widely (Gallup, MORI polls)	
Commercial firms eg A C Neilsen (of Oxford)	

PANELS - Groups of consumers record those data for

+ MINTEL REPORTS

Some sources of secondary data

(TGI Target Group Index) + KEYNOTE REPORTS + BRAD + KOMPASS
+ information on business markets

Activity 3	Go to the college, or some other local, library, and find out the following information (ask the librarian for help if you cannot find what you want):

1 The population of your local city or town.
2 The latest retail price index.
3 The proportion of married females in the population aged 30 to 39.
4 The latest index of average earnings of employees in Great Britain (whole economy).
5 The latest public opinion poll details of support for the various political parties.

Activity 3 was probably time-consuming, and not without some frustrations. This illustrates some of the drawbacks of secondary data. The main problem, however, is that the data retrieved is of an unknown quality and reliability as far as the user is concerned. The data may not be precisely what was wanted; and may not be specific enough. It may not be in the format required; it may be out of date. The conditions under which it was obtained and the sampling methods used are unknown.

Primary data on the other hand is directly generated or collected during field work or obtained by some other collection method (e.g. electronic traffic counting). Such data relates totally to the investigation in hand, and once processed, should provide information to aid decision-making.

Qualitative and quantitative data

Qualitative data is data which conveys impressions or attitudes rather than precise information. The way people see the world (perceptions), why they do things (motivations), and how they feel about things (attitudes) are of interest to the marketeer. These ideas are explored further in Block 5, but here we can note that long, in-depth interviews or group discussions can bring out feelings about, or attitudes to, products.

(*Source:* S P Schnaars and L G Shiffman, *Journal of Academy of Marketing Science* Autumn, 1984.)

American historical romance paperback novel market	
Type	Characteristics
'Movers and shakers'	Heavy cinema goers; 30 to 40 years old; least price conscious
'Isolated readers'	Less attendance at cinemas; 40 to 50 yrs.; low price consciousness; like quiet evenings at home
'Young swingers'	Frequent cinema visits; under 30; least interest in romance; fashion conscious; tired of reading romantic novels
'Laggards'	Few cinema visits; most price conscious; highly religious; over 50; least educated; lowest income

The kind of information in the example above is based on research where consumers are asked to express agreement or disagreement with statements covering their activities, interests, and opinions. This sort of information is very useful in establishing a publisher's marketing mix, but very demanding on the skills of the researchers.

Quantitative data is easy to understand: it comprises survey findings set out numerically.

Table 3.2: UK market for soup 1986. (*Source:* Nestlé)

	£ million	% Change on 1985
Liquid	150	-1%
Packet	31	-5%
Instant	54	-12%
Total	236	-4%

In effect, quantitative data records what people do: in the case of the soup market statistics, what soup they buy. We can say quantitative data is **statistically definitive** or precise.

It is clear that there is a place for both kinds of data in building up pictures of markets and the people in them who make choices.

How is data captured and collected?

There are three widely-used methods of obtaining primary marketing research data: observation, experimentation, and by survey.

1 Observation

Here the data is collected by observing the respondents, and no interviews are involved. Qualitative data gained by observation could be, for example, when researchers watch how shop assistants actually deal with customers. Quantitative data is usually a counting process. Prior to the approval of a comprehensive shopping development for a Cotswold town, the local county council monitored traffic flows in and out of the town all day, every day, for a period. All exits to the town were covered; counting also took place at key spots within the town. The development was seen as viable, and parking needs identified. In a similar way, the movement of people in a city shopping centre was monitored over a period; certain alterations were made to the layout as a result.

The undoubted merits of observation are:
1 large amounts of data can be collected within a reasonably short space of time,
2 a high degree of accuracy can be achieved,
3 cost per observation is very low (compared with interviewing),
4 the interviewer does not intrude upon the activity observed.

Against this is the problem that the data merely records what has happened; without giving an explanation as to why it happened.

Activity 4	Carry out in pairs one or more of the following observations. Record and tabulate your results.

Carry out in pairs one or more of the following observations. Record and tabulate your results.
1 Observe lunch-time refectory queues in your college (or place of work). Identify the male/female split, speed of service (i.e time of completion of being served minus time of arrival in queue), types of meals purchased. Compare the results on different days in the week.

2 Visit a supermarket (with the manager's permission), and carry out similar observations of foods bought and the speed of the check-out. You could note how much each person spends at the check-out.

3 Visit a car park on successive days. Count the total number of cars and empty spaces at hourly or half-hourly intervals. (in a small car park you could also identify numbers of different makes of vehicles and their ages.)

Experimentation

Experimentation (sometimes called the experimental method) involves trying to acquire data on how a product, advertisement, promotion, etc would fare under given conditions controlled by the experimenters. More than one form of experimentation is used.

For example, we may have developed an acceptable product, but are somewhat unhappy about its packaging. We could just decide to change it and hope for the best. On the other hand, we could select a particular area (say 50 miles radius from a city), and send products in the new package to our outlets in that area.

To check on the reception of the new pack, we would need to look at the sales figures carefully, as well as to have some 'customer attitude' surveys done. If the response seemed satisfactory, the decision could be made to 'go national', and change to the new pack throughout the UK.

A second possibility is to launch a product in a 'test market'. This could be a geographical area, or a group of specially selected people. Where geographical areas are chosen, we would need to launch the product in the normal way (eg, with advertising, publicity, sales promotion). Even if the response were good, we might need to make design changes as a result of test findings. The 'Mentadent P' toothpaste dispenser is an example of a product well researched and tested before its national launch.

Yet a third possibility is to create a model of a market to see if we can find gaps in it. Suppose we want to enter the air freshener/toilet cleanser market. We could purchase examples of every product already on the market, set them out on tables, and invite 50 or 100 users of the products to assess them. Typically, the users would be invited to list the products in order of preference, with comments as to why certain brands were preferred: would it be price, smell, ease of use, or germ-killing ability, or some other factor? (A study on these lines did actually result in the development of a new toilet cleanser.)

Asking questions (interviews, sample surveys)

A survey in which an opinion or advice is solicited from all adults in a country is called a 'referendum'. (The last to be held in the UK was in 1975 on our continuing membership in the EEC.) Another type of investigation into the whole popultation is carried out every 10 years: the Census of Population. Both of these methods of obtaining data are complicated to organize, and extremely expensive to mount.

Quite obviously, it would be impossible to interview every single person in a marketing research exercise. Instead we select a small group of people to represent the whole (or 'universe' as statisticians call it). This small group is called a **sample**; the method of selecting it is known as **sampling**.

Sampling

The most important point about any sample is that it should be fully representative of its universe. A small blood sample will tell us how someone's blood is made up, whether it is taken from an arm, leg, or finger. All the blood in a person is of similar consistency. With people it is not so easy, and great care has to be taken to ensure respondents selected for interview are truly representative of the whole.

Careful rules need to be drawn up to avoid **bias** in a sample. Suppose a sample of West Country housewives were required, and we did all our interviews in Torquay: the sample would be unbalanced, biased towards older women as a high proportion of retired people live in the town.

There are three basic methods of sampling: **simple random, cluster** (both being 'probability' or random sampling), and **quota** (non-random).

In a random sample every individual in a particular universe must have an equal chance of being selected. A simple random sample of people in the UK could mean, for example getting together lists of every adult (from electoral registers), and choosing one person in every 25 000 to interview. The difficulty would be that the respondents chosen would be scattered all over the country and difficult to find, and this would entail lots of travelling for the interviewers.

A way out is to use cluster sampling where we divide the country into areas or regions (counties are not always suitable) and randomly select two or three regions, then towns within those and finally streets within those towns. We could then, say, call on every second house in those streets. The resultant samples would be less representative than purely random ones, but would still be acceptable for market research.

Quota sampling is quite different. Here we specify in advance the types of people we need to interview. (Usually a great deal of information has been built up about the universe in advance: proportions of males to females, age profiles, and so on.) The interviewer is told how many people to find of each category: by age group, social class, or sex. Provided these conditions are observed, who the people chosen actually are, or where they live, is usually not important. They can be interviewed in some convenient central place.

The number of interviewees in each category (the 'quota') is calculated in advance to be representative of the population in the area. For example:

Table 3.3: Quota sample.

	AGE GROUP			SOCIAL CLASS			Total
	16–34	35–54	55–64	ABC1	C2	DE	
Number of females	8	12	10	8	10	12	30

We need to interview 30 females in all, and when completed, the numbers interviewed in each of the three groups and social grades should conform to the groups specified. More complicated quotas can be compiled, although they all are based on the same principles. (However, bias *can* creep in, if interviewers call on or stop people known to them, or people they instinctively like.)

Sample sizes

In qualitative research sampling is not really relevant. Small numbers of people are interviewed in depth, and results interpreted by those with some knowledge of psychology. Quantitative research (facts about the market) does lend itself to sampling.

To find out how many video recorders were sold last year, to which age groups, and to which social class – or even more useful, how many might be expected to be sold *next* year – samples of over 500 are involved. If more precise accuracy is needed, samples of 2000 or over are necessary. (Political polls, for instance, need to identify changes of 1% in party allegiance.)

It would be rare for a marketing research agency to go lower than samples of 100, even if only broad estimates were required.

<table>
<tr><td>

Activity 5

</td><td>

Obtain copies of local electoral registers for your town. (Your District Council should be able to supply these for a small charge – or you might get last year's free!)
1 Using the registers, devise a method of producing:
   a a random sample (of, say, 5 per cent of the total)
   b a cluster sample (again producing a 5 per cent sample).
2 Compare the problems of conducting interviews based on the two methods of sampling in terms of journey time and cost (say at £10 per hour), and assuming each house call lasts five minutes.

</td></tr>
</table>

Survey fieldwork and open-ended interviewing

A distinction is often drawn between **survey fieldwork** (interviewing with highly-structured question plans), and **open-ended** interviewing, which is part interview and part discussion with the respondents.

Asking questions – designing questionnaires

First look at the box below for some general hints on questionnaire design.

> Questionaire design: General Hints
>
> * Prepare a balanced set of questions
> * Prepare introductory material for interviewers' use
> * Phrase questions clearly and positively
> * Avoid imprecise terms, slang, jargon words
> * Don't suggest answers; keep questions unbiased
> * Don't ask questions people can't or won't answer

The different kinds of questions that can be asked are shown in the second box, 'Question Types'. We need a balanced mix of multiple-choice, open, probe, etc. A proper introduction for the interviewer to use should be at head of the questionnaire: 'Good afternoon. I am Mandy Jones, representing East Loamshire College. We are making a study of newspaper reading habits. Would you mind answering a few questions?'

Some agencies go much further, producing detailed guides for interviewers. The guides cover not just the introduction, but how to explain to respondents the way they came to be selected, how to react to replies given by respondents, how the questionnaire is to be completed – and even sometimes what clothes to wear!

Questions should be positive, not negative in form: 'Which is your favourite newspaper?'. Jargon terms like 'PSBR', 'cross-modular assignment', or 'white goods', should be avoided. A question which is ambiguous or imprecise, such as 'Do you live in a large house?', may have different meanings to different people.

Leading questions (which suggest or encourage certain answers) are traps for the unwary. 'You do presumably use this shopping centre every week?' can almost certainly expect the answer 'Yes!'. Slightly less obvious is 'Do you like the friendly attitude of the staff in Smith's Supermarket?'. This, too, is likely to get a high percentage of affirmative responses. (If you do have to ask questions about the staff's behaviour, better to use a 'scale' approach. This is discussed in the next section.)

A common error is to ask questions which respondents are unable or unlikely to answer truthfully. 'How many illnesses have you had in the last five years?' may get no answer, or just a sheer guess.

Types of questions

The six commonest types of questions used in marketing research are:

1 *Direct* (sometimes called 'closed'). Usually the respondent is given the choice of two answers: 'Yes' or 'No'. (Occasionally 'Don't known' as well.) 'Do you smoke?' 'Have you got a video recorder at home?'; or 'Do you normally travel by bus?' The answers provide basic facts.

Question Types

* Direct (closed)   Answers usually Yes/no; Don't know

* Multiple-Choice   Choice of one of several listed possible answers; easy to code

* Open-Ended   Respondent required to expand on choices; to give reasons; to state attitudes
                   and opinions

* Probe   Respondent encouraged to go more deeply into replies given

* Attitude Scale   Designed to gauge strengths of feelings, beliefs, attitudes towards
                   products/brands; respondent selects out of chosen adjectives, or gives marks
                   out of 10, etc.

* Bi-Polar Scale   Attitude measurement using scale with opposing attitudes at each end.

2 *Mutiple-choice.* These are somewhat like multiple-choice
questions in examinations, though not so hard! The
respondent is asked a question, the answers to which are
fairly limited, or established by previous studies or common
sense. The answers are typed, printed on the questionnaire,
and are usually coded to aid computer input.

Question: 'Which brand of washing powder did you buy last time?'

Name	Code
Ariel	0011
Daz	0012
Bold.....etc.	0013

(appropriate code is circled)

Sometimes the answers to 'reason why' questions are coded,
multiple-choice ones:

Question: 'What to you are the advantages of using a microwave oven?'

Answer	Code
It cooks the food more quickly	0031
It is cheaper to run	0032
It stops food being burnt	0033
It eliminates need for cooking utensils	0034

3 *Open-ended.* This kind of question often follows on from the two above. The respondent is required to expand on factual answers. The interviewer records what the respondent says verbatim. (This would slow down the interview if there were many such questions.) Accurate recording is essential.

Question: 'Why do you normally read...............?'

      (Title of newspaper respondent claims to read regularly)

      (Answers are written in a box drawn below the question)

Open-ended questions almost invariably finish with an instruction to the interviewer to 'probe'.

4 *Probe.* Probes are extra questions put in to get the respondent to answer more precisely, or more fully a previous question.

Respondent: 'Yes, that soap does give a good lather.'
                 ('Good' does not give us enough information—it's just
                 a value judgement.)

Interviewer (probing): 'Can you tell me in what way you think the lather is good?'

(You can see an answer of sorts was originally obtained, but the 'probe' tries to tie the respondent down. The probe is *not* a leading question; The interviewer does not suggest answers like: 'Do you mean it's foamy?' 'lasts a long time?' etc.)

A further method of enlarging an answer is to ask 'Is there anything else?', or 'What else?', after a short answer.

Respondent: 'I like Tingle toothpaste because it makes your teeth whiter.'
Interviewer: 'Is there anything else you like about Tingle?'

5 *Attitude scale.* One way of measuring peoples' attitudes about products, brands, services, etc. is to ask them to respond in a

measurable way. Verbal scales are normally used on cards containing such phrases as:

> VERY LIKELY
> QUITE LIKELY
> NEITHER LIKELY/UNLIKELY
> RATHER UNLIKELY
> VERY UNLIKELY

> Question: Please look at this card and tell me which of the phrases best expresses how likely you are to buy the cheese you have just tasted?'

Marking scales are probably more familiar to you if you ever watch international ice-skating on television (where competitors are 'marked' out of 6 under such headings as 'artistic impression'). In research into attitudes and opinions, respondents are asked to 'mark out of 10' some quality or other of a product. A computer magazine rates video games under such headings as 'sound', 'graphics', 'playability', 'value for money', and 'overall impression'.

6 *Bi-polar scale.* This is another way of gauging attitudes. The respondents are shown cards with two statements, one a very positive statement, the other the contrasting negative, with a seven-point scale between.

> Example: _____
>
> | Removes stains | 1 | 2 | 3 | 4 | 5 | 6 | 7 | Does not remove stains |
> |---|---|---|---|---|---|---|---|---|
>
> Interviewer: 'I have a scale here with two phrases describing Acme washing-powder at each end. If you think the left-hand phrase best applies to Acme, indicate box 1. If you broadly agree, indicate the appropriate box. If, however, you think the right-hand phrase applies, again indicate the appropriate box. Now tell me how you feel about Acme and the way it removes stains.'
>   (The interviewer notes the box indicated.)

Order of questions

Whilst there could be good reasons in particular surveys for varying the order given below, most workers in the field would accept the following general rules:

1 Ask one or two general, bland, factual questions easy to answer. ('Is this your first visit to the Southgate Shopping Centre?'), to relax the respondent.
2 Move into direct, and/or multiple-choice questions about past events or regular habits (What make of TV set have you got in your home?'). Present respondent with lists or 'prompt' cards (pieces of stiff card listing the alternative answers in alphabetical order).
3 Follow up with one or two probe questions to expand on individual points.
4 Next, introduce attitude measurement questions (if needed). Either attitude or bi-polar scales may be used.
5 Any open-ended questions, and those asking for personal information, should ideally be left until the end, including those about age and social class. (The latter can be disguised by asking about jobs.)

Pilot questionnaires

Even if a group of you were to work on a questionnaire for some time, the chances are there would still be room for further improvement. The standard approach is to try out on a small sample what has been agreed so far. Problems like respondents misunderstanding questions, or taking offence at certain phrases, can then be dealt with. At times there may be too many questions in a survey. Those taking part in the pilot survey should attend a conference when all the difficulties encountered can be considered, and a final version agreed.

Practical matters

Before going into the field, there are a few other considerations to bear in mind.

1 It is advisable for all interviewers to have some form of identification. Many research firms insist on the use of identity cards with photographs.
2 Visual aids to jog a respondent's memory are useful. 'Prompt cards' shown to respondents, with mutiple-choice alternatives clearly printed in large letters, assist replies considerably. Attitude scale questions can be facilitated by the use of 'shuffle packs'. (Each card in the pack carries one of the scale statements. Shuffled, and presented to respondents in a random order, they are a good method of establishing attitudes.)

3 'Routing statements' may be needed. These apply where there are questions which do not have to be answered if the answer to a previous question goes a certain way. For example: Question 3, 'Is your television a full colour set, or a black and white one?' Question 4 might apply to colour television viewers only, and question 5 to black and white viewers. The routing statement after question 3 would then read: 'If 'yes' to colour, go to question 4: If 'yes' to black and white, go to question 5.' (Sometimes this process is called 'question skipping'.)

4 A special 'Thank-You' card, leaflet, or letter handed to respondents on completion of interviews is general practice in good surveys. The reasons behind the use of research can be explained as well as the objectives of the particular survey. An assurance should be given that all replies are 'confidential', and that the respondents will not be 'sold' anything.

| *Activity 6* | Either one or both parts of this activity could be attempted. Please note the second part is a very extended activity involving field work, and will take several weeks to complete. It is also really designed for group, rather than individual, work.

1 The sample questionnaire on page 68 was designed by some students to help establish the commercial and financial viability of starting up a travel agency in the upper Thames Valley. It was used in four market towns within a 30 mile radius.

Discuss the questionnaire: its layout; the sequence, type, and wording of questions. Would it be clear to you how to use it, if you were an interviewer? As a respondent would you find it easy to answer the questions? If you wanted to carry out a similar survey in your area, what changes would you make?

2 Design a balanced questionnaire, and carry out appropriate interviews (bearing in mind the points considered in this block), on *one* of these topics:

a Smoking amongst young adults (16 to 25). Whilst the final make-up of the questionnaire is your decision, topics you could include are: the percentage of young adults who smoke (split into males/females); daily consumption, brands, etc. Non-smokers can be asked why they do not (or have ceased to) smoke (eg, because of price, fear of lung cancer, pressure from others). Note attitudes to banning advertising, or even the sale of cigarettes; extra price penalties; no smoking in offices, etc.

b Television watching, all ages. Here you could include: hours viewed each week; favourite channels and programmes; personalities liked/disliked; type of set (owned, rented); remote control or not; attitudes to violence and sex on TV; use of video recorders.

c College facilities (interview full/part-time students and staff). List facilities (eg, library, refectory, student areas, labs, computer networks), and establish the amount of use (by course, sex, full/part-time students, etc.). Attitudes towards and suggestions for improvement.

d A topic of your own choice. (See the next section.)

Note that it will be necessary to pilot the test, and for the main survey it is suggested a minimum of 100 interviews be done by each group. See below for data processing and final report. Also note refusals where they occur.

Types of survey

There are different kinds of survey. They include:

1 *Product tests* to determine users' attitudes to various products. Actual samples can be left to try: interviews take place after some weeks.

2 *Usage, habit, and attitude surveys* to establish why people buy (or do not buy) various products, brands, and their like and dislikes.

3 *Advertisement tests* to measure the effectiveness of newspaper magazine, and television advertisements.

4 *Pack testing* of changes or proposed changes in the design or quality of product packaging.

5 *Continuous surveys* obtaining data over a period of time (say one year) about the usage of, and attitudes towards, products. (Suitable people are engaged to complete diaries with details of purchases and how products are used. Very useful for basic food products like flour, margarine, etc.)

6 *Retailer surveys* to obtain details for manufacturers on customers buying from retail outlets. Also to find out how shop managers view their suppliers.

MARKETING QUESTIONAIRE
****

DATE   /   /   LOCATION _____

QUESTION _____   INTERVIEWER CODE _____

<u>REMEMBER:</u>   MAP
            SHOW CARD
            LETTER

INTERVIEWER: "Good Afternoon, I'm from West Oxfordshire College. We are conducting a survey
            in connection with a marketing project. Would you mind answering in complete
            confidence a few questions?"

SPECIFY

1. Where do you live?   [MAP]   _____
            Woodstock   _____
            5 miles radius   _____   _____
            Elsewhere   _____   _____

2. Do you ever go on holiday?   _____
            No   _____   (END)
            Yes   _____   (CONTINUE)

3. Who chooses your holiday in your family?   _____

4. How often a year, do you go on holiday?   _____
            Less than once   _____   _____
            Once   _____
            Twice   _____
            More than twice   _____   _____

5. Where did you last go on holiday?   _____
            United Kingdom   _____   _____
            Europe   _____   _____
            United States   _____   _____
            Elsewhere   _____   _____

6. Do you normally? [SHOW CARD]   _____
            A. Make own arrang.   _____
            B. Travel agency   _____   _____
            C. Tour Operator   _____   _____

7. Why do you choose (Answer 6)?   _____
        _____
        _____

8. Do you know of a travel agency in Woodstock?   _____
            Yes   _____   _____
            No   _____

9. Do you think it would be useful to have a further, independent travel agency in Woodstock? (Circle)
    [SHOW CARD]
            VERY   1   2   3   4   5   NOT AT ALL

10. If there were one, would you use it?   _____
            Yes   _____   Go to 12.
            No   _____

```
QUESTION              INTERVIEWER CODE

11.  Where do you think it should be situated?    _____
                      Close to here               _____
                      Centre of town              _____
                      Side street                 _____

12.  Which age group are you in?  [SHOW CARD]     _____
                      A.  16 – 24                  _____
                      B.  25 – 39                  _____
                      C.  40 – 59                  _____
                      D.  60 +                     _____

13.  What is your occupation?          _____

[GIVE COPY OF LETTER TO THE RESPONDENT AND THANK FOR HELP]



INTERVIEWER'S QUESTIONS

14.  What sex is the respondent?                  _____
                      Male                         _____
                      Female                       _____

15.  Socio-Economic group of respondent           _____
```

7 *Shop audits* counting of stocks of particular product
lines (both on shelves and in stock rooms) and recording of
deliveries. Sales over a period can be calculated from this
data. (Firms paying for this research often want to know
about competitors' sales, as well as their own.)

8 *Omnibus surveys* to save on both time and money, groups of
questions about different products or services are included in
one questionnaire. (Costs can then be shared between
several clients.) Omnibus surveys are often conducted at
regular intervals with, of course, different sets of
respondents on each occasion.

Other research methods

The most important are those shown in the box below.

Method	Uses	Advantages/ Merits	Disadvantages/ Problems	Comments
1 Telephone	To contact large numbers of people at same time. When respondents are at a distance from interviewers (and each other).	Takes very little time and is inexpensive. Can be timed to coincide with events (Have you seen our advert on TV?).	Lack of face-to-face contact. Cannot use prompt cards, pictures, etc. Not everyone on the telephone (biased sampling?).	Increasing use of telephone in M R. Good for industrial MR.
2 Direct Mail	When respondents are difficult or inconvenient to contact.	Low cost. No interviewer bias. Mailing lists can be bought easily.	Still difficulties in getting a totally reliable mailing list. No guarantee that replies are truthful. Questions must be few and simple. Low response rate.	People replying may be unrepresentative of the sample as a whole.
3 Counting/ observation	When numbers of people doing various activities are required.	Cost very low. Bias not a significant problem. High degree of accuracy obtained.	Very limited types of data obtained. Only notes what happens: not why.	Sometimes done mechanically (eg electric cords on road surfaces counting vehicles passing).
4 Self-Completion	To get data on purchasers of products. Forms included with instructions, guarantee cards, etc.	Response rate can be higher than Direct Mail, prizes if offered for completion and return. Little cost.	Those completing not likely to be representative of the universe.	Used by magazines to get data on their readers and by manufacturers of consumer items.

Some research methods (other than Test Marketing and Face-To-Face contact)

1 *Telephone.* This method is disapproved of by some marketing research agencies, and the association of Professional Opinion Polling Organizations, on the grounds that the use of the telephone has a built-in bias in favour of higher-income households. However, an increasingly large share of the MR market (possibly as much as one third), is taken up by telephone research.

Agencies in this field claim their sophisticated computer programs provide suitable samples, and the progress of the survey can be tightly controlled (all researchers work in the same room). Charges are as low as 10% of amounts charged for face-to-face interviewing. Up to 40 calls per researcher per day can be made.

Against this, it can be argued there is no visual contact with respondents, no opportunity to use visual aids, no real feedback about the respondent's personality. And current estimates show 19 per cent of UK households are still without telephones.

2 *Direct Mail.* Since no interviews are involved, this method is cheap, with few bias problems. If respondents are scattered widely, then direct mail becomes a viable choice.

Whilst mailing lists can be bought easily, they quickly become out of date. The rate of response can be as low as 5 per cent, but improved responses can be engineered by using reply-paid, stamped addressed envelopes and by having a limited number of simple questions, with a 'personal letter' from an executive of the enquiring organization.

3 *Counting observation.* Already discussed in this block.

4 *Self-completion.* Research, particularly into the social class, age, and sex, of purchasers of household equipment can be easily and cheaply carried out. Pre-addressed, simple questionnaires on reply-paid cards invite purchasers to give information about themselves.

Summary of skills

The intention of the study in this Block is not only to learn facts about marketing but also to develop skills which will be of use in the business world.

Skills

Skill	*Activities in which skill is developed*
a Learning and studying	All activities
b Communicating	All activities
c Identifying and tackling problems	1,2,4,5,6
d Information gathering	2,3,4,5,6
e Working with others	All activities
f Numeracy	5,6
g Design and visual discrimination	6

Block 4
Making Sense of Researched Data

Introduction

So far you have gained an insight into how marketing research is organized, and have discovered some of the ways in which a survey is planned and conducted. The current task is to make sense of the data obtained, to analyse and incorporate it within an acceptable format for management to consider — that is, to present it as a formal marketing research report.

Part of the data processing activity is forecasting trends. We shall examine this aspect as a separate topic.

Research, like any other business activity, has to be paid for. You will need to become aware of the kinds of cost involved.

Anyone who has carried out marketing research will have encountered problems and difficulties. In the final part of this block you will be looking at these problems, and other constraints affecting research.

Collating data

With multiple-choice questions, or those with attitude or bi-polar scales, it is easy to code each answer (See Block 3, *Marketing through Research*). Even with open-ended questions there could be five or six 'popular' answers which again could be coded. All this makes data collation a simple, if routine, task. Agencies these days have appropriate computer programs to simplify the process even further.

Some agencies use questionnaire forms specially designed for OMR (optical mark reading). The interviewer marks responses on the questionnaire with a soft pencil. (Each possible answer has a rectangle on the right of the questions e.g. ☐ Each chosen answer is recorded by drawing a line across the rectangle: ☐. The OMR equipment 'reads' the mark, and the data is passed to a computer for processing.

Where the work is done manually, all the forms need to be checked, then analysed one question at a time. The percentages of each option chosen can be calculated.

Open-ended questions are more difficult. All you can do here is to summarize the points made under four or five headings.

Interpreting the data

The collated data then needs to be interpreted for the eventual reader, with any recommendations that might be appropriate. Layout is important: lots of lists and tables tend both to mystify and bore the client. It is essential that data is organized into a form easily understood by the reader. Simple tables are useful, but it is better, to use techniques you should be well acquainted with by now: pie-charts, histograms, line graphs, and bar charts. These are used to illustrate percentages or highlight trends. (More recently, use is being made of animated computer graphics.)

Activity 1	Using the survey completed for Activity 6 (2) of Block 3, *Marketing through Research*:

1 Collate, review, and analyse the data.
2 List the findings.
3 Prepare visual aids to illustrate the findings.
Remember the use of colour, shading, etc. with charts, graphs and diagrams.

A marketing research report

Most marketing research reports are not written for experts and specialists in marketing. When companies commission research it will be general management (accountants, directors, senior managers) who are likely to read it. Care has to be taken to submit the report in such a way that it is readable, easy to understand, and has an air of authority.

Whilst you will have had previous experience in report-writing, there are features of marketing research reports you should note.

Marketing research report

Title page:	Title of report; name of client; name of agency
Contents page(s):	Includes list of Appendices

Preface:	Description of problem to be investigated
	Purpose of report
	Synopsis of main findings, conclusions, recommendations
	Glossary of special terms used
Terms of reference:	Numbered, precise, and crystal clear
Structure and Programme of Project:	Stages of project-history or its progress
	Research methods used
	Sources of primary data
	Sample size and composition
	Fieldwork programme
	How data obtained was analysed
Findings:	Data revealed by research considered relevant and significant
Conclusions:	All based on findings
Recommendations:	If any; if applicable to particular survey
Appendices:	More detailed account of the sampling method used, including how it came to be chosen, and its level of reliability
	Copies of any questionnaire used
	Detailed analysis of statistics and tables; charts, diagrams, to illustrate references to other material

Outline of a marketing research report

The report layout

1 *Title page.* Besides the formal title of the report, both the name of the client (or sponsor) and that of the agency (or people carrying out the survey) should appear on this page.

2 *Contents page.* This *is* needed. Busy executives may only want to refer to particular parts of a report, or a specific graph or diagram. (With reports you prepare, page numbers might have to be left until the report is completed.)

3 *Preface.* This is, in effect, a general introduction to the report. It explains to the reader the details of the problem upon which it is hoped the research will shed some light, or details the mutually-agreed objectives. For example:

Before launching a new version of your computer
program, you wished to know which features current

> users preferred left unchanged, which were no longer
> needed, and which extra features should be provided.

The preface will then go on to describe how the agency
identified the users' views.

A synopsis, a very brief précis of the main findings,
conclusions, and recommendations (if any), follows. This is
to enable a busy manager to understand what conclusions
have been drawn from the research, without having to
plough through a lot of detail first. (The detail of the report
may be passed on to marketing or sales staff for a closer
evaluation.)

Finally, it is suggested that a glossary of unusual terms used
(with brief definitions) should appear at this stage.

4 *Terms of reference.* No report should be without terms of
  reference.
  Preferably each separate term should be numbered.

> 1 To describe the problem as presented to us.
> 2 To explain how we tackled the problem; the methods
>   and techniques used; sources of data, and details of
>   sample size and composition.
> 3 To detail the fieldwork programme, and the results
>   obtained; to explain how the data was analysed.
> 4 To set out the findings of the research, with our
>   conclusions.

(The report should by now have strict guidelines and should,
section by section, follow the pattern laid down.)

5 *Main body of the report.* Here terms of reference numbers 2
  and 3 will be covered. (Note all this part will be strictly
  factual.)

6 *Findings.* This section is a summary (possibly with a
  commentary) of the data revealed by the fieldwork. (The
  details will usually be left to Appendices, though if some
  data is particularly vital or significant it would be quoted in
  detail at this stage for emphasis.)

7 *Conclusions.* As with all conclusions in reports, these should
  follow logically from the findings.

8 *Recommendations.* Not every report will contain
  recommendations. Where they *do* appear, they should
  follow logically from the findings. (A great deal will

depend upon the original terms of reference. If an agency is commissioned just to provide data, say about reactions to certain advertisements, it will be up to others like the client or his advertising agency to decide on what action to take.)

9 *Appendices.* All the technical data can be included here: sampling methods and their degree of reliability; a copy of each kind of questionnaire used, and an analysis of respondents' replies; charts, diagrams, tables, and lists.

Any references to published sources should be given.

Activity 2	Individually, or in groups of three or four, write a complete report on Activity 6 (2) of Block 3, *Marketing through Research* incorporating the detail already prepared as part of Activity 1 in this block.

Forecasting Techniques

Data and information which are up-to-date and relevant are essential in good decision making. Where routine decisions are taken about *the present* (shall we re-order stock today?) the data required is usually easily available, and up-to-date. Decision making is straightforward: we can often leave it to a computer system to handle. When we look at less routine decisions (which are likely to be **planning decisions**: shall we revamp our product, or replace it with a new one? how many shall we plan to make for the first run? shall we persevere with a loss-making product for another year?), we realize that they are about *the future.*

The future is by definition uncertain, and anything that can be done to make it less so is welcome. Forecasting attempts to do just this. Forecasting techniques are of two distinct types: the first we might call **formalized considered opinion,** and the second group is based on an assumption that the future will resemble the past. (This group mostly consists of statistical formulae, operating on known data.)

Synthetic forecasting

The verb **to synthesise** (from which **synthetic** is derived) means 'to combine separate items into a whole'. In synthetic forecasting, then, forecasts are built up by taking data and information from a variety of sources. Suppose we need to predict the money value (for next year's budget, for example) of the total product sales of our organization Product Engineering Ltd.

This diagram sets out the various sources of data and information.

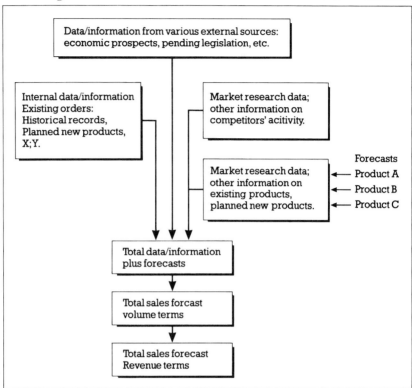

Product Engineering Ltd.
— Demand Forecast

Looking at the diagram we can see data/information is available from three sources:

1 *Internal to the company.* This would include definite orders on the books relating to the budget period (very firm data); records of past sales for trends upwards, steady, or downwards (useful guidance data); knowledge of progress towards the launch of new products X and Y (fairly reliable), and knowledge of what the total capacity would be (fairly firm).

2 *Marketing information.* Some information will be obtained by **market research** on competitors' activity (firm), and sales potential for products X and Y (customer surveys). An assessment of the firm's advertising programme will give some estimate of expected effect on demand.

Sales force opinion will be canvassed. Every sales representative will be invited to make sales forecasts, product by product, in his/her territory. (The reliability of such forecasts will depend upon the calibre of the sales people, their knowledge of the market, and the number of customers. It is a good method where the market has a few, very significant customers.) Similar estimates will be canvassed from export sales staff and overseas agents.

Test marketing (the 'pilot launch' of a product in a small area of the country to see how it sells) could be a useful source of extra information, particularly for products X and Y.

3 *External information.* This is secondary data, as mentioned in Block 3, *Marketing through Research.* Government. department publications, newspapers, TV, etc. provide data and information on the economy in general. Of particular relevance are proposed tax changes, interest rate fluctuations, government initiatives and interventions.

All this information will now be collated; eventually a sales forecast will emerge. Skill is required at this stage: no one source is likely to give a trustworthy or complete assessment of the future.

Analytic forecasting

This form of forecasting essentially makes predictions based on the past. The different techniques all rely on obtaining precise information on past outputs and sales, and calculating trends in, or projections into, the future. It looks quite scientific but there are two drawbacks: first it is assumed that the marketing environment will not change fundamentally—which may turn out not to be true, and secondly, much of the data available will not be current. Techniques include:

1 *Extrapolation* (projecting forward.) This can take various forms (one of which is illustrated below.) Company 'X' finds that its sales graph since 1985 has moved steadily upwards. In 1990 it bases forward estimates on the same upward trend.

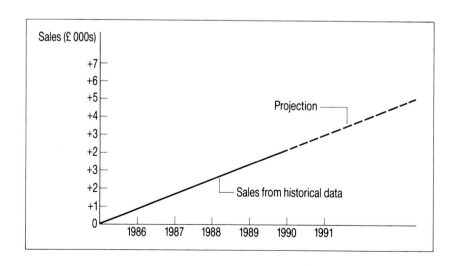

2 *Averages* Taking past monthly sales, and 'averaging' the last 12 for which there are data, provides us with an average monthly sales figure. Provided sales are steady, this could be useful to predict from, but many product sales can have wide monthly fluctuations and seasonal variations. Past experience could be used to add or subtract from the arithmetical average to arrive at a better estimate. (With the '12 month average' system, as each new month's figure becomes available we jettison the oldest figure, leaving only 12 at any one time.)

A way of 'smoothing out' the fluctuations is to take averages of averages by using 'QMAs', or quarterly moving averages; that is, we take three months' totals at a time. This method helps to identify underlying trends up or down.

Activity 3	Table 4. 1 shows the monthly sales over two years of Whizzo, a soap powder, in thousands (000s).

Table 4.1: Sales figures — Whizzo

Month	Year 1	Year 2	Month	Year 1	Year 2
Jan	22	22	July	25	26
Feb	24	26	Aug	16	18
Mar	20	24	Sept	14	20
Apr	18	20	Oct	26	26
May	24	28	Nov	21	22
Jun	18	20	Dec	24	26

1 Using these figures calculate the average monthly demand (AMD) from January to December for both Year 1 and Year 2.
2 Calculate, using the 'moving AMD' method, forecast sales for July (ie by using the average of the figures July Year 1–June Year 2), August, and December for Year 2. Compare the variances between the forecast and the actual sales.
3 Calculate QMAs for Year 1, and use these as predictors for Year 2: compare these figures with actual quarterly sales. (Again note the differences.) Then work out a suitable percentage figure (which would represent the underlying upward sales trend) to apply to the QMAs to bring them close to the actual figures.

A third method is to give more weight (or importance) to the most recent figures; the **exponential smoothing** technique. To make a prediction for the future (P) three items of data are needed. Two are from the immediate past: the estimated sales in period 'O' (the preceding or 'old' period); the 'old' (or preceding) forecast; and the actual sales in period 'O'.

The third element is a **smoothing factor** 'X' (which is normally between 0.1, and 0.3). The formula is:

Forecast for 'P'$=$(X) (latest actual sales, period '0') $+$ (1–X) (old forecast),

where P $=$ next period, 0 $=$ last period, and X $=$ the smoothing factor.

Applying the formula to Whizzo, assume the forecast for July last was 20 000 packets; and the actual sales were 18 000, we get:

$$\text{Forecast for August} = (0.2 \times 18) + (0.8 \times 20)$$
$$= \quad 3.6 \qquad + \quad 16$$
$$= \quad 19.6 \text{ (thousand)}$$

3 *Correlation* Correlation is a method used when a firm believes its sales vary with some quite independently calculated figure — such as the UK Gross National Product (GNP) — especially if there is a time lag between the two variables. It might be found, for example, that when GNP increases by 3 per cent, Whizzo's sales increase the following period by 2 per cent.

Predictions can then be made. This is a method to be treated with extreme caution. Causal relationships of this kind are difficult to prove; and again there is the assumption that the future will resemble the past.

Marketing research costs

The costs of marketing research will differ from one organization to another; a great deal depends upon how research is handled. Costs tend to collect under three main headings:

1 *Fixed Costs* A totally organization-based marketing research operation is very expensive. There will be a need for permanent staff (manager, assistant manager, executives, clerks, statisticians, fieldwork supervisors, etc.). Contracting out

to agencies as and when required will reduce fixed costs (of, for example, a manager, assistant, and a secretary) to a small percentage of the total.

2 *Semi-Fixed Costs* Subscriptions to (market research) journals, and membership of marketing research associations come under this heading, as well as some research which is organization-based, (ie, regular or continuous work plus training costs).

3 *Variable Costs* Each individual study done as a separate *ad hoc* activity, whether organization-based or contracted out will be a variable cost. (It will include briefing sessions for field supervisors; the briefing and training of field workers, fees and travelling expenses, paid either direct or as part of an agency fee.)

Problems and constraints in marketing research

1 *Errors* There are many potential sources of error in marketing research. The sample of population chosen for investigation may be incorrectly identified or too small, or the questions they are asked may be incorrectly phrased.
2 *Bias* Not only can bias be found in questions, but also in interviewers who might prefer to interview some kinds of respondents rather than others. Respondents may well give the sort of replies which they feel will be acceptable to or which will not offend the interviewers.
3 *Constraints* Money and time are the most significant constraints in marketing research. An under-funded (and possibly-understaffed) survey; one carried out with too small a sample, or done with too little preparation, or done with undue haste-all will stand every chance of producing inaccurate results.

| *Activity 4* | Consider Activity 6 in Block 3. Either individually or in groups, examine the problems and constraints you faced in doing this piece of marketing research. In particular, make a list of what you felt were: 1 The significant problems or constraints encountered. 2 How you overcame them (or failed to do so). Finally, indicate: 3 How reliable you feel the data you obtained was. 4 What changes, if any, you would make if you were to carry out a similar survey in the future. |

Summary of skills

The intention of the study in this unit is not only to learn facts about marketing but also to develop skills which will be of use in the business world. This section at the end of each block indicates the skill areas covered by each activity.

Skills

Skill	Activities in which skill is developed
a Learning and studying	1,3
b Communicating	1,2,4
c Identifying and tackling problems	All activities
d Information gathering	1,4
e Working with others	All activities
f Numeracy	All activities
g Design and visual discrimination	1,2.

Block 5
How Purchasing Decisions are Made

Introduction

Successful marketing of products or services depends upon a variety of important factors. Amongst these is the ability of a supplier to identify correctly (and in advance) the needs and wants of customer — by marketing research perhaps; or the ability to supply attractive products and services at competitive prices to meet the needs and wants identified. An obvious essential condition is the presence of a sufficiently large number of potential customers or buyers with enough cash or credit resources to make purchasing decisions. But very important to suppliers is *how* and *why* do purchasing decisions come to be made?

If suppliers could answer these questions correctly then they would be in a very favourable situation indeed. At best they could predict what purchasers would do in any given set of circumstances, and therefore create the most favourable environment for the sales and marketing effort. At the very least they could make informed and correct decisions as to the precise way in which products or services should be offered or promoted — that is, they could design the ideal **marketing mix**.

This block introduces you to some of the current theories and so-called 'models of purchasing behaviour', which attempt to explain both human motivation and the factors and influences which effect purchasing decisions. It looks at the way particular selling techniques are used to persuade or induce customers or buyers to make favourable purchasing decisions.

Customers, buyers and consumers

These three words are often used in ordinary conversation as if they had the same meaning. In a marketing context, each has a precise and different meaning.

Customers are people or organizations who make contracts or agreements to buy goods or services from some other source. You and I are customers when we buy groceries or petrol, or visit the dentist. Organizations like firms or hospitals are customers when they buy raw materials for production, or drugs for use with patients, or when they use a security service to deliver cash for wages. (There are other kinds of customers who neither retain nor use the products or services they buy: wholesalers, middlemen, retailers, and agents buy from one type of source and resell to others.)

Buyers might be thought to be the same as customers. In fact this is the *job title* given to an employee within an organization entrusted with the specific responsibility of *organizing the purchase* of everything the organization might need: raw materials for production, stationery and office equipment, or motor vehicles for delivery purposes. So whilst from a *legal* point of view the organization employing a buyer would be the customer when a purchase is made, it is the buyer who actually places the order. Buyers are normally very skilled and experienced people, who are allowed to exercise considerable discretion in making substantial purchases. Selling to such people is a totally different operation from selling to the individual customer.

Consumers (sometimes called 'users' or 'final users') are those individuals, organizations, or parts of organizations who use, use up, or 'consume' products and services — just like you and I do when eating a packet of crisps, or travelling by train. Customers and consumers *can* be one and the same; but usually consumers 'consume' products and services bought for them by someone else. Children who receive presents from, or are clothed by, their parents, people who read magazines brought into the home by friends, or a maintenance department which gets through a batch of machine tool spares every month — all these are 'consumers' in a marketing sense.

Consumers *are* important. True, they don't necessarily *make* purchases, but they can (and often do) strongly *influence* what is bought, when it is bought, and where it comes from. Any enquiry, then, into purchasing behaviour must take into account consumers as well as customers.

Influences on purchasing decisions

Any decision a person makes is affected by an assortment of influences. Consider the cases of a 16-year-old faced with choosing between offers of a job or a full-time place at college to gain further qualifications; a 25-year-old contemplating a proposal of marriage ; a 55-year-old weighing up an offer of early retirement. In each case, major influences are likely to be **economic** (the financial costs and benefits of each course of action both short- and long- term); **psychological** (what kind of personality the individual possesses, what beliefs he or she holds, what driving motives or ambitions he or she has; or **social/environmental** (the social group the person comes from, the life-style he or she leads or aspires to, and what immediate family and friends, or even workmates, advise).

Organizational buying decisions are a little different: for professional buyers, **economic** factors assume on the whole greater importance; but buyers are people, and as such are influenced by relationships with sales personnel, and the pressures of the environment—other executives, for example, urging the purchase of goods quickly and 'never mind the price'.

The diagrams on the next pages show the individual as a customer (or consumer) and the organizational buyer, surrounded by a host of influences, some indeed conflicting. Perhaps you can see that there are both similarities and differences between the two. How many can you spot?

| *Activity 1* | Singly, or in groups, consider the following situations: |

1 Assuming you are 16 years' old, faced with choosing between staying at school to do 'A' levels, going to college to take a BTEC National Course, or leaving to find a job (with you hope, day-release for a National Certificate Course), make a list of *all* the influences and considerations you feel would have a bearing on your final choice. (Or which did so, if you have already made such a choice.) Try and group these influences as far as possible under the three main headings — **economic, psychological**, and **social/environmental.** (If you find any influences which don't seem to fit these general categories, to which other headings would you allocate them?)

2 Assume you are 20 years' old, live at home, and your

family have just moved to an area not served by public transport. You need a car or motorbike to get you to work. Make a list, grouped under headings as above, of all the influences you think would affect the final choice of vehicle, and where you get it from.

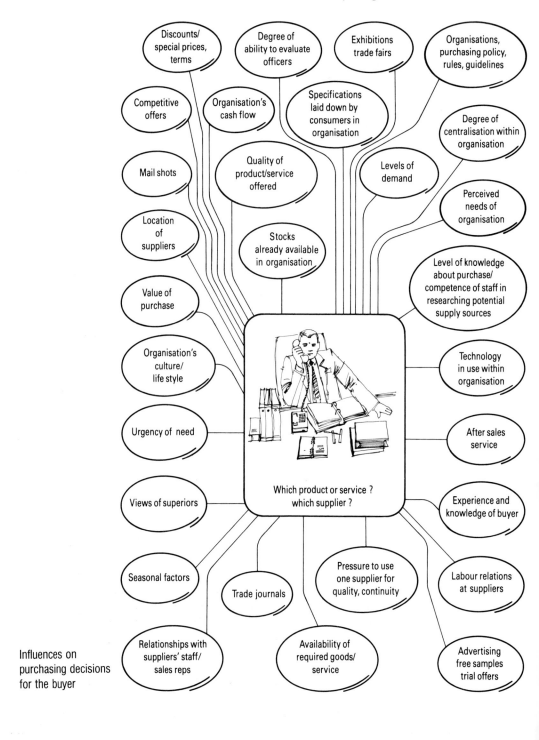

Influences on purchasing decisions for the buyer

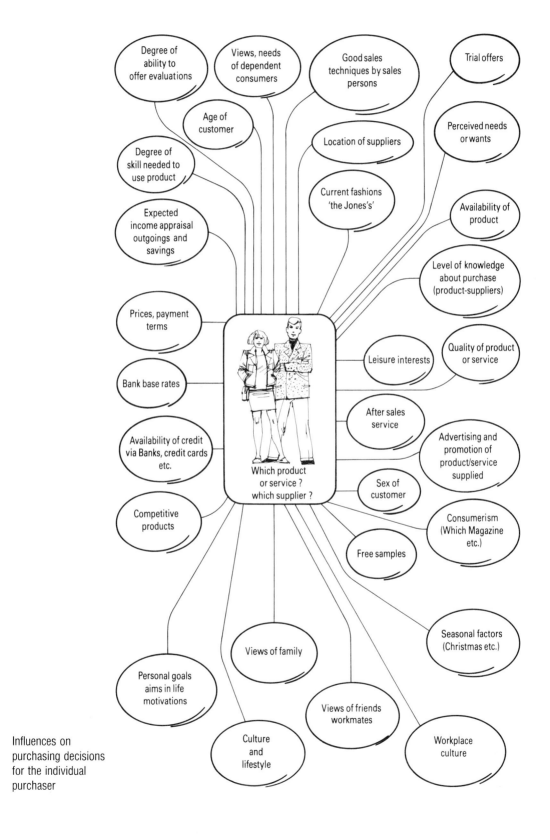

Degree of ability to offer evaluations

Views, needs of dependent consumers

Good sales techniques by sales persons

Trial offers

Age of customer

Location of suppliers

Perceived needs or wants

Degree of skill needed to use product

Current fashions 'the Jones's'

Availability of product

Expected income appraisal outgoings and savings

Level of knowledge about purchase (product-suppliers)

Prices, payment terms

Leisure interests

Quality of product or service

Bank base rates

Which product or service ? which supplier ?

After sales service

Advertising and promotion of product/service supplied

Availability of credit via Banks, credit cards etc.

Sex of customer

Consumerism (Which Magazine etc.)

Competitive products

Free samples

Seasonal factors (Christmas etc.)

Views of family

Personal goals aims in life motivations

Views of friends workmates

Workplace culture

Culture and lifestyle

Influences on purchasing decisions for the individual purchaser

Economic influences

Before considering some important economic influences on
buying decisions, it is worth looking at three mistaken ideas
about individual customer behaviour, arising from
assumptions made by nineteenth century economists. These
economists looked at their own purchasing behaviour, and
assumed that everyone else (rich or poor, young or old, clever
or otherwise) was as rational as they (the economists) were
at making choices. They eventually arrived at the following
conclusions (amongst others):

1 People are *rational* about choices (that is they consider
  carefully the pros and cons of buying particular goods and
  services).
2 People buy goods and services which will be useful to them.
3 People plan spending carefully so as to maximize the total
  benefits to be obtained (in terms of goods/services
  purchased) for a given amount spent.

It is clear that these assumptions are not necessarily true:
people do buy things they don't want (and sometimes don't
need). The lowest price is not always the ruling factor.
Many purchases, we say, are 'made on impulse'. In an
industrial/commercial context you might well think that
these assumptions held. But an examination of purchasing
decisions made by organizations reveals that even they are
not always rationally made.

The influences which are significant include:

1 The general economic situation

When the national economy is booming, people will tend to
spend more, particularly on household items. Conversely,
when the economy is depressed they will tend to spend less.
(Both these tendencies have been reinforced in recent years by
direct government intervention: alterations in interest
rates and the amount of borrowing allowed in the public and
private sectors, and variations in tax levels, direct and
indirect.)

People also seem, in times, of high inflation, to spend what
money they have more quickly, fearing its value will fall if it
remains unspent. They also become keener to borrow, with
the knowledge that their debts will decrease in real terms as
the value of money falls.

2 *Purchasing power*

People cannot spend what they do not have (or cannot borrow). Thus an individual's **purchasing power** depends upon the amount of money left over after all taxes and other deductions have been made from income; also subtracting all other regular outgoings (rent, rates, mortgage, and HP payments), but adding the amount of credit that can be drawn upon. (As you saw in Block 3, *Marketing through Research* it is useful for marketeers to classify people into different categories, each of which is likely to have different levels of purchasing power.)

Having purchasing power implies having a choice: not only between products, but between different versions of the same product.

3 *Credit availability*

It is hard to imagine a world without credit, but the increase in its availability in the last 20 years has been spectacular. (One in three adults in the UK has at least one credit card. We owed £22 000 million in 1986, and the total increases yearly.) Not only has the *amount* lent multiplied many times over, but the *forms* in which credit is available have also increased: Access and Barclaycard, other credit and charge cards, hire-purchase, budget accounts, 'revolving credit', overdrafts, and personal loans from building societies. The increasing amount of mortgage advances has helped the boom in home ownership. In turn, the demand for houses forced their prices up much faster than inflation. The result: millions of householders have an asset worth far more than the outstanding mortgage on the property, which extra value can be turned into cash by means of a second mortgage.

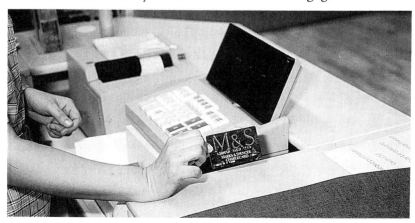

It's easy to use a credit card for purchases.

The important message here for marketeers is to be able to offer appropriate payment or purchase funding schemes, not only to promote the sales of products and services, but to meet or do better than the deferred packages of competitors. (Tesco now takes credit cards for food purchases.)

Strangely, the rate of interest charged does not seem, in itself, to put people off borrowing, provided the weekly or monthly payments can be spread over several years, and therefore the regular outgoing does not appear large.

| Activity 2 | A selection of methods of obtaining credit or borrowing facilities has been mentioned above. |

1 Look at each form of credit/borrowing method mentioned (and any others you can find) and make quite sure you understand clearly what each is, and how it functions. (For example, what exactly is meant by **revolving credit**, who offers it, what conditions do the lenders lay down, how expensive is it in interest terms?) It may be necessary to research in the library, in the pages of *Which?* or in financial publications.

2 You can extend this activity to preparing a portfolio of leaflets advertising literature, and application forms for credit cards, mortgages, etc.

3 Many of the credit facilities mentioned are more applicable to individual purchasers. What forms of credit are available to business organizations? (Don't forget to include such methods as issuing debentures, lease-buy arrangements, and delaying payments to suppliers.)

4 Price

Price and pricing are complex topics (already briefly discussed as one of the '4 Ps' in Block 2, *More about Marketing*). Here we will look at price as related to purchasing behaviour.

Economists have long maintained that the cheaper a product becomes, the greater will be the demand for it; and conversely, the more expensive it is, the less will be the demand. (That is assuming all other demand factors remain constant.) Whilst this generalization has a lot of truth in it, it is not the whole story.

Individual customers and consumers, as well as industrial/commercial buyers, often regard price as a mark of quality. In the early 1970s a well-known firm of lock makers put on the market a front door lock which was strong and reliable: a deterrent to intruders. Unfortunately it did not sell well. After taking advice, the company completely 'revamped' the packaging and general presentation. The lock was then relaunched at more than twice the original price. At the earlier, lower, price customers did not accept it as being the quality product it in a fact was. At the new, higher, price with more 'prestigious' packaging, it became much more acceptable.

In other situations price can be relatively unimportant: where delivery or immediate possession is an urgent requirement; where a product is new and 'trendy'; or where a particular price level is perceived to be the 'going rate'.

Considerations of these kinds must not be taken to suggest that people never want to buy low-priced goods — although it may be necessary to disguise them as 'bargains' or at 'sale' price (in itself attractive because it *is* low), with the higher 'crossed out' recommended retail selling visible price as a reassurance of quality! Some goods may indeed be offered *below* cost — that is, below the price the supplier has paid to possess the goods in their present form. Such goods are called **loss leaders**. Used widely in grocery shops and supermarkets, the hope is that, once enticed into the store by the promotion ('this week's special offer'), shoppers will put in the trolley not only the offer goods but enough other items to produce an overall profit at the check out.

Price cuts may be used to attract customers to switch brands, or to launch a new product or service. For example, in the summer of 1986 the then new BR Network South East was inaugurated with a special introductory offer on 'Network Day' of unlimited travel within the region (including the Underground) of £3 per head.

Industrial and commercial buyers are of course price conscious, often working to strict guidelines, budgets, or limits on expenditure, and will, for example, be looking for quantity discounts. Suppliers will often quote 'special prices' for uneconomic small orders in the hope of getting large repeat orders which would be more profitable. (Loss leaders in another guise!) A more aggressive version is to sell at cost (or even lower) to gain or maintain market share, when there is a glut of a product on the market. This policy has been widely used in the 1980s in the retail car market (where, for long periods, few cars were ever sold at list price), and in the oil industry when oil companies extracted and sold oil from expensive North Sea locations below the full cost of extraction. OPEC also used the same tactic in 1986 to keep market share.

Other price considerations are:

Price plateaux. There is some evidence that for many products or services there is an upper level of price beyond which people are reluctant to purchase. For a long time the 20p price level for tabloid newspapers (eg the Sun, Mirror) was a barrier that publishers were uneasy about breaking. **Psychological pricing** is a trick frequently used by suppliers when they price products just below the plateau level. £14.99 for a pair of jeans or leisure shoes means the £15 barrier is not breached.

Competitors' prices. What competitors charge cannot be ignored – especially if a firm wants to sell at a higher price than that charged by the majority of them. Once a recognized market price has been established, customers, consumers, and buyers will resist paying more than what they perceive as the 'going rate'. To get over this problem it is necessary to change the product in some way, so that in the eyes of potential purchasers it has a new feature, an extra benefit, or some exclusive quality which justifies the extra payment.

The 'going rate' can also be used as a price 'marker' from which to price downwards (though care must be taken not to make an operation unprofitable by doing so). When the *Today* newspaper was launched in 1986, it was priced at 18p as an

extra attraction to a market used to a 20p level. (However, after only a few weeks an upwards adjustment to 20p was found to be necessary.)

'Creaming off'. The launch of a revolutionary new product can be both an expensive operation (heavy development and pre-launch promotion), and a very profitable activity. Customers may well be prepared to pay a high price for the novelty value or the prestige of owning something avant-garde. The (now) humble ball-point pen, sold weekly by the million, began life soon after the second World War as a prestige object, and was in real terms hundreds of times more expensive than it is now. As sales increased the 'exclusivity' disappeared, and prices fell; but the initial price made the manufacturers a fortune. A second profitable phase followed as the appeal widened.

Activity 3	1 Visit a local shopping area on your own or in small groups, and choose three different types of retail outlet (for example a supermarket, a furniture and a clothes shop). In each case record how price is (or is not) used as an inducement to purchase, and compare the practices used by the different outlets. 2 Carry out a smaller exercise, this time looking through local newspapers, comparing how price is used in advertisements for cars, houses, and electrical goods. 3 Part-time students could analyse their organization's approach to pricing.

Psychological influences

This major heading covers a wide range of factors which have been identified as having some effect upon purchasing behaviour. Descriptions and explanations of these influences mainly involve drawing on ideas and concepts derived from the behavioural sciences. A major difficulty is that, whilst some generalizations about groups of people can be made, the behaviour of individuals is often complex and not easy to predict. You would be wise to be careful about accepting theories or models of behaviour which claim to have universal application.

Behavioural scientists argue that the range of buying choices open to people is dependent upon individual, internal (psychological) processes. These scientists would suggest that, to make sense of peoples' purchasing choices, you need to look at the way they perceive the world, the beliefs and attitudes they hold, and their motives for doing things. You also must consider the standards of behaviour (called **norms**) to which they subscribe; or what they believe to be normal or usual behaviour within a community or social group. We shall consider all these.

1 *Perception*

Perception is the process of making sense of the world around us. Every moment of our lives we are subjected to numerous external stimulation via our senses. It is impossible for us to note, record, and evaluate all of it. The best we can do is to make a *selection* of the data received, and base our view of the world (perceptions) upon that. (This has implications for advertisers: we ignore most of the advertising messages we receive!) Perception can be influenced by where we start to look; by expectation or desire. If we are looking for a particular tin of baked beans on a shelf, we will undoubtedly find it more easily if we know what it, or its label, looks like.

The main elements of perception which help us to group the data we do select are:

a **Proximity** (or nearness). We have a tendency to believe that things which are near to each other 'belong' to each other. Seeing one reminds us of the other. Marketeers use this idea of association frequently: leading sports personalities are often associated with specific products, and companies vie with one another to sponsor sports meetings, test matches, or football clubs, to be associated with something popular and successful.

b **Similarity** (or likeness). This is the tendency to group items which appear to be similar together. Advertisers make use of similarity to encourage (and occasionally discourage) associations between products (or services) and particular groups of people: 'Elegant old terrace awaits elegant young buyers', 'Beans for beanpoles' (advertising weightwatchers' Heinz Beans).

c **Continuity** is another grouping activity in which separate elements (such as a series of dots) can be visualized as a straight line, circle, or square. It is closely related to **closure** (or completeness, or symmetry) where our minds 'fill in' gaps in data which appear to be missing. A clever device is to get advertisement readers to supply missing letters, syllables, or whole words: 'Schhh! . . . you know who!'.

2 *Attention*

You have already noted that we can only process a small amount of the data available to us at any one time. We are likely only to attend to what interests us at the moment: we glance at the television to watch the climax of a race, the winning goal, the final shot – and then go back to reading the paper or talking to someone. We say our attention *wanders* from one thing to another.

The factors which lead us to attend to one thing rather than another are first **objective** (that is they relate to the nature of the event or data being scanned), and secondly **subjective** (that is they relate to feelings and emotions within ourselves).

Objective factors include **intensity** and **size** (loud sound; bright colour) which attract attention. **Change**, **position**, and **movement** (neon signs, moving displays in a shop window) are all important. So is **repetition** (like the famous 'My Goodness, my Guinness!' advertisements, which acted as purchasing 'reminders' – but the message was shown in different situations which combined repetition with **novelty**). People are normally curious about anything new, and may even buy it just because it *is* new. (Potential readers clamoured for the first edition of *Today*, for example.) Thus 'new' is one of the most popular words used to influence buying behaviour – along with 'Improved'.

Subjective factors are those instinctive feelings, acquired tastes, views, and interests which largely dictate to what we actively direct our attention. Fear, sex, curiosity, maternal instinct; the wish to be successful, glamourous, trendy – any or all of these can arouse, and direct, our attention. Customers, consumers, and buyers will be more interested in advertisements for products or services in which they already have an interest – and will be more likely to purchase them.

3 *Attitudes*

A complex topic, much of which is very theoretical (and open to argument). For our purposes we can define an attitude as a **position taken** or **viewpoint held** about:

a an idea, doctrine, or principle – moral, religious, political, etc.

b people and their behaviour.

c things, including products and services.

We can therefore talk about our attitudes to privatization, people who smoke in public places, or buying products made in foreign countries. All our attitudes have been learned over time (usually from others, and at an early age), are long-lasting, and difficult to alter. There are some areas, however, in which people have only vague, imprecise attitudes; or even no attitudes at all.

From a marketing point of view, attempts to create attitudes where none existed in any meaningful form, can be very rewarding-as pressure groups such as CND, the Consumer Association, or those connected with the 'natural food' movement (pure food with no additives, etc.) have demonstrated. (The number of 'believers' in 'healthier eating' doubled between 1983 and 1985.)

Other campaigns aimed at attitude-changing in the 1980s include British Rail advertisements stressing the roominess, comfort, and freedom from strain provided by rail travel, to try and persuade both air-shuttle and car drivers to change their travelling habits; British Nuclear Fuels PLC issuing invitations to the public to visit Sellafield in the wake of the Chernobyl disaster to reassure Britons of the safety measures taken in our nuclear energy production. There was also for a time a fascinating battle between Qualcast and Flymo to try and convert gardeners to (or from) buying 'hover mowers'. Other, typical, ways in which attitude-change is attempted are where stress is laid upon qualities or characteristics of a product known to be important: ('additive free'; 'can be cooked in a microwave'; 'soluble in water' (of junior paracetamol). Again there is the use of **image building** in which a total package is offered of a sound product, excellent after-sales service, and friendly, helpful staff. The latter (used by both the RAC and the AA) is a more long-term attitude-change approach.

What is quite clear is that an unhappy experience with a product or service will produce an adverse reaction in people –

Advertisement campaigns aimed at changing attitudes.

a change in attitude against the product or service. Any anxieties a purchaser might have about a choice made – especially if the purchase were expensive (a car, a computer, or a house, for example) – will be heightened by finding favourable reports about rejected alternatives later. Where a product is bought regularly, the effect on future sales could be serious. The message here is not to make exaggerated claims, which cannot be substantiated, for products.

Activity 4	In groups of three select at least two quite different advertisements from:

In groups of three select at least two quite different advertisements from:
1 a Sunday newspaper's colour supplement
2 a woman's magazine
3 a trade or professional magazine (eg New Scientist or Marketing)
Through discussion, analyse and evaluate each advertisement in terms of:
1 the elements of perception (use of proximity, similarity, etc.)
2 the attention-getting strategies used (intensity, size, sex).
3 the extent to which any degree of attitude-change is attempted.

4 Motivation

You will probably by now have come-across the subject of motivation in the context of 'getting the best out of people' (at work), by recognizing their needs and wants, and then providing means of satisfying them. However, motivation has a much wider application than just the work situation – after all, work cannot supply *all* our needs. (Nor does everyone 'work' in the employment sense.)

You will remember that in Block 1 we discovered that the task of marketing in an organization was first to identify or anticipate customers' needs, then to satisfy them efficiently, and at a profit. Can you see the similarity in the two situations – work and marketing? Both aim to identify needs and satisfy them. Thus motivation in buying behaviour is a very similar process to work motivation.

In this block we shall only look at two motivation theories, being the two most applicable to marketing: Maslow's *Hierarchy of Needs* (1943), with two derivatives, Alderfer's *ERG Theory* (1969), and Pope's *Seven Deadly Sins*; and Vroom's *Expectancy Theory* (1964).

Motivated behaviour can be described as having four stages: Stage I is where a need or want is noticed, identified, or arises. (You suddenly feel thirsty while on a walk on a hot afternoon.) The response (Stage II) could be to make for the

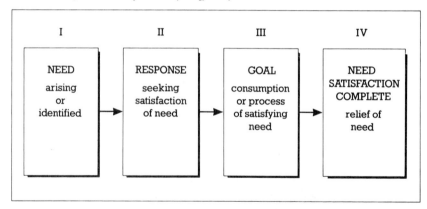

The process of need satisfaction

nearest place where soft drinks are sold, and to buy a can of fizzy lemonade. Quickly opening it and drinking it, you pass to the consumption stage (Stage III – Goal Achieved). Feeling refreshed, your need has been satisfied; your thirst quenched (Stage IV). Maslow's *Hierarchy of Needs* assumes the Need → Response → Goal → Need Satisfaction model is a correct one, but goes on to examine needs more carefully, splitting them into five broad categories, as shown in the diagram below.

The 'Level 1', **physiological needs,** are the most basic, and according to Maslow, require regular satisfaction. This being the case, instead of suddenly becoming thirsty, and being caught unawares, you could plan ahead and buy your lemonade before you set out. However, some walkers will not be so organized, and any soft drinks sellers in the right place at the right time will benefit.

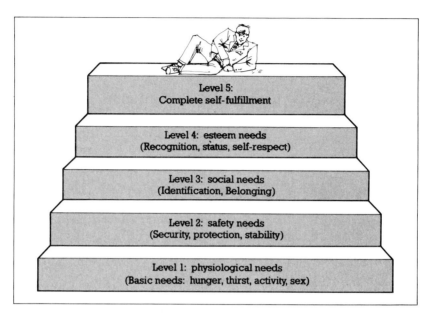

Maslow's hierarchy of needs

Maslow believed that the *order* of the levels of need is important, maintaining that as needs on one level are satisfied, so those on the next level surface, become dominant, and require satisfying. When Level 1 needs are satisfied, Level 2 needs will surface – and so on. Only *unsatisfied* needs motivate people to do things (including purchasing goods and services).

A major division is found between Levels 2 and 3. Below Level 3 are the physical needs for the maintenance of life. Safety needs are great motivators: the need to have an ordered life, a safe place of one's own to live in, provision for the future. People strive hard for these goals.

Above Level 2 are the **psychological needs**. The need to belong, to be identified with others, is a strong one (Level 3), as is the need to give and receive affection. Again, people want respect, to have status in their group (Level 4); to feel important, to be wanted and useful. At Level 5 the need to develop the whole personality, to be creative, to make the best use of our talents emerges.

Maslow's theory, whilst incomplete and open to criticism, is still a useful explanation of a wide spectrum of behaviour. It has great relevance for marketeers. Identifying which needs are important for particular individuals or groups means we will know *what* to offer (or *how* to offer what we have). A soft drinks manufacturer might seem only to satisfy Level 1 needs, but if he realizes that his potential market consists of people wishing to 'get on in the world' (Level 4,) or social status), then he will feature his lemonade in glamorous, up-market surroundings, with the implication that only people of distinction use the product. (There was once an advertisement which read: 'Top People Read *The Times*' which had a similar intent.)

The DIY market has homed in on Level 5 aspirations: a whole range of offerings to the amateur builder, decorator, or home improver is available, from near ready-made equipment just needing final assembly, to kits involving hours of planing, shaping, painting, and varnishing. Advertising dwells partly on price with a Level 5 touch ('. . . a craftsman finish at a price you can afford . . .'), but also stresses ease of home assembly, the pride of achievement in completing the job, or the approval of others ('. . . give your wife the kitchen of her dreams. . .').

Alderfer compresses the five Levels into three: **existence needs** (Levels 1 and 2); **relationship needs** (3 and part of 4), and **growth needs** (part of 4 and 5). He then adds that these needs are either **chronic** (there all the time), or **episodic** (only there part of the time). It is important for marketeers to realize that the approach to customers will need to be different in the case of purchases made only occasionally.

Pope's 'Seven Deadly Sins' theory is deadly simple! He maintains that the basic motivators are: **pride, covetousness** (wanting something possessed by somebody else), **lust, anger, gluttony, envy**, and **sloth** (the Biblical list). It is not difficult to find a multitude of advertisements where the persuasive approach touches upon one or more of these 'sins: 'At Sainsbury's you don't have to get up early to buy fresh doughnuts', '*Lumière* is a dazzling new *Rochas* . . . an appealing combination of freshness and sensuality', or even 'Selecting the right venue for the ultimate gastronomic experience is hard enough . . . thank goodness one doesn't have to worry about the aperitif'.

Vroom's 'Expectancy' theory of motivation, developed to explain work motivation, suggests that the level of job performance depends partly upon the effort put into the job, which, in turn, depends upon the value of the rewards offered (as perceived by the worker), and the probability (as perceived by the worker) that extra effort will bring the desired reward. By making appropriate substitutions we get a model such as this:

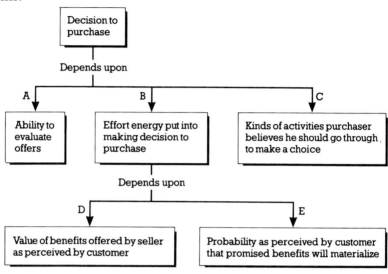

An 'Expectancy' model of purchasing motivation

A great deal depends here on both D and E; and the clear implication is that exaggerated claims (or claims the purchaser suspects *might* be exaggerated) are counter-productive in the long run. Also, if the benefits offered don't seem attractive, or 'different', the purchaser may decide not to buy. Marketeers keen to avoid this happening will try and out-class the competition by offering products or services with clear-cut differences (which are stressed as benefits).

The AA and RAC, on the face of it, offer very similar services. However in recent campaigns, whilst the RAC stressed their ability to attend to breakdowns with a high degree of promptness, the AA dwelt on their size, ability to have more patrols on the road, and *their* record of having attended more breakdowns in a year than their competitors.

| *Activity 5* | In groups of 3 or 4 work out which motivating factors you would use to appeal to potential customers/buyers in organizing campaigns to sell:
1 A computer dating service
2 A 49cc two-stroke 100 mpg moped with a 2-speed automatic gearbox and a 4-litre petrol tank at £299.99. (Price includes Road Fund Licence, number plate, 6 months' warranty, and 'L' plates.) |

3 A new range of culinary sauces (chilli and garlic; lemon and herb; spiced peppercorns).

4 A wall-safe, which when closed looks like a twin three-point 13 amp plug socket. Price £27.50.

5 A new after-shave for men, using very expensive perfume oils, selling at £14.95 for a 200ml. bottle.

Social and environmental influences

Another wide classification. Human beings are frequently in contact with others. To get what we want from others, we have to learn what kinds of behaviour are acceptable to them: their likes and dislikes. A consequence of this is that we will tend to conform to the ideas, attitudes, values, and life-styles of the groups with which we associate most. This leads to the existence of groups or classes of people with similar tastes, attitudes, and outlooks on life. The members of these groups are constantly interacting and exerting pressure (often subtle and unnoticed) upon each other to maintain a common set of values. The result is consistent behaviour.

Activity 6	1 As a class or large group discuss what you feel are the common characteristics of the group to which you belong at college. How far do you agree that the group acts as some kind of influence on each individual's behaviour? What happens when one member 'gets out of line'? 2 In small groups consider the other groups to which you belong – family, church, youth or sports club, political party, etc. Do these influence you in any way? How?

The fact that there are groups with definite and distinctive characteristics (age, sex, income level, education/qualifications, jobs, geographical origin, etc) is of profound significance to marketeers. It enables them to target groups with specific advertising, promotions, offers, products, or services. This is called **market segmentation** and is discussed later.

We shall need first, though, to look at **roles** and **status** within groups, and then go on to learn something of the structure and operation of the more important types of groupings/classifications used in marketing.

1 Roles

The word **role** reminds us strongly of actors – people with parts in a play or soap opera, say, who make sure they 'get inside' the part or role they play. 'Dirty Den' has to be convincingly devious; 'Bet Lynch' needs to look the part of a pub landlady. We say that the actors 'learn' their roles. So it is with us. It may surprise you to realize that we are all in a sense actors, with roles in our daily lives: we play the parts of children or parents; students or lecturers; customers in a supermarket; workers or bosses; the joker in the group, or the counsellor to others. We often move (without noticing it) from one role to another.

Each and every role has accepted ways of behaviour associated with it: overstep the limits to that behaviour, and it becomes a matter for comment or criticism by others in the group. When we get a new role (promotion at work, say), we immediately look around for clues and cues from others of the same grade to follow – which may mean wearing different clothes, not arriving late, or not having lunch with ex-colleagues.

2 Status and social class

Some roles are considered to be more important or **superior** to others (for example, that of a college principal, a managing director, or a committee chairman), whilst some are rated as less important or **inferior** (that of a porter, an operative, or a committee clerk). The degree of importance is usually dependent upon the power the role-holder has, and the wage, salary, or income he or she commands. We call this degree of importance the role-holder's **status**.

The idea of status ties in with that of **social class** which you met in Block 3, *Marketing through Research* in connection with marketing research (see pages 51–3). Social class is a term used to describe groups of individuals sharing common characteristics such as inherited wealth, particular types of jobs, and status. Some American studies carried out in New England, such as Lloyd Warner's, suggested that people in the same social class had similar buying habits, and that these habits varied from class to class. Other studies indicate that social class can be useful in predicting attitudes to products like cars, furniture, and clothes; and services like credit cards. For example Warner's study, *Social Class in America* (1960), suggested breakdown of buying habits by social class:

> Upper middle class
> Spend much on their houses and home fittings, live in *high class* neighbourhoods: have expensive furniture: often go to theatres and concerts.
>
> Lower middle class
> Live in good houses, but in less up-market neighbourhoods. Buy good furniture and clothes, but not from *high class* stores. Probably have a savings or deposit account.
>
> Upper lower class
> Live in small houses in less desirable areas; probably own an up-to-date model, medium range car; and a large TV set.

This research is not necessarily accurate for the UK in the 1990s, but the evidence suggests that differences *do* exist. That is why marketeers, when planning campaigns or launching products often take care to 'pitch' the appeal to specific groups. Marketing research may well be undertaken to find which newspaper, magazine, or TV region would be the most suitable to use to advertise to whichever group.

Note: There are drawbacks in pinning too much faith in social class as a guide to individual buying habits: there are poor earls, old-age pensioners who win the pools, and 'working-class' families with two, three, or even more wage-earners.

| *Activity 7* | In groups consider the problems of **social mobility**: people moving up (or down) the social scale. Do they change their habits as they rise or fall? Do pools winners behave like those who are rich from birth? Does a bankrupt ex-millionaire adopt working-class attitudes? |

3 Life-styles and market segmentation

Because of these difficulties in using social class in planning marketing campaigns, marketeers have turned to what is fashionably called 'life-style marketing'. A series of profiles of different kinds of people has been developed. The elements include **activities** (work, hobbies, sports, etc); **interests** (family, home, job, food community, etc); **opinions** (about themselves, social issues, politics, education, etc); and demographic details (sex, age, income, occupation, house, etc). These are known as the 'AIO' measures, from the initial letters of the first three elements.

Various attempts have been made to classify life-styles. A particularly notable example of this appears in *Marketing*, 12 June 1986 with Ken Crofton's 'On the trail of the Yuppie'. In *Marketing Times* (May–June 1976), R Bartos compared four categories of women: the stay-at home housewife, the housewife who plans to work, the working woman who says 'It's just a job', and the working woman who believes her work is a career. McCann–Erickson (advertising agents) have different lists for men and women. The following is a sample:

Men	Women
Avant-guardians	Avant-guardians
Pontificators	Lady righteous
Chameleons	Hopeful seekers (like to be always right)
Self admirers	Lively ladies
etc	etc

Lady avant-guardians are, for example, trendy, active, and sociable; somewhat 'liberal-left' politically; they buy products which are up-to-the-minute and fashionable, and have an independent life-style.

Taylor Nelson's 'Monitor' Unit has a different list which includes *self explorers, social resisters, experimentalists,* and *conspicuous consumers* (19 per cent of the population according to them).

These types are gathered into three broad groups: **sustenance motivated** (Maslow's Levels 1 and 2), **outer-directed** (concerned with material progress, 'getting on', and status (Level 4), and **inner-directed** (concerned with esteem needs; some Level 4, but mostly 5).

Activity 8	Find out all you can from other sources on 'life-style marketing'. (Try to obtain the *Marketing* articles 'On the trail of the Yuppie' and 'The Affluent Sociables' (issue 12 June 1986), and:

1 Discuss whether the life-style classification is a useful one in identifying groups of people with different buying habits.
2 Taking any of the lists you discover in the literature, analyse at least three advertisements – one in a colour supplement, one in a woman's magazine, one in a sports magazine – to see if there is any use of the life-style approach. If not, discuss how this approach might be used.

Market segmentation also makes use of life-style marketing. (This is the dividing up of a market into clear-cut and independent sub-groups of customers, with a view to choosing one or more sub-groups as a target market, with its own special marketing mix.) Market segmentation follows the basic definition of marketing; it attempts to match customers' and buyers' needs more accurately.

Types of marketing segmentation include:

a **Geographic** – for example, different foods, and wines for different areas.

b **Demographic** – age, sex, stage in life cycle. ('Young marrieds' are heavy purchasers of consumer durables and furniture.)

c **Socio-economic** – some evidence of contrasting types of expenditure, but UK marketing researchers tend to regard this segmentation as being of only marginal practical interest.

d **Life-style** – swingers, yuppies, punks, rockers, achievers, Sloane Rangers, etc

e **Volume of use** – heavy, medium, light, and non-users of products/services.

f **Benefits offered** - for example, lines of skin care products for those with dry/greasy skins.

g **Women's interests** – magazines for working women; Royal Bank of Scotland operating branches staffed by women to serve female customers.

Activity 9	Consider the 'life style' idea below which is based on some American findings:

1 **Bachelor stage:** young, single people

2 **Newly-wed/living together:** young, no children

3 **Full nest 1:** young marrieds/live-ins, with youngest child less than six

4 **Full nest 2:** as above, but youngest child over six

5 **Full nest 3:** older couples with dependent children, perhaps still studying

6 **Empty nest 1:** older couples, childless or children all left home

7 **Empty nest 2:** older couples, chief breadwinner retired

8 **Solitary survivor 1:** single/widowed person in work

9 **Solitary survivor 2:** as above, but retired

a Try and work out for yourselves (assuming the nine types mentioned come from a similar background to yours) what the earnings levels are for each type; and what take home pay might be spent on.

b What are the particular problems faced by people at each stage, which could affect purchasing activity (eg retired people experiencing a drop in income)?

h **Students** – banks, for example, look at the future potential of students/undergraduates who, they hope, will stay with them after graduation. Low interest loans are 'loss leaders' here.

After researching the chosen market segment, appropriate products and services can be devised with corresponding advertising and promotion.

| Activity 10 | Assume you work for a company which has just developed a new dried skimmed-milk powder with low fat content and added vitamins. A 200g tin sells for 65p (at 1988 prices) retail. |

Discuss:
1 Which particular group of people (ie which market segment) would be attracted by your product?
2 How you would design your advertising to appeal to that market?

i **Culture** – a culture can be a set of values handed down from generation to generation within a country or group of countries eg 'Western' values). There are also 'sub-cultures' – the 'Rock' movement, 'Goths', and 'Hell's Angels'; or strongly nationalist movements. Culture can also have a religious basis.

Models of individual purchasing behaviour

So far you have examined various ideas about the influences on buying behaviour put forward by a variety of people. To try and make sense of these ideas, you will need to consider several *models* of individual buying behaviour. None, however, is a total explanation of what you must have already realized is a very complex activity.

1 System-based models

You noted a basic systems model in the process of need satisfaction. A slightly more elaborate version is given here. It assumes a series of variables affecting buying decisions, which act as **stimuli** (or initiators).

Another version of the above is to have:

a **Stimulus variables** (as inputs) which are social/ environmental. They include:
      Products, advertisements, stories in the papers,
      Relatives, friends, workmates,
      Psychological needs.
b **Response variables** (as outputs) which are the observable reactions of individuals to the stimulus variables. They include:
      Discussions with sales people,
      Buying,
      Making objections, asking questions.

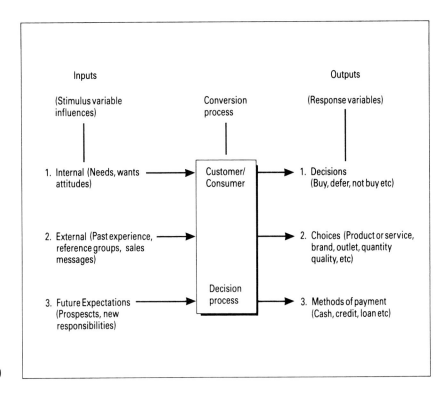

Buying process:
systems
model (variables)

c **Intervening variables** (to be found in the
'Customer/Consumer' box):
    Attitudes, beliefs, perceptions and aspirations,
    Motivations, moods, habits.

Both these versions can be further simplified to:
    EXTERNAL STIMULI ⇒ **INTERNAL STIMULI** ⇒ **DECISION**

2 Howard and Sheth model

Another 'systems' model. More complicated, but in essence
it suggests:
a **Inputs** which are the awareness of:
    some aspect of the product or service (quality, price,
        delivery)
    the social/environmental factors (class, family, culture,
        friends)
    the financial situation (availability of funds to purchase).
b **Conversion process** is first a search for, and processing of,
    data and information about a product or service. It leads to
    getting an idea of, and learning more about, the product or
    service, and how to assess its usefulness (choice criteria).

c **Outputs** are:
>   intentions, decisions
>   attitudes to the product or service purchases.

3 New product purchasing

The so-called **adoption process** models attempt to explain how new products (new, that is, to the customer) are bought. They have the following pattern:

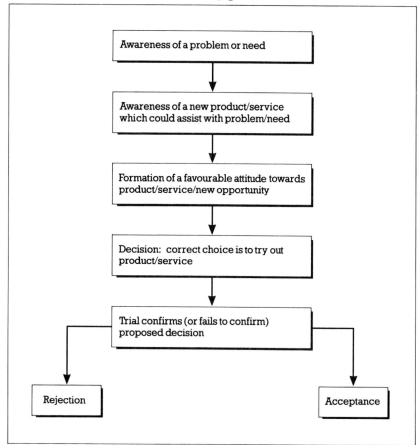

Choosing
a new product

Activity 11

1 In small groups, select a purchase made by one of you recently, and by looking at the models above, decide which one most accurately describes what actually happened. Would you make *all* purchases the same way?

2 In the same groups, discuss and list all the possible reasons why a potential customer might reject a product or service after an initial trial. (Choose a particular product or service known to you if you feel this will help you.)

3 When you have finished (2), try and classify your list under the following headings:

Product failures
Marketing failures
Customer attitudes (to product, brand, manufacturing, or service provider)
Outside influences (eg another, better product or service comes on the market)

4 *Decision-making based*

Some models view the purchaser as a 'rational' individual who does not 'buy on impulse'. Such models follow the traditional six-stage decision-making process, which you probably will have met already:

Step 1 Identify the problem or need.
Step 2 Gather all the relevant facts on product/services, and ways of satisfying the need.
Step 3 Analyse and evaluate the information obtained.
Step 4 Review all the possible options.
Step 5 Chose the best option, product, or service.
Step 6 Evaluate the choice after a lapse in time.

Note Step 5 could involve rejecting *all* the options in favour of a complete rejection of purchasing, a deferment, or starting from Step 2 all over again.

5 *AIDA and the sales approach*

A very simple model of the buying process taught for nearly seventy years to sales representatives. It maintains that a **prospect** (a potential customer) can be persuaded to make a favourable buying decision.

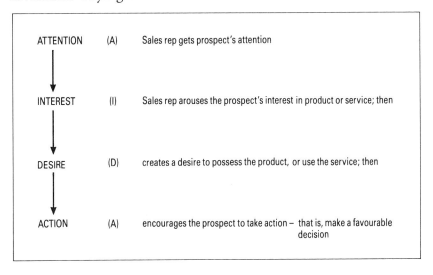

ATTENTION (A) Sales rep gets prospect's attention

INTEREST (I) Sales rep arouses the prospect's interest in product or service; then

DESIRE (D) creates a desire to possess the product, or use the service; then

ACTION (A) encourages the prospect to take action – that is, make a favourable decision

The Aida process

This model assumes the prospect to be somewhat captive; and under the influence of, and guided by, the sales representative throughout. (It is the 'ideal' situation from a salesperson's viewpoint.) In the real world, people do not always fall for salespeoples' charm. They may buy, but very unwillingly (because they feel compelled to); or fail to buy things they would in fact like to possess very much (perhaps because of other, more pressing, needs).

Organizational buyer behaviour

As you will remember from the remarks at the beginning of this block, organizational buyers have a very different role to play from that of the average individual going out shopping. Buyers rarely buy for themselves; nearly every purchase is for some other department, function, or person within the organization. Thus whilst the purchasing is done by individuals (the buyers), it is done in conjunction with other people working within the organization, who are in turn affected by the sort of environmental forces you will have come across in other studies. Organizational buying can therefore be influenced by individuals or groups of individuals, by general organization rules or policies; and/or by the economic and other influences on the organization.

Some other major differences between individual and organizational purchases are:

1 **Length of pre-purchase period**. As many people may be involved with a purchase, such as technical, research and development, marketing and sales, and production planning staff, and so on, the period from an initial enquiry to a potential supplier to the placing of a firm order for an item could be months – even years.

2 **Frequency of purchase/size of orders.** You probably shop monthly, weekly or even daily, and buy in small quantities. Buyers purchase at much less frequent intervals (the precise intervals will be largely dictated by re-ordering formulae outside our scope here), but usually in much larger quantities. Money values of orders can exceed tens of thousands of pounds.

3 **Direct purchasing.** Organizational buyers do purchase from middlemen (eg wholesalers), or local shops for small items, but in the main they deal direct with manufacturers, main dealers, or importers.

4 **Precision of requirement.** The buyer lays down the precise specification of the raw materials, sub-assemblies, or the type of service required (often after advice from others within the organization), and the required rate and method of delivery.

5 **Negotiation.** Buyers will negotiate over such matters as price, levels of discount, quality, and availability of items required. These negotiations can extend to agreements on forward commitments many months ahead.

6 **The organizational purchasing process.** A further difference between customer/consumer and organizational purchasing is that in the latter there is much more emphasis on planned decision making, often in accordance with laid-down procedures. In fact models of the organizational buying process are very like the well-known decision-making model. A fairly standard model is:

> 1 *Anticipation/recognition* of a need or problem. (Examples: the stock of a particular item is nearing the re-order level; a change in production methods necessitates new equipment and/or different qualities of material.)
> 2 *Working out* the quality, quantity, and general characteristics of the required product/service. More applicable to new products or equipment to be purchased. With *re-buys* – that is repeat orders – for existing purchases, this stage is a formality.
> 3 *Arriving at* precise descriptions and specifications for required products/ services.
> 4 *Search for* and contact with potential suppliers; including an assessment of their technical ability to supply.
> 5 *Evaluation* of offers and proposals from potential suppliers. (Again, 4 and 5 could be a formality in the case of re-buys from reliable suppliers.)
> 6 *Selection of supplier* and laying down of order processing routines. (May need to use more than one supplier for continuity of materials; or to 'play off' one against another.)
> 7 *Feedback evaluation* of supplier performance.

7 **The DMU (Decision making unit).** The DMU is the short name given to that group of individuals in the organization who have a hand in a purchasing decision. It will not always be the same group. The Board of Directors might authorize, say, the purchase of a £2 million item of plant. (They, in turn, might be influenced by technical or

production staff; and the buyer's own opinion.) A new lathe costing £40 000 might be authorized by a General Management Committee under the guidance of the Works' Director. An operating manager might order a special jig or tool worth £500, in collaboration with the buyer.

The product characteristics, assessment of the technical abilities of potential suppliers, evaluation of samples offered, and the eventual feedback evaluation might well be carried out by technical personnel. The buyer, in contrast, might have complete control over the search for suppliers, sending out enquiries, choosing the eventual supplier (with the approval of technical personnel), and handling re-buys.

The message here for marketeers is to ensure that sales representatives see the right people, according to the technical complexity of the product or service, the value of it and the degree of newness or innovation in the enquiry. Of course, protocol may demand that an initial contact is made through the buyer.

| *Activity 12* | In small groups decide who would be the major buying decision-maker, who would make recommendations, and who would conduct the buying negotiations in the following situations:

1 The purchase of a set of 100 VDUs linked to a central database with facilities such as electronic mail, etc, for a large firm having an extensive manufacturing plant (with roboticized production lines), offices, and sales showrooms on a single site.

2 The placing of a maintenance contract for repair and upkeep of 100 electric typewriters situated in the Business Studies Department of Wessex College of Further Education

3 The routine replacement of a sales representative's company car (Ford Sierra), after completion of 25 000 miles' travel, with a new model of the same make.

If there is time, also consider in each case with whom the sales person from a potential supplier would do best to conduct negotiations after the initial visit to the buyer.

A sales representative selling direct to organizations would do well to create a check-list to assist the search for the most useful contact at any particular stage in negotiations. This check-list will vary from product to product, and industry to industry, but would be on the following lines:

---

1 Who starts off the enquiry in the first place?
2 Who lays down the precise specifications of what is required including quantity (and perhaps price limits)?
3 Who looks for potential suppliers? Does he/she try one, two, or more sources?
4 Who sends out the enquiries?
5 Who evaluates the samples/free trials/quotations/estimates/tenders? What criteria are used to judge price, technical excellence, quality, delivery, etc?
6 Who authorizes the purchase to be made? (A key question – this is the first part of the most important decision.)
7 Who chooses the actual supplier(s)? (Second part of the most important decision - more than one supplier may be chosen.)
8 Who evaluates supplier's (or suppliers') performance
9 Who authorizes repeat orders?
10 Who decides if a change of supplier is required?

Purchasing risks

For organizational buyers, all purchasing carries risks: of ending up with unsuitable products or poor service, or paying over the odds, and so on. This is especially the case in the international money markets, or when buying basic commodities such as metals, coffee, or wool. Whether or not the buyer perceives that there is a risk in placing an order, the seller's marketing and sales strategies should be aimed at trying to reduce the feeling of risk-taking.

The most extreme situation is the purchase of a highly technical product, new to the buyer's organization, which even technical personnel cannot assess with any degree of certainly. Here the strategy is to send technical people to the prospect to 'teach' the technical aspects of the product, and to give them more confidence in it.

Another example is where the buyer's organization is uncertain of the way the sales of *its* product will fare; and where, therefore, buyer is reluctant to commit his firm to a large order. A good strategy for a supplier is to get a **letter of intent** stating that the complete requirements for the parts needed would be obtained only from that supplier, and for the supplier, in turn, to supply a smaller quantity if sales of the article are lower than target.

Anything a supplier can do to remove the feeling of risk is an aid to getting favourable purchasing decisions.

Summary of skills

The intention of the study in this unit is not only to learn facts about marketing, but also to develop skills which will be of use in the business world. The section at the end of each block indicates the skill areas covered by each activity.

Skills

Skills	*Activities in which skill is developed*
a Numeracy	2, 3, 9
b Learning and studying	2, 3, 8, 9, 11
c Identifying and tackling problems	1, 5, 7, 9, 11
d Design and visual discrimination	3, 4, 8, 10
e Information gathering	2, 3, 4, 8, 9
f Communicating	All activities
g Working with others	All activities

Block 6
Marketing Communications

Introduction

In this block you will examine the role of communications in marketing, though the emphasis here will be on impersonal methods of communication, such as advertising. (This topic is a substantial one, covering the part advertising agencies play in assisting organizations with the creation and production of advertisements; the advertising budget, and how it might be calculated; and the various media used to carry advertising messages.) You will also be looking at other ways of putting over a marketing message – sales promotion, PR (public relations), and lobbying.

The activities in this block cover: consideration of advertising objectives; preparing an advertising brief; budgeting for advertising; media evaluation in various forms, including by cost; a sales promotion investigation; and aspects of public relations.

Communication

You will have looked at communication channel models in the first year of your course. We shall now need to adapt them slightly to explain the use of communication in marketing.

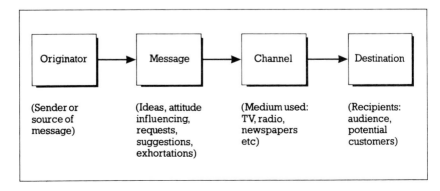

Communication in marketing

Have you noticed that the 'feedback element' is missing in the diagram above? As you will see, most marketing communication is *one-way* and/or *impersonal:* addressed to the market (or the world) at large. Feedback is difficult to establish, except perhaps by careful measurement of sales against levels of advertising or marketing research.

The following diagram shows the variety of marketing communications. They are divided into two basic categories: **impersonal** (addressed to large numbers), and **personal** (messages addressed to particular individuals or small groups).

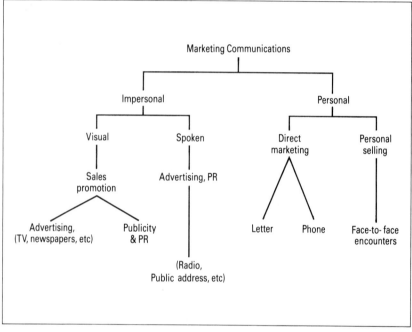

Marketing communications

Most of the impersonal methods of marketing communication are examined in this block: personal methods are covered in Block 7, *Direct Marketing*.

| *Activity 1* | Singly, or in groups, consider whether personal or impersonal methods would be better for communicating with potential customers about the following:
1 A new, 'hi-tech', very specialized, expensive piece of equipment to be used in a factory,
2 A reduction in the price of a popular soap powder,
3 A BTEC National Course,
4 A brand new four-bedroom detached house in two hectares of land,
5 A fizzy drink,
6 The opening of a new, unisex hair salon. |

Whatever your answers were, the established view is that personal communication (selling) is more suitable for situations where there are many risks (including financial ones) for the purchaser making the buying decisions: new equipment, a new house, a new motor bike. The opposite is true for cheaper, easily available consumer products (or services) with low risk factors: here mass, impersonal, methods are more appropriate.

Some of you will perhaps have realized that *both* methods have a part to play in the same marketing/sales situation. The new house can be advertised in a newspaper (impersonal), but it will be eventually sold by a personal visit to the property, accompanied by an estate agent's representative. A BTEC National Course can be advertised in a newspaper, or feature in a prospectus sent to a local firm, but it is better explained to employers, potential trainees, or prospective full-time students by appropriate college staff.

Whatever the actual communication mix, remember personal messages (especially face-to-face ones) are normally much more expensive than impersonal ones.

Impersonal methods

There are two categories of impersonal methods: **visual** and **spoken**. Of the two, the visual kind are both the more important, and the more widely used.

Advertising (visual)

The many definitions of advertising you can find in books all stress one point: it has to be paid for (by a firm, sponsor, or some other body such as the government). The American Marketing Association defines it as: 'Any paid form of non-personal presentation of ideas, goods or services by an identified sponsor.' The British Code of Advertising Practice talks of '. . . paid for communications, addressed to the public, or part of it, with the purpose of influencing the opinions or behaviour of those to whom they are addressed'.

Advertising objectives

The objectives of advertising are many. Here are some of them.

Greengate
T S B
Curry's
BISTO CORNFLAKES
HARP
Bri. J CAR
CONF.
Pepsi / Coke
CARS FREE INSU
Phone No ??

> To create awareness of an organization
> To create a company image
> To stimulate and build an initial demand (for a product or service)
> To remind customers about a product or service
> To increase sales (of existing products or services)
> To provide technical information
> To develop and maintain customer loyalty
> To stress the unique selling features of a product (what makes it different from all the others)
> To announce special offers
> To stimulate enquiries (for the sales force to follow up)

Activity 2	Individually, or in groups carefully examine a weekend colour supplement, a fashion magazine, a daily newspaper, and any publication aimed at young people. Compare the purposes of the advertisements in each publication, under: 1 the headings given above (where applicable); and 2 any other headings which occur to you. You might also consider whether the advertisements achieved their apparent objectives. If there is time, in a general session you could draw up a list of the six most popular objectives identified.

Categories of advertising

In completing Activity 2, you might well have decided that the objectives of advertisements depended upon the latter's type or category. **Product advertising** seeks to promote the sales of new or existing products in one way or another. **Institutional (company or organizational) advertising** promotes the seller, the *image* of the provider; builds goodwill. (See if you can find in your library the newspapers for a few days after the 'Zeebrugge' disaster, with P&O advertisements stressing that they (P&O) were 'now at the helm'. This was a short-lived attempt to 're-market' Townsend–Thorensen: within weeks the tarnished image of the latter was eliminated altogether.)

Another contrast exists between **manufacturers' advertising** (with the accent on the **products**, and not on where they can be bought), and **retailers' advertising** (with the accent on the **sales outlet**, and less on individual products).

Differing advertising approaches

Finally, there is the distinction between advertising to the consumer (*'buy and enjoy'*); to the retailer (*'buy and resell at a profit'*); to the industrial buyer (*'use this in your firm'*); and to professional people like doctors (*'prescribe this pill for your patients'*).

| *Activity 3* | Review what you did in Activity 2. Try and re-classify the advertisements already examined under the categories discussed above. |

Advertising through agencies

If you or I have something of moderate value for sale (a second-hand bicycle, a home computer, or a transistor), we could well decide to put a card in a local shop window, or advertise the item in a newspaper – that is, to do the job ourselves. However, if the item for sale is, say, a house (a much more valuable asset), then it is more usual to go to an estate agent who would handle all aspects of the sale, including generating the sales literature and the newspaper advertising.

Some small firms who advertise on a limited scale do indeed deal direct with advertising media (that is, with providers of the means of advertising, such as newspapers, magazines, or ITV); but most organizations of any size (including the Government) rely heavily upon **advertising agents**.

The advertisement below, clearly describes the work of an advertising agency. Do you remember Claire Rowlands from Block 1, *Introducing Marketing*? She was an **Account Executive** with Musad, which means she would work in the **Account Management** section. The **creative staff**, working in the **Creative** section, prepare the text and layout of advertisements, and the **studio** prepares the **art-work** (sorting out the type-styles, illustrations, photographs, etc, and planning the finished appearance).

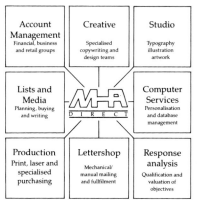

MHA. The complete direct advertising agency where nothing is left to chance.

Account Management Financial, business and retail groups	Creative Specialised copywriting and design teams	Studio Typography illustration artwork
Lists and Media Planning, buying and writing	*MHA DIRECT*	Computer Services Personalisation and database management
Production Print, laser and specialised purchasing	Lettershop Mechanical/ manual mailing and fullfilment	Response analysis Qualification and valuation of objectives

MHA. One of the largest of Britain's independent direct advertising agencies. Growing fast. Uniquely, we control a client's campaign from conception to completion using our in-house services. In this way the creative concepts from our international and national award-winning creative department are translated perfectly into action and sales.

Our clients include:
The Royal Mail, British Telecom, Citroen UK. Montblanc, Nestle, La Manga Club, Welbeck Financial Services.

You can call Ian Minors, MD. now on 01-898 6064.
MHA Direct, Norcutt House, Norcutt Rd., Twickenham TW2 6SS.

The structure of a marketing organization

The **lists and media staff** plan the bookings, and purchase space (or time in the case of TV) in appropriate media (and check that the advertisements appear exactly as ordered). Note MHA have a **response analysis** service which researches into how effective the advertising has been in achieving the objectives set for it.

For TV or cinema advertising, some agencies will have their own **production** facilities; while others will contract out this work to specialist agencies.

How agencies are paid

Many years ago, the forerunners of advertising agencies were sellers of advertising, acting on behalf of newspapers. They worked on a commission basis (ie they were paid a percentage of the advertising revenue they generated). From what you have learned so far you can see that the role of the agencies has changed greatly: there are new activities such as suggesting advertising objectives, preparing advertising campaigns, producing the advertising, and doing post-campaign research. However, agencies still receive commission on the advertising they place with the media.

Commission alone (even at 10–15 per cent) is not enough to yield a worthwhile profit where the client requires services other than just the purchase of media space. Thus such work as **copy preparation** (preparing the text of an advertisement), **artwork**, and **campaign planning advice** will definitely be charged to the agency's client. (So diverse are these extra services that some agencies could be better described as 'marketing agencies'.)

The legal status of agencies

The status of an advertising agency is often misunderstood. The term **agency** itself is not strictly correct: an advertising agency is *not* the *legal agent* of the advertiser; but is a business in its own right. Thus an agency is responsible for settling accounts rendered by media owners for space purchased.

Selecting an agency

Selecting an agency to do your advertising is rather like selecting a firm to build an extension to your house. You would need to get quotations from several different builders, but none of them could quote until they had visited the proposed site and got a clear understanding of what you wanted them to do. After this, technical representatives would want to discuss with you the style and quality of the materials to be used. A very crucial question would be how much you would be prepared to spend on the work.

In the same way you would approach a number of agencies (either from past experience, recommendations from business contacts, or by going to the Advertising Association or the Institute of Practitioners in Advertising) and get an idea of what they offered. They would first need to know how you see your company image and style; what you want to achieve with your advertising; where and when you propose advertising; and how your intended campaign would fit in with your other marketing activities. They would also need to have an indication of the annual budget (ie the amount of money set aside for advertising).

Selecting an agency: 10 Questions to be asked

1 What is the quality of top management?
  (Qualified; with drive; reliable?)
2 What about other staff?
  (Qualified; is agency prepared to recruit specialists?)
3 Is the agency creative, imaginative?
  (Example of past successful work available? Who does the work?)
4 Is it committed to research?
  (Is marketing research done, pre- and post- campaign? Is it 'in house' – done by the agency – or bought out?)
5 Is it in current touch with the media?
  (Experienced with the media you want to use? Up-to-date with circulation details, and readership/viewer profiles?)
6 Can it plan good campaigns?
  (Records of past successes; can it produce an integrated plan? Does it understand *your* market?)
7 Has it a good image?
  (Is the general 'feel' of the place purposeful and confidence-building?)
8 What services can it offer?
  (What about PR, exhibitions, brochure preparation, video-making?)
9 How does it charge?
  (Commission, fees; cost per hour; mixture?)
10 Is it recognized?
  (Member of an advertising association?)

It is essential to explain to the agencies all they need to know about you and your organization. At meetings with them you would be looking for that group of people who seem best to understand your problems; who have experienced staff, and with whom you get on well.

A normal practice is for competing agencies to put on formal **presentations** for prospective clients, during which the main proposals are outlined. At such presentations you would need to question agency representatives very closely to find out how well they have understood your needs. The final choice would also involve talking to other clients of the agencies considered, and evaluating the quality of work done for them.

| *Activity 4* |

Divide into three groups. Two groups are to represent the Account Director and staff of competing agencies, Adgrab and Connem & Twistem. The third group represent **either**:

1 *(This option for full-time students, or those not employed.)* The senior management of your college, about to brief an advertising agency on taking over the college's advertising and publicity next year. (This group would be able to bring to this activity knowledge gained from looking at the college's marketing mix.) You are particularly keen to upgrade the college's image, and improve the advertising for specific courses. You are dissatisfied with your present prospectus, and course leaflets – as well as those for short courses and leisure provision. You wish to advertise one particular course nationally (you decide which one); **or**

2 *(This option for part-time, employed students.)* The senior management of a local company represented on the course, about to brief an advertising agency on taking over the company's advertising next year. You are particularly keen to upgrade the company's image, and improve the advertising for particular products/services. You are dissatisfied with your catalogues, brochures, leaflets, and company stationery. You wish to advertise one product/service abroad.

In the case of either option, the brief should also set out all the information on your organization that you think the agency would want to know about you.

The groups representing the competing agencies should each prepare a list of the information you would like to know about the client company/college, and prepare some ideas to meet the client's needs.

Finally, in a general session, the two lists prepared by the agencies can be compared; and matched against the client's questions and needs.

The advertising budget

Setting an advertising budget is no easy task. Since there is
no known relationship between money spent on advertising
and the resulting level of sales, and formula for budget-
setting will be less than scientific. The most popular formulae
include:

1 *The inspired guess*. Here a figure is plucked from the air
   (eg £50 000), and this is the amount spent. Not
   recommended.
2 *What can be afforded*. A projected budget for next year is
   drawn up without any figure for advertising. The
   projected net profit is examined, and a decision taken
   on what will needed for distribution to shareholders
   and/or to be put to the purchase of new assets. What is
   left over will be allocated to advertising. (The real
   problem here is that the actual amount could vary
   considerably according to the success or failure of the
   firm. An increase in sales could generate by the year end
   a sizeable slice of revenue to spend on advertising. A fall
   in sales could reduce the figure available to zero – after
   money has in fact been spent! Where sales are falling,
   there could be a good case to increase, rather than
   decrease, advertising.)
3 *What was spent last year*. It is easy to allocate what was
   spent last year, plus (possibly) a percentage for inflation.
   If the original figure was an inspired guess, the original
   sin is perpetuated! In any event, market conditions may
   change significantly from year to year; and advertising
   may need to change too.
4 *What competitors are spending*. Even if you can find out
   what competitors are spending, no two firms are alike,
   or have the same costs, products, and sales. Such
   comparisons are dangerous. Worse still, competitors
   may have fixed *their* levels of expenditure in a
   haphazard, rule-of-thumb way. (There is no doubt,
   however, that if competitors were to double their
   advertising expenditure overnight then a drastic reappraisal would have to be made.)
5 *A fixed proportion of expected sales*. A method which looks
   attractive, but also has its problems. Certainly it is better
   to base proposed expenditure on expected sales rather
   than on past ones; and even if sales do not reach the
   projected target, the advertising budget will not be

affected during the year. But if sales *increase*, there will be no ability to build on more success with more advertising; or to capitalize on some fortuitous happening. Again, the fixed percentage figure could have been chosen arbitrarily; and the resultant budget be far from what is really needed to do the job properly.

6 *What is needed to achieve advertising objectives.* (Sometimes called the 'task method'.) This leads to a much more realistic approach. After setting the advertising objectives, what is needed to achieve them is carefully mapped out. This task would include complete campaigns, run-of-the-mill brochures, leaflets, mail shots – everything coming under the heading of advertising. All the work needed is costed out realistically. If there is adequate money available, the plan is adopted. If not, then it is amended to suit what *is* attainable, with some of the less important objectives shelved for the time being.

To consider advertising as a *proper cost*, rather than an optional extra, results in it being dealt with on a par with other costs like wages and materials.

7 *The Amalgam Method.* Possibly the best approach is to cost out using the *task method*, then to match this figure against competitors' spending to see if there is a big imbalance, and finally to consider at what stage products and services are in their individual *life cycle*. (Please refer back to Block 2, pages 34–7).

Note: advertising expenditure will be very high at the immediate pre-launch stage of a new product or service, and possibly in the early part of the decline stage. A steadier level of expenditure could be expected during naturity; and towards the end of the decline period all advertising could be discontinued.

| *Activity 5* | Assume, as a group, that you have been given an assignment to organize an evening disco on the premises of a local sports club, which can hold about 120 people. You want to make as much profit as possible (by selling lots of tickets, at £2.50 each) to hand over to a worthy charity. You decide that outgoings are to kept at a minimum – some of you feel that advertising expenditure should be limited to £10.

Suggestions have been made about advertising in the local papers, and on the local radio. Other people favour printing 1,500 leaflets for door-to-door distribution; and hiring a public address system on the day. Yet others want to visit local schools with leaflets. An outsider has suggested that a large banner strung across the main street might be effective . . .

Meet as a group in committee to finalize the advertising budget for the event. (You may include or exclude any of the suggestions made; or choose alternative ideas. But remember the need to maximize profits!)

Advertising media

The term **media** is used in marketing to mean the various channels of communication utilized in advertising. (A single channel is called a **medium**.) Advertising media include TV, newspapers, weekly and monthly magazines, radio, cinema, and outdoor posters, hoardings, etc.

Newspapers

The UK is very well covered by newspapers (both daily and weekly, national and local). The United Kingdom as a whole is a reasonably compact unit with good road/rail communications, and British people are avid newspaper readers: the total average daily sale in late 1986/early 1987 was 14.7 million.

[*Source:* ABC]

Average daily paper circulations 1986/7

(in million copies)

Express	1.713	Telegraph	1.132
Mail	1.718	Financial Times	0.198
Mirror	3.121	Guardian	0.498
Star	1.296	Independent	0.289
Sun	4.012	Times	0.450
Today	0.298		

[*Source:* ABC]

Average Sunday paper circulations 1986/7

(in million copies)

Mail on Sunday	1.633	People	2.959
News of the World	4.947	Observer	0.772
Sunday Express	2.206	Sunday Telegraph	0.707
Sunday Mirror	3.019	Sunday Times	1.188

Still a very attractive medium, in 1986 advertising revenue grew by 20% in the quality daily market (ie the *Telegraph, Financial Times, Guardian, Independent, The Times*) to a total of £263.5 million well above the rate of inflation. The popular (tabloid) papers were up by 10 per cent to £235.8 million. Statistics are available on the **readership profiles** of these papers which identify typical purchases. Decisions can then be taken on whether to advertise in any or all of them, based on this information (and on the rates charged). Advertisers in general seem to have a preference for the quality papers: all have about 80 per cent of their readers in the ABC1 social class grouping, and obtain most of theincome from advertising.

This medium is very flexible. Advertisements can usually be placed at extremely short notice. (Good examples were found in the 1987 general election campaign period.) National or regional coverage can be obtained quickly. Free papers go to virtually every home in large areas of the population. By 1987, they had gained nearly 29 per cent of all regional newspaper advertising.

Many papers are willing to include 'new stories' (called editorials in the trade) about new products, or moves to new premises, when firms place large advertisements.

There are definite 'days' for certain kinds of advertisements: mail order products are best advertised on Saturdays and Sundays, for example, when people have more time to read newspapers.

Circulation (the number of copies sold per issue) and **readership** (the number of people who actually *read* the paper) figures, and **profiles**, as well as advertising **rates** are vital pieces of information to be taken into account before buying space. (These figures change over time, and care should be taken to obtain up-to-date statistics before final decisions are made.)

Display and classified advertising

Display adverts are more expensive, but provided they are not lost in a forest of competing similar advertising, they can be very effective and eye-catching. The top left or right of the front page alongside the newspaper masthead (title), is a prime – and expensive – spot.

On the other hand, classified advertisements – just a few

Display and
classified advertising

lines of type under category headings – are the life-blood of
local papers, particularly weekly ones. Advertisers can be
reasonably certain that most readers interested in a particular
category of offer or service (eg *articles for sale*) will read their
advertisements.

Sunday newspapers

These papers are not just glanced at, but read at leisure.
More attention is paid to advertising. Although colour
printing has now become commonplace in newspapers, the
Sundays have an accompanying (free) colour magazine, with
plenty of opportunity for high quality advertising.

| *Activity 6* | In separate groups examine one quality Sunday paper (plus magazine), one local weekly, and one tabloid daily. |

1 Estimate the percentage of each taken up by
   advertising.
2 Estimate the balance of display to classified in each
   paper.
3 Compare the quality of colour adverts in newspaper
   with those in the magazine supplement.
4 By research, compare the costs of display and classified
   adverts in each of the three papers.

Magazines

Magazines are quite different in size and appearance from newspapers. There are five major categories:

1 **General magazines.** These are aimed at mass markets. Many cater for women (though men do read them too). *Nova*, *Cosmopolitan*, and *Woman's Own* are examples. All have much longer **reading spans** (time taken after purchase to read through) than newspapers (usually discarded after 24 hours). They can be re-read over many months.

   Most are published monthly, with advertising bookings closed well in advance of publication. Items advertised include household goods, luxury items, and clothes.

   Other general magazines cater for men (eg *Arena*, fashion dominated; and Q, a guide to modern music).

2 **Specialist magazines.** A feature of the last decade has been the enormous increase in specialist magazines with two, three, or even four covering specialist hobby or leisure areas such as photography, railway modelling, DIY, or particular sports. Most brands of leading home computers have magazines devoted to individual models.

   Advertisers tend to be suppliers of equipment or services relating to the subject matter of the publication; and articles include news about new products and/or critical reviews. Readerships are highly specific, and the ratio of advertising to articles, letters, etc can be as high as 50 per cent.

3 **Retail and Trade magazines**. A fairly wide group. The *Brewers' Guardian,* the *Grocer*, magazines for farmers, electrical retailers, booksellers – all serve different but specific readerships. Advertisers tend to be manufacturers wishing to inform the retail trade of new products or promotions, about advertising campaigns to be aimed at the public, or to offer products/services to assist the business.

4 **Professional magazines.** Many professional associations have their own magazines/publications. The majority are circulated by post, and postage is included in the annual subscription. The membership **profile** is normally well documented. As the circulations are 'controlled' (ie copies only go to members) advertisers can be very confident that only a specific audience – lawyers, accountants, supervisors, chartered surveyors, etc – will be reading the advertisements. Advertising can be very specific too.

5 **Give-aways.** The last few years have seen the arrival of free magazines, given away in the public places – especially at railway and tube stations – and aimed at the female ABC1 16 to 30 age range. *Girl About Town,* for example, has an average 125 000 copies distributed each week in the London area. It contains articles on films, music, TV, cosmetics, clothes, eating-out, and sport. Advertising covers holidays, hairdressers, beauty products, and flats; but the main emphasis is on secretarial, word processing, and office vacancies.

Activity 7	Visit a local newsagent in groups. Note all the magazines displayed. Analyse them under the categories discussed above; and advise suitable sub-categories (eg travel, transport, computers). Which category has the greatest range? Compare the prices of competing magazines. Prepare a short report on your findings.

Television

Most people in the UK have access to television – 98 per cent of all households have the use of a set; the majority of which have colour/Teletex/Oracle. Research has found, however, that the ABC1 group tends to watch less TV than C2DE viewers; and that the former watch BBC more than ITV.

Not surprisingly there is a continual battle between the BBC and ITV for viewers. Advertisers on TV, of course, want large audiences, but in 1986 the BBC captured well over 50 per cent of the viewers on several occasions (during snooker championships, for example). Worse still, a national survey in 1985 found nearly 20 million adults 'sometimes' missed seeing adverts, even when tuned to ITV. 4.1 million (9.4 per cent) 'skipped' adverts 'almost always'!

ITV stations cover some 13 regions. Advertisers can choose to advertise locally or nationally. Additionally, most regions now offer test marketing with local campaigns. Marketing (August 1979) reported in detail on this development. For example, Grampian TV launched *Hothouse* in 1983. In this region, products are placed in large Gateway stores in agreed positions. Careful checks are kept in sales, and on those of competitors' products. TV advertising is then introduced, aimed at specific customer groups, and advertising effectiveness monitored.

Central TV attempt to relate advertising to sales with their service *Adlab*. 1000 housewives keep records of purchases which are later matched against advertising dates.

TV advertisements can be as short as a few seconds; or longer, in multiples of 15 seconds. The rates charged will vary from region to region and from hour to hour. As ITV gets closer to a 24-hour day, seven days a week, the choice of times increases. (Particularly important in the recent past has been the post 9.30am slot. Soap opera watchers are replaced, after 10.30am, by the younger retired; and non-employed housewives.) Coupled with the ability to advertise for seven minutes every hour, the longer day can now make available over two hours of advertising.

Continuous research is now being done into the effectiveness of both newspaper and TV advertising. (See *Marketing*'s weekly *Adwatch* reports on the previous week's Top 10 remembered advertisement.)

Since the 1950s television has changed the face of marketing. It offers colour and sound to illustrate the message. Musical **jingles** are used to develop an awareness of a particular product (**brand identity**). Because one advertisement follows another in rapid succession within a 'natural break' period, all messages (to be successfully remembered) need ideally to be presented in short, sharp, even stark, terms.

Activity 8	Obtain the most up-to-date data you can on the comparative costs of advertising in a quality paper (eg *The Times, Telegraph*); a tabloid (*The Daily Mirror, The Sun*); and in two ITV regions in different parts of the UK. Compare the figures. Which is the more expensive – a full page in either category of paper, or one minute of prime time evening television, say between 7 and 10pm? Why?

Commercial radio

Radios Normandy and Luxembourg began life before the Second World War, but until pirate radio arrived in the 1960s, few people listened to radio advertisements. Since 1973, however a whole network of commercial radio stations has developed. At first, all stations covered concentrated areas of population, such as BRMB does for Greater Birmingham. Later there were amalgamations such as GWR

The studio of a local commercial radio station

(Great Western Radio), based on Radio Wiltshire (Swindon/Bath) and Severn Sound (Bristol). GWR serves a large area, not all concentrated, from West Oxfordshire to North Somerset.

Audiences are young people (though the numbers in the 16 to 24 age range are expected to fall by 1.5 million in the next five years), housewives, and people driving to and from work. Profiles differ from area to area, but females dominate, with a larger proportion of C2DE listeners. Advertising is limited to nine minutes per hour.

The attraction for listeners is a constant supply of music, news about local events, and 'open-line' chat-shows. For advertisers, the cost of preparing commercials is minute compared with a TV production.

Problems faced by the industry include the fact that firms advertising nationally tend to prefer to organize their sales territories to correspond with ITV regions, and these often bear little resemblence to the catchment areas of commercial radio stations. As a result the stations have to depend on local advertisers for the greater part of their income (up to 60 per cent).

Many stations sell their own 'airspace', and do not have large marketing/sales forces to exploit the potential in each area. Despite these drawbacks, by mid-1987 revenue was increasing steadily, and running at an estimated £24 million annually.

Activity 9	Spend two hours on different evenings listening to one or (if possible) two independent radio stations.

1 Estimate as accurately as you can the percentage of the time taken up by national news, local news, music, sports,' phone-ins, and advertising.
2 Note the different kinds firms advertising: are they national or local for products and services?

An optional extra activity would be to obtain details of advertising rates from two commercial stations. Compare the rates charged with those for television.

Outdoor Advertising

Outdoor advertising includes a much wider variety of media than posters and hoardings: flashing signs, buses with advertising slogans, taxis, tube trains, delivery vans with a snappy message – all are outdoor communications. (Not forgetting the placards carried by demonstrators!)

Posters, though, are the most important. There are over 130 000 poster sites in the UK, varying in size from 5ft × 3ft 4in to giant hoardings, all serving the same function: **reminder advertising** – that is they **remind** people of a product or an advertising campaign, or they reinforce a more detailed TV or newspaper message.

One exception to this practice is where companies are breaking into new markets, and want to explain who they are and what they do. When the products are eventually launched, potential customers will be aware of them. (In recent years, Japanese companies like Sony, American ones like Pepsi-Cola, and British Airways have all conducted poster campaigns in China to prepare the way for future business.) Poster messages have to be short and to the point; people on the move have little time to take in more than one line of text. Whilst **production** costs are high, **overall** costs are much lower than for television messages.

The cinema

A supremely important medium before the advent of commercial television, the cinema declined thereafter until mid-1980s, since when it has had something of a revival. Large cinema complexes housing several screens are opening throughout the UK. Slough's Maybox 10-screen 'movie-theatre' (with double 'love seats' for courting couples, who make up 29 per cent of the audience) and Nottingham's Showcase 11-screen cinema both opened in 1987, at a time when annual audiences were climbing above 73m. A well-made film still attracts the public.

Advertising time is normally concentrated into a single session. The industry is dominated by two companies who act as 'advertising agencies' – Pearl and Dean, and Rank. Time is sold in multiples of 20 or 30 seconds.

Cinema advertising has all the sound and colour of television, plus a larger screen. Specific advertisements can be created (with high production costs); or 'off-the-shelf' advertisements can be used (eg for new cars), to which the names of local distributors/retailers are added.

Audiences tend to be in the 15 to 24 age group, particularly people on dates, the engaged, or young marrieds. This group has money to spend, and advertising tends to concentrate on such items as soft drinks, confectionery, cosmetics, clothes, and consumer durables such as washing machines, cars, and motor bikes.

| *Activity 10* | Many of you will visit the cinema from time to time.
1 Find out how many of you in the group go to the cinema:
   a often (say once per week, most weeks), |

    b sometimes (say once or twice per month),
    c rarely (say two or three times a year)
    d never.

2 Visit a local cinema. Make a particular effort to make a note of the advertisements you see on your visit.
    a Attempt to classify the advertisements you remember seeing under product/service headings. Do they resemble the list above?
    b Did you feel that they were more or less effective than equivalent television advertisements?

Sales promotion (visual)

You encountered promotion as part of the **marketing mix** in Block 2, *More about Marketing*. **Sales Promotion** is an aspect of promotion, and whilst some would restrict the use of the term to mean just 'in-store merchandising' (that is, the way goods are presented for sale), most would agree that it covers a variety of forms of impersonal marketing communication.

For our purposes, **sales promotion** can be defined as 'the activity of making special and specific offers to an identified group of customers (the **target market**), for a limited time, to influence the behaviour of those customers'. (Note that these offers may be to induce people to buy goods 'on trial', to buy greater quantities of an existing line, to pay more quickly, or to buy at particular times (eg 'off-peak') – in fact, they cover a wide selection of aims.)

A very special kind of sales promotion can also be found aimed at a firm's own staff, rather than at the customers. Salespeople reaching a particular target sales figure might win a prize – eg a week end for two in Paris. Sell more than anyone else, and win a Concorde holiday in America. Wholesalers and retailers can also, be targeted in a similar ways.

Types of sales promotion	
Price reductions	Trading stamps
Coupons (ie 'money off next purchase)	Free gifts (eg software with computers)
Competitions	Retailers' discount/
'Two for the price of one'	commission

Free admission (to exhibitions)	Trial offers
Free delivery to the door	Free training/advice on usage
	In-store demonstrations

Activity 11

1 Either singly or in groups visit a local shopping centre, and make a list of all the varieties of sales promotion you can identify. In each case try and work out what the objective was – to introduce a product, to get repeat business, to clear out old lines, to meet competition, etc. Make a report on your visit, showing findings *and* conclusions.

2 Alternatively, part-time students could choose to look at their own organization's sales promotion methods.

3 All students could examine college sales promotion for, say, short courses. What new methods could you come up with?

Quaker Oats have run promotional campaigns for over 80 years. Each has had specific objectives, such as to increase sales of a line significantly; to launch a new product; or to regain lapsed customers. Famous promotions have included free bone china cereal dishes (1960), the 'Honey Monster' (1976), and the 'photo jigsaw' offer (1985). Naturally most of their promotions have been aimed at the young consumer: eg stickers which could be collected and exchanged.

Within retail outlets, sales promotion is often carried out by teams of sales merchandisers to promote products at the point-of-sale (POS). The Market Research Society found that 20 per cent of all purchases made by housewives were actually decided upon in the shop, where goods were displayed. These merchandisers visit stores, taking with them POS material (showcards, mobiles, etc), cleaning up dirty or dusty shelves where 'their' product is to be displayed, and ensuring that adequate space is available for stocking.

Some merchandisers also take orders for fresh supplies (checking stock levels in the process,) and give advice on new products, national promotions, and coming advertising. (Valuable marketing research on retailers can be done at the same time.) CPM (Counter Products Marketing) and FPS (Field Promotions Services) are two leading merchandising team providers.

Industrial goods manufacturers also use sales promotion as part of the marketing mix. Trade-in allowances for old models, free staff training (eg when purchasing new computer system), and special credit terms all play their part.

Public relations

Public relations (marketing the organization's image to the public) can be divided into **press relations (publicity)**, by which an organization aims to obtain editorial or free coverage in a news story about itself; and **non-press relations** (open days, stands at exhibitions, providing prizes for local charities, sports days, etc). Note that **editorial** coverage is not only *free*, but will be more convincing to readers than advertisements (even though *you* wrote the story!).

Think of the number of times in a TV news bulletin or 'chat show' that firms or show-business people 'get a mention'. Politicians, authors, and entrepreneurs (like Richard Branson) love to get this free editorial, especially when they are allowed (encouraged, even!) to mention their latest book, film, or pop record. Reviewers of books, plays, or films do publicize the products reviewed, and can materially influence sales. No wonder a whole industry has grown up devoted to the promotion of people, products, organizations, and ideas.

Schools and colleges like to see stories highlighting good exam results, field trips abroad, sports days, new courses, or successful charity fund-raising. Such stories do not get published without much calculated effort on the part of the institution concerned. Staff will have cultivated relationships with journalists and provided all the details of the stories (and often the pictures). Commercial and industrial organizations (or their agents) use similar tactics, albeit on a larger scale.

Activity 12	1 Look through the last twelve months' back numbers of local newspapers, and identify stories appearing about:
	  a your college, and local schools,
	  b local firms,
	  c your local MP.
	Compare the amount of coverage in each case, and the topics written about, and evaluate the amount of good publicity gained thereby.
	2 Find the person in the college, or where you work,

who is responsible for public relations. Try, by
interview, to establish what the job entails, and how
the job-holder gets on with the media.
3 Write a **press release** (your version of the story) on
some aspect of your present course.

Public relations is really on art, not a science. Establishing or
re-establishing a reputation within a community calls for great
skill, especially if you work for, say, a firm like Union
Carbide (the Bhopal disaster), Townsend-Thorensen
(Zeebrugge), or London Transport (King's Cross). British
Rail has spent a great deal in recent years trying to overcome
the image of a worn-out, over-priced, unpunctual, old-
fashioned transport system. The stress now in PR campaigns is
on modernization, speed, and comfort. More information
(by loudspeaker systems and computerized displays) is being
given to the public on train movements. Proper apologies
are being made for lateness or other inconveniences. Similarly,
in mid-1987, British Telecom was making strenuous efforts
to repair its tarnished image of a company which was
unreliable, over-priced, and was poor at servicing.

| *Activity 13* |

Assume that there was a disturbance at a local disco last
week, and (totally incorrect) allegations were made in a
local newspaper that some of your fellow students were
involved.
Prepare either:
1 a letter addressed to the editor of the paper from the
   Principal; or
2 a statement from the chairman of the students' union,
   attempting diplomatically to put the record straight.
Note that attacking the paper would normally be
counter-productive.

Lobbying

Lobbying — the art of influencing those with political
power — is a special branch of PR. Companies that need to
persuade not customers, but legislators, to amend the law in
their favour, to get concessions from the EC, or to further
their interests by, for example, going ahead with (or
cancelling, as the case may be) the Channel Tunnel, can no
longer rely on the efforts of a captive MP on the board.
Political consultants are now acting for water authorities,
banks, British Airways, and companies like Plessey. Whether

the subject is home audio-taping, water privatization, or air-line mergers, lobbying goes on. It is commonly agreed that the 1986 defeat of the Sunday Trading Bill owed a lot to successful lobbying.

Some agencies prefer to contact the appropriate civil servants; others see the need to talk to a minister direct. However, the main effort goes into establishing a 'target market' of MPs who are likely to be favourably inclined to what a company (or organization, or foreign interest) is trying to achieve, or would like to see happen. These MPs are then well-briefed, with the hope that they will influence others.

Summary of skills

The intention of the study involved in this unit is not only to learn facts about marketing, but also to develop skills which will be of use in the business world. This section at the end of each block indicates the skills areas covered by each activity.

Skills

Skills	*Activities in which skill is developed*
Numeracy	5, 6, 7, 8, 13
Learning and studying	2, 4, 5, 6, 8, 11, 13
Identifying and tackling problems	1, 4, 5, 12
Design and visual discrimination	6, 10
Information gathering	2, 3, 4, 5, 6, 7, 8, 9, 10, 11, 13
Communicating	All activities
Working with others	1, 2, 3, 4, 5, 6, 7, 9

Block 7
Direct Marketing

Introduction

So far you have been looking at **impersonal** methods of putting over a marketing message. There are, however, complementary (though very different) **personal** ways of getting a message across. The person-to-person contact (either face-to-face, or at a distance) does have an added, pyschological ingredient, one normally missing from the large-scale, mass-appeal approach of advertising, sales promotion, or publicity.

With personal contact the target market is very small, often just one person. Each unit of that market can be made to feel he or she is being approached as an individual. We call this **direct marketing**.

You will look at the most important methods used in direct marketing, including face-to-face selling and selling at a distance by letter or telephone.

Finally, this Block shows how the various different communication methods can be integrated into the planning of a single campaign. You will be invited to examine some recent campaigns; and then to devise one for yourselves.

Direct marketing

This area of marketing used to be totally dominated by personal, face-to-face selling. Now more attention is being given to (and vast sums of money spent on) other selling techniques such as **telemarketing** (marketing by telephone) and **mail-shots** (letters targeted at particular groups of people).

Personal direct marketing: Selling face-to-face

It is impossible to write a universal job description for a sales person. Products and selling situations vary so much: showroom staff selling on their 'home ground' have a different task from that of a sales representative visiting new customers at *their* places of business. Consider the following examples:

1 *The retail trade.* Even here contrasting situations prevail. Salespeople representing food, confectionery, or soft drinks manufacturers could well make a dozen or more calls a day if their customers are small, independent retailers. Primarily **order-takers**, these reps (acting rather like the sales merchandisers in the larger outlets) will often check the shops' stocks of their lines for the manager; suggest re-order quantities, look at display material, reposition stock; and give advance warning of national advertising campaigns. In-depth technical knowledge of the product is not really required.

The rep calling on the head offices of retail chains will make fewer calls and have fewer customers, but will call more regularly and see very senior executives. The discussions will centre round quality, packaging, delivery arrangements, quantity discounts, and national promotions.

2 *Consumer durable stockists.* Consumer durables are normally sold to the public in specialist outlets (electrical shops, audio centres, car showrooms etc). With a call average of, for example, ten per day, besides taking re-orders, or orders for new products, a representative could spend time dealing with queries and complaints (passed on from the stockists' customers), introducing new lines, and passing on a certain amount of technical information.

For some products there may be a need to train shop personnel on the features of the latest model, and how best to communicate its benefits. The need for technical knowledge is clear.

3 *Products and services for industry.* Many of these products and services are sold direct from maker to user. (Examples: industrial heaters, pumps, steel sheets; plating services.) Manufacturers' representatives will need some technical knowledge, both of their own products and services and of how they are used by their customers. They must also be prepared to handle some enquiries for non-standard items.

Some products are not sold direct: these are mostly sundries and small general products (machine oils, nuts and bolts, hand tools). Such items are sold by manufacturers to **distributors** (wholesalers). (Distribution channels are covered in detail in Block 8, *Marketing Distribution.*) Thus for these products reps will call on relatively few customers, and deal in large quantities. The talk will be about delivery details and discounts. In contrast, distributors' salespeople will make about as many calls per day as the retail sales reps, and will be selling a wide range of products from different suppliers.

4 *Specialist products and services for industry.* Salespeople working in this part of the market are more likely to be called **technical representatives**. They will be selling direct to industrial users products such as large machine tools or purpose-built plant (e.g. for acid dipping), or specialist assistance like security services. Technical reps will obviously have considerable knowledge of their own products and services, but an essential extra requirement is the ability to understand customers' needs and wants, and to match them with their own firms' products and services.

Normally, technical reps will meet their customers' technical or specialist staff. Discussions may take many hours, and be followed by further discussion and research back at their own companies. A series of calls over many months may be necessary even before a quotation or tender is submitted and more again before a contract finally negotiated. No wonder the daily call rate will be very low.

Selling skills and strategies

Many manuals have been written on selling skills and strategies – the two are interlinked – so here we will only note the essentials of the selling task.

---

1 *Pre-call*
 To find out as much as possible about the (potential) buyer/customer.
 To identify buyer/customer needs.
 To identify those benefits in which the buyer/customer will be most interested, both of product and back-up service.
 To find out what competitors are offering – their benefits, strategies, and weaknesses.
 To evaluate what results the buyer could get by using our product/service.
 To plan what to say, what to show (samples, leaflets), what to do.
 To have 4 or 5 definite aims for the call.
 To make a telephone appointment whenever possible.

---

2 *At the start of the interview.*
To arouse the buyer's interest as soon as possible.
To show or demonstrate the product if at all possible.
To stress the benefits of the product/service, using the customer's own language/jargon, set against his/her buying needs.

3 *As the interview progresses.*
To watch for *buying signals* (how much is it?, what can you offer?, can it be supplied in other colours/finishes?). To try and get a decision at this stage.

4 *Overcoming objections*
To identify the real reasons for an objection ('too expensive' may mean 'we can't afford it').
To vary the package - discounts (as a last resort), credit facilities, special offers, free extras etc, - to get round the objection. (Objections can be buying signals as well as signals of uncertainty. Reassurance is vital).

5 *Clinching the deal*
To turn attention into interest, interest into desire to possess; to convert desire to possess into conviction to purchase and conviction into action (by writing out the order).
(As with any other communication, care needs to be taken to involve the customer in a dialogue, ie two-way communication.)

Costs in direct selling

Remuneration of personal selling staff and the extra costs involved in employing them are a considerable expense. Add together a salary, commission, bonuses; a car and its running expenses, parking fees; the cost of hotels, meals and entertainment of prospective customers; office support services; and a firm could easily spend £200+ on a technical representative's overnight visit to one customer 100 miles away.

No wonder managements of firms have been looking for many years for cheaper ways of selling.

Some considerations of selling face-to-face

Advantages	Disadvantages
1 Can respond immediately to questions	1 Cost of salary and support services
2 Can identify customer needs more accurately	2 Cost of commission payments
3 Can select appropriate benefits to push	3 Cost of travelling
4 Can deal with objections on the spot	4 Cost of meals, hotels, etc.
5 Can ask for the order	5 Customer contact time small compared with travelling, waiting about, recording result

Activity 1

Singly or in groups assume a senior lecturer in your college visits a large hospital complex 20 miles away, to discuss an enquiry about training your local health authority's clerical staff to program data into a new computer network.

Two hours are spent in travelling, and two hours talking to the health authority executives. A further two hours are needed the following week in demonstrating the college's training facilities and finalizing the course programme. (These last two hours are in time when normally the member of staff is teaching; someone is therefore brought in to 'cover'.)

Calculate the cost of getting the order. You will need
a To find out the salary of a senior lecturer at the top of the scale.
b To establish a 'daily rate' (possibly by dividing a by 52 × 5).
c To establish an 'hourly rate' (possibly by dividing b by 6).
d To establish the 'category III' cover rate per hour.
e To find out the current travelling rate per mile paid to lecturers.

Direct marketing by letter (direct mail)

Personal selling, to be successful, needs an **offer** (a product or service to sell); a **target market** (a customer to talk to); and a **sales approach** (as indicated above, based on the classic formula: **attention, interest, desire, action**). Alternative direct marketing methods must have the same mix to be successful. In the case of direct mail, the target market is the essential ingredient: in this selling technique, the target market is the **mailing list**. Use the wrong list, and you waste time and money.

Direct mail has been around for decades, with companies like *Reader's Digest* using printed letters (which at first sight looked as if they had been typed). It was the introduction in the early 1970s of typewriters which used punched tape to produce 'top copies' of the same letter in hundreds (with individual addresses added), which spurred on many firms to try this medium. To begin with, direct mailers ploughed through directories and the *Yellow Pages* entry by entry to compile their lists.

The technology improved rapidly. Now, large address databases can be kept, and appropriate market sectors quickly extracted and printed. A recent estimate suggested the cost of capturing one name and address on a data base was only 13p. *Readers' Digest* claim to have the address of *every* household on its books. British Database have processed the entries from *all* the *Yellow Pages* for the UK, and hold the complete postcoded address and telephone number of some 1.5 million UK businesses. (15 000 entries are checked and updated weekly.)

With 'mail-merge' facilities, messages can be personalized quickly, and even graphics added – such as a map showing the addressee the location of the mailing firm's nearest outlet. Another idea has been to attract potential or light users of products or services with personal inducements, larger than those offered to regular customers. Thus the process of targeting individual customers is becoming more and more sophisticated. Desktop programs enable mailing campaigns to be carried out 'in house' (by the firms themselves), and there are companies willing to sell lists of customers. (Many 'controlled circulation' magazine publishers have set up divisions offering to rent out their readership lists. From time to time readers are asked to fill in 'registration cards' which do marketing research into readers' jobs; company details, special responsibilities, etc. The AA won the Database section of the 1987 BDMA/Royal Mail Direct Marketing Awards for using its database of members to market products tailored to their needs. 20 000 mailings were sent to those who could make use of an independent financial advisory service.)

Consumer durable manufacturers often invite customers to fill in 'product registration cards' after purchase. These can be used to build up a database of product users.

However, larger companies would prefer to 'contract out' such work. Specialist agencies now handle the preparation of the target list, and compose the message. Nine million shareholder addresses were obtained for BP to use in its privatization campaign. The British Gas share register was offered in 1987 by British Investor Database at £400 per 10 000 entries.

Some of you will already have heard of the '80/20' law (or Pareto analysis). This also seems to hold good in marketing for most firms: that is, 80 per cent of sales come from 20 per cent of a firm's customers. Finding that 20 per cent and mailing them regularly should not be a difficult task: the appropriate records exist already.

| *Activity 2* | In groups decide upon the best way to create address list databases for your college to use in mailing: |

In groups decide upon the best way to create address list databases for your college to use in mailing:
1 details of your day release and short courses for industry.
2 details of the leisure courses you offer.
3 details to parents in the area with children in school 5th forms about a college open evening, with an invitation to see the facilities and courses on offer.

A direct mail campaign

The shape of any campaign will to a great extent depend upon the product/service being offered. There are few restrictions on the colour, shape, or size of the material; and a mailing can be timed to coincide with seasons or special events. The target market or the end objectives (introducing a visit, testing reaction to a product, getting donations to a charity) will also affect the layout and approach. An example was the 1987 Yorkshire Bank campaign aimed at 17- to 25-year-olds, introducing them to the Solo account. A major feature was the inclusion in the letter of a pre-recorded tape, with the benefi humorously discussed by Rory Bremner. The tape also formed part of a competition. The accompanying literature was expressed in a straightforward, adult manner, which research had suggested was the best option.

Essential points to remember are:

1 *Wording.* Best short and to the point (many mail shots are far too long, far too wordy), Stress *you*: don't use *I* or *we*. Try and excite interest and curiosity to get people to read on. (A sealed, personally addressed envelope marked 'strictly private and confidential' can be intriguing, as was the Yorkshire Bank tape.)
2 *Ease of reply.* Make it simple. Easy to fill in coupon, reply-paid or *Freepost* envelope, already addressed.
3 *Incentives.* Offer some inducement to reply: mystery gift, automatic entry to a prize draw; opening trial offer.

4 *Invite action.* Urge immediate response: offer only open for a limited time, special discount for an early reply.

5 *Use key words.* Announcing, new; new improved; offer closes 30th June; send no money now; free; save (money, time, effort, worrying); amazing savings; major breakthrough, exclusive, no obligation.

6 *Stress benefits.* Appeal to the target market's needs/wants.

| *Activity 3* | Full-time students should design, in groups, a direct mail campaign to local industry, to get them interested in using a new training suite/conference centre facility just completed in your college. You will need:
a to draft a 'selling' letter,
b to decide what other material should be included.
Part-time, employed students could do a similar exercise on one of their own products or services. |

Telemarketing (telephone selling)

The idea of ringing people up to sell them something, or to get an appointment for a salesperson to call, is not new: what is new is that people in their own homes are being contacted about a variety of products and services: replacement windows, double glazing, insurance, even book club membership. Larger firms involved in take-over battles have used telemarketing to persuade shareholders either to support or oppose bids.

In 1987 telemarketing agency business was estimated at about £40 million per annum; and increasing. Additionally, companies are running their own, in-house, telephone sales teams. One problem emerged in 1987 however: the Office of Fair Trading became concerned about the making of 'unsolicited calls', and about how the phrase was to be defined. Regulation by agreement with the telemarketing agencies is technically possible, but it would be difficult to police in-house activities.

Successful operations call for the use of small teams of highly dedicated staff, sticking to carefully prepared 'scripts' (like actors) and getting plenty of encouragement from supervisors. For a short campaign (for example, to get respondents to allow a representative to call), it can cost several thousands of pounds to hire an agency. (The actual price will depend upon the complexity of the operation, plus a 'per call' fee.) An in-house operation (including initial consultancy advice, training, wages, clerical support, and BT's charges) for six full-time staff could cost in the first year upwards of £200 000.

An interesting development in telemarketing has been to turn the idea on its head: instead of ringing up prospects, get them to ring *you* – free. The favoured method for **inbound telemarketing** is to place an advertisement on television in a 'prime time' slot, or less often in a newspaper (or with Heineken, on the product itself) giving a number to telephone for futher details – or whatever the promotion is. BT offer telemarketeers both the *Freephone service* (via the operator the average call cost is about £1.50), and *Linkline 0800*. This latter allows the customer to contact the advertiser direct. Whilst rental charges are higher than *Freephone, Linkline 0800* is charged at lower rates; more appropriate for large response calls.

Door-to-door leafleting

Door-to-door leaflets were once regarded as the 'poor relation' of other methods, but they are now a growth area also. Design is a key factor (very similar to newspaper ads) but distribution can be varied. A charity or small firm can send people on foot to deliver locally at very low cost. Others use the GPO, or have the leaflets inserted in a free newspaper (about £9 per thousand plus cost of leaflet in 1987).

The uninformed view is that people dislike leaflets: don't read them, don't act upon them. But note that in 1987, Millward Brown's survey revealed only 14 per cent of housewives leafleted by a specific agency declined to read the message; on the other hand, 57 per cent 'usually looked through' and read items they found interesting. 70 per cent approved of free samples through the letter-box.

| Activity 4 | Devise the text of an A4 leaflet advertising your college's autumn programme of evening classes, to be delivered door-to-door in your locality. Suppose you had to arrange to have them delivered. Compare the costs locally of hand delivery, and using free papers. |

Road shows

In recent general elections the 'battle buses' of party leaders travelling round the country were constantly seen on TV. They *did* have some PR value, but bore little relationship to the company **road show**. This is now a formidable and flexible communications tool. Annual expenditure on shows was estimated at £15 million in 1987. ASDA–MFI before their management buy-out in that year) ran a travelling exhibition

with a fashion show and cookery demonstrations thrown in, and made the admission charge to the show a donation to Esther Rantzen's *Childline.* The firm were convinced that the exercise was worthwhile, despite the cost of £0.75 million. Road shows have also been used by Fisher-Price (toys); Imperial Tobacco (cigarettes); and British Airways (pre-privatization). British Rail have a travelling exhibition train service, with enough different coaches to include catering and receptions as well as space for exhibitions.

The real virtue of this medium is that a message can be put over in a series of different localities; and at the same time company representatives can mix with potential buyers.

Exhibitions

Exhibitions can be defined as showing, displaying, or representing facts, features, or aspects of products or services in public. They can be **static** (unmanned, with an *impersonal* message); or **active** (manned, with a genuinely *personal* message). As with other marketing communication methods, an exhibition should be regarded as part of a larger marketing programme. Thus in deciding whether to take part in an exhibition, you would want to see if and how it would fit within and complement your existing sales promotion programme.

Different categories of exhibitions can be identified: they include those for industrial equipment, and associated goods and services; commercial and office equipment; domestic and kitchen goods and appliances; toys; clothing and fashion; agricultural equipment; and educational, leisure, and sporting interests.

All these occasions provide organizations with an unusual selling situation where customers come and see *them*, as opposed to *their* visiting the customers. The person-to-person contact has a much more positive impact upon customers than advertisements or mail shots.

Some objectives of taking an exhibition stand

To get orders on the spot

To give potential customers a chance to see, hear, touch, taste a product

To see what competitors are doing

To introduce a new product or service

To create contacts for the future

To encourage local agents

To give your own staff a wider sales experience

General exhibitions (eg Ideal Home) do bring in large crowds, but a large percentage of visitors may well not have any need for a manufacturer's particular product. **Trade exhibitions** (the Toy Fair), where manufacturers invite distributors and retailers to see the wares, do have a higher percentage of 'target market' visitors. **Private exhibitions** (on your own premises for example) mean displays can be permanent and cost minimized.

The design and erection of a stand at a major exhibition is best left to specialists, but the layout is something the exhibitor can control. A well-illuminated stand, with room in which to move about and a quiet area for discussion is desirable. Position, too, is important: probably best near an entrance or exit, catering area, or a bar; and on a main 'people traffic road'. (Some hospitality may be needed which cannot be catered for on the stand.)

Sponsorship

Sponsorship, that is, supporting or subsidizing some activity with hard cash in return for publicity and/or free exposure in the media (and especially on BBC TV) is big business. In 1987, expenditure on sponsorship was estimated at around £190 million, plus as much again on advertising the fact that the sponsorships existed. This sum only covers big firms supporting major activities such as the Boat Race (Beafeater Gin) or the Football League (Barclays Bank), or a person such as Nigel Mansell (ICI Fibres). Tens of thousands of smaller sponsorships, like those of 'under 15' seven-a-side football teams (or just of individual players) by local firms increase this amount considerably.

By far the greatest sponsorship expenditure is on sport. Major events – test matches, athletics meetings, horse races – and individual players not only draw large crowds, but they are also televized. Cameras focus on '*Suntory*' notices in the World Match-Play Championships, and on cars and drivers at Grand Prix Motor Racing events, where nearly every visible square inch of each car and each driver is covered in logos, trade-marks, and brand names.

Sponsors' typical objectives

1 To create or increase awareness amongst consumers of sponsor's company, products, brands, services.
2 To improve the company image in the minds of consumers.
3 To increase goodwill amongst wholesalers and distributors.
4 To strengthen the company image within the local community.
5 To improve employee morale and strengthen their loyalty.

Whether sponsors get 'value for money' is hard to assess. Chosing the right area to sponsor is important. The question to ask is 'Where can I find my target market? If the answer is 'Watching snooker on TV at the weekend', then sponsor televized snooker. (Snooker costs about £4500 per hour, but your company's name is seen about 5 minutes every hour.)

If you sponsor an event, you will always be there at the end presenting cheques to the winners. Sponsoring a team or individual carries more risk; although including the firm's name in a horse's name (Everest Double Glazing, Sony, and Next do this), or a boat's (White Horse whisky's 'White Crusader' in the last America's Cup qualifiers' races) does entail frequent mentions – whether they win or lose – over a period of time. Benefits to sponsors include:

1 *Customers and staff*. Ability to hand out complimentary or discount tickets for events. Entertainment facilities. Photographs taken of those present. Opportunities to promote the products, hand out leaflets. Staff can be involved in the arrangements and get to meet VIPs.
2 *Publicity*. Media coverage in the run-up to the event; coverage of the event, and reports afterwards. (Particularly the local press, radio and television.) Advertisements, banners, posters for the event. Especially with charity-linked events, personal appearances of 'show biz' notables are real bonuses.

Arts' Sponsorships (backed by the government-funded *Business Sponsorships Incentive Scheme* – BSIS) raised £7 million for the arts in the first 1½ years of the scheme. Awards matching those of industry are made by the BSIS to a maximum of £25 000. Sponsorships cover opera, drama, exhibitions, etc.

Sponsors get a relatively cheap platform for PR, promotion, and unusual entertainment opportunities. All receive free publicity through the Office of Arts and Libraries, and commemorative certificates from the Minister for the Arts. Firms such as Mobil, BP, FJC Lilley, and Marks and Spencers are leading arts sponsors.

Activity 5	1 Investigate how *one* of the following is sponsored, and, as far as you can, what is entailed:

1 Investigate how *one* of the following is sponsored, and, as far as you can, what is entailed:
   a the nearest county cricket team to your college,
   b the nearest Football League team,
   c Boris Becker,
   d the London Marathon.
2 In 1986 Embassy spent £350 000 sponsoring snooker; £131 000 on bowls, and £52 000 on darts. Discuss in groups why they spent so much on sponsorship. Would they not have been better off using the money on 'straight' advertising?

Integrated marketing campaigns

A marketing campaign needs a carefully balanced 'mix' just like any other aspect of marketing. The search is for that blend of advertising, sales promotion, and packaging, which both achieves the overall objectives of the marketing plan and harmonizes the different activities into an integrated promotion.

John Smith's Strong Ale promotion: a case study

An example of the unified approach was the 1986 promotion by the brewers John Smith, which won the Institute of Sales Promotion's Grand Prix. The campaign's objective was to get potential customers to try the beer out: research had indicated that once people had tasted the brew, they would re-purchase – despite it being more expensive than other brands.

The cans were offered in packs of four with a *double* promotion. First, a '40p off' coupon could be traded in against the next four-pack purchase. Secondly, there was a *Trial of Strength* challenge. The strong ale concept was developed into a challenge to both retailers and customers to demonstrate how strong they were. All they had to do was to tear paper replicas of the cans in half: unfortunately for

them a special 'tear-proof' paper was used which made the task very difficult indeed. 'Winners' were promised a free can.

Advertisements were placed (with accompanying replicas) in magazines read by the perceived 'target market'; and 'couponing' was undertaken, immediately prior to Christmas (an ideal time to launch a drink). Before the launch date, retail buyers were mailed with replicas and the challenge: those 'passing the test' were awarded special certificates.

The campaign was very successful.

Heuga, UK, manufacturers of carpet tiles, faced quite a different problem. Innovators in the market in the 1960s, they found in 1983 their products were considered 'worthy, but old-fashioned'. The sales message of that era stressed the virtues of durability and flexibility, and was very product-orientated. The office trend in the 1980s was to regard carpets as an essential part of the overall design. Heuga asked the question you have met before: 'What business are we in?', and decided the answer was 'In the interior design one'.

Advertising agents were engaged, and a campaign mapped out. The objective was to convey the message that Heuga UK were not only part of the interior design industry, but also leaders in the field. Using display advertising in architectural and design magazines, new product developments were highlighted. (Fashion photographers were used to help sell the design image.) The 'target market' were architects and designers (who would, Heuga hoped, specify and/or order Heuga carpet tiles), and specially prepared brochures were mailed to them.

Designing a marketing campaign

So far in the these last two blocks you have considered different elements in the marketing communications mix; and how some of these elements can be effectively combined. In this final section, the aim is to consider the overall design of a marketing campaign. The example chosen is that of a new product. Where a campaign relates to an existing product or service, Stage 1 can be omitted.

Throughout the following stages, the chosen example is that of the launch in 1978 in the UK of Krona margarine.

Stage 1: a gap in the market

The development of a new product is often a consequence of realizing that there is a 'gap in the market' – a possible need, which hasn't been spotted before, for some particular product or service. Naturally research will be necessary to establish that the suspected gap does indeed exist; and to identify as precisely as possible the target market.

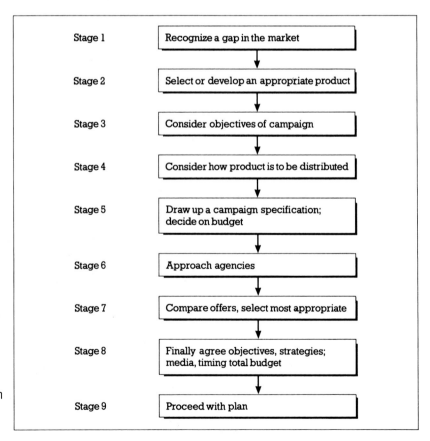

Planning and executing a marketing campaign - new product launch

> In the late 1970s the price of butter was rising; and sales falling. A margarine manufacturer, Van den Berghs, a member of the Unilever Group, was aware that an Australian associate company had developed a margarine which seemed to resemble butter in appearance, taste, and texture. If a similar product could be made in the UK, a market surely existed of those people who preferred butter, but who could no longer afford to buy it on a regular basis. Research confirmed this opinion, but it was finally decided to consider the 'target market' as *all* housewives.

Sometimes, especially where a chosen product or service is substantially different from a company's existing range, it may be necessary to look at the firm's 'image', and revise or update it.

Stage 2: an appropriate product/service
Where no product/service exists to occupy the gap or suit the target market, one must be developed, or adapted to fit the bill. (Where there is already an apparently suitable product lined up, stage 2 can be largely omitted; but even here, it does make sense to be totally sure about the target market and product suitability before embarking on an expensive campaign.)

> Van den Berghs developed a product in the UK, similar to the Australian one, which they called Krona.

Stage 3: campaign objectives
You have already considered campaign objectives in the previous Block, when looking at the work of an advertising agency. As our chosen model is the launch of a new product, it is obvious that the two major objectives here are to introduce a new product to the target market, and induce that market to try it!

> Van den Berghs decided the 'marketing mix' would be:
>
> | | | |
> |---|---|---|
> | Product | — | to look, and taste, like butter (ie this was the USP, the 'Unique selling point'). |
> | Price | — | to be cheaper than butter; but more expensive than other margarines (to give it a *quality product* look). |
> | Place | — | prevailing method; that is to sell it in the same way as other margarines, via shops, supermarkets, etc.) |
> | Promotion | — | a budget of £1.5m : target market all housewives |

Stage 4: distribution decisions

At this stage, decisions on distribution are taken. (These kinds of decisions are considered in more detail in Block 8, *Marketing Distribution*, but essentially manufacturers have the choice of selling direct to users or via intermediaries such as agents, wholesalers, retailers, etc.) The campaign strategy may well have to take into account that the goods will have to be 'sold' to the intermediaries. A separate, subsidiary, promotion campaign aimed at the intermediaries may be essential, timed in advance of the main campaign.

> In the case of Krona, as noted above, the distribution decision was to go via intermediaries. However, in 1978 it was felt that the intermediaries would not need to be specially targeted with a promotion, but that they would see the TV advertising aimed at the final customers. Today there is a definite preference to 'pre-promote' products to the trade.

Stage 5: campaign specification

Finally the pre-planning stage is completed by drawing up a draft campaign specification – setting out how it is felt the campaign should be conducted. This will need to be costed, and a budget figure established. (See earlier comments on this process in Block 6, *Marketing Communications*.)

> Van den Berghs, had, as we have seen, fixed a budget of £1.5 million, with a 'target market' of all housewives, for the period of the launch. However at this stage it was decided to use a 'test market' first, made up of the Westward and Harlech TV regions. (About 10 per cent of the total UK population lived in these chosen areas in the late 1970s.)
>
> TV would be the *sole* medium: it had a wide immediate coverage, and was seen by the majority of housewives. Short, concentrated bursts of advertising would be used.

Stage 6: approach to agencies

This stage was covered in Block 6, *Marketing Communications*. Agencies are invited to look at the company's draft plans, and after due consideration, submit their (competing) proposals.

Stage 7: choice of agency and campaign preparation

As you noted in the previous block, the agency which seems to offer the most appropriate detailed proposal, within the agreed budget, will normally be chosen.

The chosen agency will:

1 Investigate the client's business (if a current working relationship is not ready in existence).
2 Review the client's initial draft campaign objectives and specification. (Modifications may be suggested, final agreement obtained, and related to the quoted budget.)
3 Prepare individual advertisements. (As well as attempting to achieve the overall campaign objectives, each advertisement will have subsidiary objectives, such as developing curiosity, changing cherished and long-held opinions, attitudes, etc.)
4 Consider the layout of each advertisement (TV, radio, newspaper, magazine). There is a need to consider the following guide-lines:

    Developing a focal point – to get attention.
    Determining the approach – documentary, humorous, glamourous, etc., and the use of 'voice-overs' and 'jingles'.
    Keeping the wording simple – appealing to basic emotions (fear, need for security, love of the family etc.). Using short words; short sentences.
    Appealing to the senses (eg a small sample of perfumed paper to smell).
    Mentioning the product's name, again and again and again.

5 Link together succeeding advertisements with a common theme, so that they relate. (The same message can be repeated, eg, against varied backgrounds: repetition aids retention.)
6 Place advertisements with the media.
7 Keep the client informed throughout, and send copies of proposed layouts for final clearance.

In the case of Krona, a particular problem was a statutory requirement which prevented any non-butter product being compared with butter. The plan developed was to film a (then) well-known and admired BBC male reporter talking in a factual, documentary manner (in a supermarket location) about the way in which a brand of margarine had been successful in Australia. He mentioned people there were soon convinced it wasn't margarine at all – which remark was in fact true.

The commercial went on to say a similar margarine, Krona, was now on sale in the UK. By these means all the regulations were observed, yet a message *did* get through –

and this was established by subsequent research – which was variously interpreted as: Krona was like butter; was an alternative to butter; or at worst, closer to butter than any other margarine.

The result was Krona became a well-known brand within weeks. People bought it, and went on buying it. A very satisfactory campaign.

| Activity 6 |

Consider the following situation. (Please note the companies involved are entirely fictitious.)

Parfumeries Lyon SA entered the UK market two years ago very successfully with a wide range of up-market perfumes, colognes, and deodorants for the younger ABC1 woman. Their UK agent commissions some research, and is advised there is a potential *male* market in the same age range (16 to 30 years) for many of the products, particularly deodorants. The research discovers, however, that many respondents are concerned about the use of aerosol cans, in view of the discovering that the earth's ozone layer is being steadily depleted by the use of the propellant gases.

Parfumeries Lyon decide on a (hand-operated) pump-action spray method of forcing deodorant droplets out of the container. They are open to advice as to whether to use a glass bottle (plain or coloured), or a plastic or metal container. The retail price of the 200g container is envisaged as being in the £3 to £5 price range to give it a more 'exclusive', up-market appeal, though it could still be sold at a profit for a retail price of £2. Zenith Advertising are finally chosen to design and carry out a marketing campaign to launch the range, starting with the deodorant.
Zenith are advised that a budget of £1 million is available, to be spent over a period of four months starting at the next pre-Christmas season. Parfumeries Lyon feel TV advertising is *their* number one choice, though possibly backed up by suitable advertisements in magazines read by the target market, including Sunday supplements. Possibly some in-store promotion in large department stores would be desirable.

Working in groups of three or four, assume you are the directors/creative staff of Zenith. This is the largest contract you have landed to date, and you are anxious to make a good impression. It is early May.

1 Design an overall marketing campaign for the product; *and*
   a Suggest a name for the product (you may need to test out some names by marketing research).
   b Design the appearance of the bottle/container chosen (again consider research).
   c Work out the TV advertising proposal in detail – that is, if you agree this is the best medium. Set out timing , dates, lengths of slots (find TV costs); and the same for newspaper magazine advertising, explaining which publications you would use and why.
2 Write a formal report to the directors of Parfumeries Lyon SA, setting out your proposals in detail, including advertising costs; drawings or mock-ups of containers; draft advertisements. Ask for the client's final approval. the client's final approval.

Guidance notes:
1 You will charge the client £200 000 (to come out of the total budget) for the services rendered in *a*, *b*, and *c*, over and above media purchase costs.
2 You may consider other forms of promotion.
3 Research may be done amongst students as well as the general public.
4 You may need to consult specialist texts on creative copy-writing, advertising, TV commercial production, or successful advertising campaigns.

Summary of skills

The intention of the study in this unit is not only to learn facts about marketing but also to develop skills which will be of use in the business world. The section at the end of each block indicates the skill areas covered by each activity:

Skills

Skill	*Activities in which skill is developed*
Numeracy	1, 6
Learning and studying	All activities
Identifying and tackling problems	1, 2, 3, 4, 6
Design and visual discrimination	3, 4, 6
Information gathering	1, 2, 4, 5, 6
Information processing	2, 3
Communicating	2, 3, 4, 6
Working with others	1, 2, 3, 4, 6

Block 8
Marketing Distribution

Introduction

While a product is still being prepared for launching into a new market, consideration is given to the *way* the product will reach its market, ie how it will get the customer. (As you saw in Block 7, *Direct Marketing*, advertising and promotion strategies may need to take account of distribution policy at an early stage.)

In this block you will be introduced to the role of distribution within the place/availability part of the marketing mix; and the concept of **physical distribution management** (PDM).

Next, channels of distribution (sometimes called the **chains of distribution**) are examined. You will be able to consolidate your knowledge of the operations of such distributive organizations as agents, middlemen, wholesalers, retailers, and dealers. Examples of such organizations are examined, including a wide range of retailing companies. You will compare distribution methods such as franchizing, mail order, and party selling.

You will then consider the distribution choices available to a manufacturer/producer, and how the products themselves may dictate the choice of channel – though you will see that different producers of similar goods may well choose dissimilar channels.

As with other areas of business, considerable changes are taking place in customers' distribution preferences; and some recent trends are highlighted. Finally, you will need to think about the *costs* of distribution, which for some products are considerable.

The role of distribution

Whilst some products are sold where they are produced (a farm shop, or a factory showroom, for example), most are required to be available at a distance from the place of production. The principal function of distribution is therefore to ensure that the

'right product is available at the right time'. (See Block 2, *More about Marketing*.) Distribution is consequently an
essential part of the marketing mix. Put another way, distribution ensures a firm's outputs are made available to customers as and when they are required: it is a *customer service*, which is customer orientated, with the aim of customer satisfaction.

Significant elements of successful distributive services

Frequency and regularity of delivery	Quality of packing: ease of handling
Speed of delivery (door-to-door time)	Accuracy of paperwork, invoices
Orders delivered to 100% of quantity required	Good communications networks, internal and external speedy 'returns' service, and action on queries
Reliability of delivery (delivery when needed)	Stocks in hand for emergencies
Delivery to chosen locations	Ability to anticipate demand in advance
Night, week-end deliveries	Credit facilities

Looking at the list can you see that there are at least four ways of grouping the different services to customers? First there is the **carriage** or **transportation** ('right place at the right time') group. Benefits such as deliveries at night (when loading/unloading problems are much reduced) come into this category.

Next there is the **goods handling** group, dominated by the benefits of easy handling. Packaging specially design to meet customers' needs; the use of well-stacked standard pallets which take up less space; bar codings on products; 'inner' packages suitable for display at the point-of-sale, and economical with space – all make significant contributions to good customer service.

Thirdly comes the **storage** or **stock-holding** group. Holding stock in readiness for customers is becoming increasingly important to retailers, for example, where they do not want to be bothered with the inconvenience (and expense) of keeping large amounts of stock in storerooms at the rear of their premises. (B & Q, the DIY store, for example, feel their strength is in retail presentation and selling; and not in warehousing.) Retailers look to suppliers to make small and frequent deliveries to keep products flowing through the store. Industrial customers too, for reasons of space (as well as of cost) need this kind of service: Austin Rover normally hold only a few days' supply of bought-in parts, relying on suppliers to deliver to strict schedules which match the planned flow of products through the factory. (All this can lead to a very close integration of supplier and customer.

The **communications network** is the vital fourth grouping. Prompt advice on deliveries, on any problems experienced (eg delays due to adverse weather en route); frequent contact by sales representatives to discuss ongoing developments; swift action on complaints, return requests, and suggestions – all help to maintain confidence and lasting goodwill.

| *Activity 1* | Forming into an even number of small groups, one half of you act as customers, the others as suppliers, in the following situations:

1 A canned food manufacturer supplying a chain of 20 supermarkets in North East England which chain has a head office but no central warehouse.

2 An expensive restaurant which prides itself on (and maintains its reputation through) the excellent quality and freshness of all the food cooked and served, and which deals with a local greengrocer.

3 A newsagent in a very busy seaside town centre which stocks a wide variety of international, national, and local papers (the latter from as far as 100 miles away) and a comprehensive up-to-date range of magazine and paper-back novels (mostly aimed at holiday-makers), and which is served by a local wholesaler.

Work out, in the case of the customers, which distribution benefits you will need your suppliers to provide; and which benefits you would want to be able to offer to your customers, as suppliers. In a general discussion later on, the groups can compare their ideas and see how closely or otherwise the lists match.

Physical distribution management (PDM)

The necessity of having a set of elements which provide a vital service and customer satisfaction inevitably leads to a further essential requirement: the integration of all the separate elements under a unified control. Variously called **integrated** or **physical distribution management**, the overall aim is to ensure that the supplier builds and maintains an efficient and harmonized distribution system. Any supplier has four major tasks in respect of distribution:

1 To set up and maintain an efficient stores/warehousing system for finished outputs (whether of goods of his own manufacture or those of other organizations), and with an appropriate stores/stock control system.
2 To set up an maintain a well-organized handling, loading, and despatch system.
3 To set up and maintain an efficient goods despatch documentation system.
4 To evaluate, select, and operate the most suitable transportation system to get the goods quickly to the customers, yet as economically as possible.

(As you will see later, the supplier may contract out one or more of these tasks such as the actual delivery of the goods, to other organizations to handle.)

If the various tasks are administered by different departments: stores coming under the purchasing function; order processing under sales; and transport choice decided by a transport manager, for example, conflicts and communication problems are inevitable over time. It makes sense (to some organizations at least) to integrate the tasks, and to appoint a **distribution supremo** to control the whole. Titles given to this individual include **Distribution Manager**, **Physical Distribution Manager**, or even **Director of Logistics!** (Logistics is derived from its use as a military term meaning moving and quartering troops.)

The development of PDM has now resulted in the setting up in Corby of the Institute of Physical Distribution Management to help popularize it and facilitate its further growth.

Channels of distribution

You can see from the diagram that there are six major **channels** of marketing distribution. It must be stressed at once that each *channel* or **chain of distribution** is not necessarily the route taken by the *goods* as they pass from manufacturer/importer to the final consumer, but is, specifically, the route taken by the *legal title to the goods.* (See notes about Agents, and below.)

The journey taken by the *goods* is called the **physical movement**.

You will be considering the various stages in the chain of distribution in more detail later in this block, but more immediately you will need to note the following terms used in distribution:

1 **Middleman**. Someone, or a business, whose role in distribution is to assist the sale or purchase of goods or services; to act as a link between sellers and buyers.

2 **Agent**. A middleman. Someone or a business whose role is to negotiate a sale (or purchase) of goods or services, but who never owns the title to any goods being sold eg, estate agent). Usually works for a fee or commission.

3 **Wholesaler**. (Sometimes called a **merchant wholesaler**.) A middleman. Someone or a business whose role is to purchase large quantities of goods from a range of manufacturers, then offer retailers a wide variety of choice – goods readily available from the large stocks held (with a willingness to sell on products stocked in smaller quantities than the original manufacturer would be prepared to supply); provide a delivery service and credit facilities. (A few are 'cash and carry' only, ie supermarkets for retailers.)

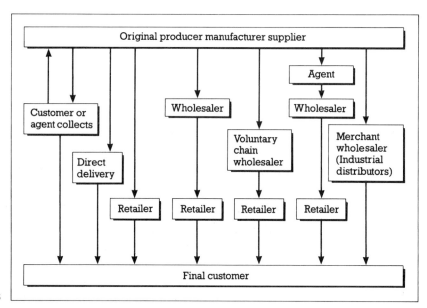

Major marketing distribution channels

Notes:
1 Agents do not own the goods at any stage.
2 In any channel, the actual movement of the goods from one part of the chain to the next can be effected by some outside agency, eg BR, the Post Office, a haulage firm. Again, these transportation agents do not own the title to the goods.

4 **Voluntary Chain Wholesaler**. A wholesaler who is linked
to (and possibly financed by) a group of independent retailers,
such as VG, Spar, etc., who can thereby act together to buy
stock at lower price – in view of the larger orders placed by the
wholesaler with manufacturer – or even to retain sources of
supply where suppliers only wish to supply bulk orders.

5 **Retailer**. Someone or a business whose role is to purchase
finished goods (usually in reasonable quantities) from
manufacturers, agents, or wholesalers, and resell such goods
primarily to the general public for non-business use; *or* to
provide a service like dry-cleaning, shoe-repair, or
hairdressing, to the general public.

(Retailers *do* sell to businesses – newsagents deliver papers to
firms, for example, but normally this activity only represents a
small part of their turnover.) Because the average retail sale is
comparatively small, the costs incurred per sale are greater than
those of wholesalers. Retailers may also offer customers advice
on product choice; credit facilities; delivery services; after-sales,
back up, and repair services; as well as in some areas preparing
(food) items for sale.

The retail trade

Most of you will by now aware that there are different kinds of
retailers, so the following is only a short summary of the
commonest types of them.

1 **Independents**. The 'corner shop' is a typical independent; as
is a small group of shops under one owner. Nowadays facing
severe competition from supermarket chains and multiples
(see below), especially in town centres. The reaction has been
for many independents to join voluntary chains (see above).

2 **Multiples.** Retail organizations with, say, more than ten
branches. Typically multiples sell a fairly restricted range of
goods – electrical household appliances, for example. (There
has been, however, a tendency for product ranges to increase
over a period of time.) Shop fronts and exterior signs have a
high degree of standardization; as have shop layouts, colour
schemes, notices, price tickets, staff uniforms. Typical
multiples include Rumbelows, Currys, Dixons, Boots, W H
Smith.
Some are even more limited in product range: Freeman
Hardy and Willis sell footware and associated products;

Sketchley concentrate on dry-cleaning and small clothing repairs. (This latter sub-group are sometimes called speciality stores.)

3 **Variety chains**, Retail organizations which have much in common with multiples in respect of a common **corporate image** but they stock a very wide range of goods – electrical items, gardening equipment, food, clothes etc. Examples include Woolworths (though recently this chain has reduced its range) and Marks and Spencer. The latter is an excellent example of a chain which demands from its suppliers goods of the highest quality, competitively priced, delivered to schedule, to help make and keep customer loyalty.

4 **Department stores.** A survival from the Victorian era, these large multi-floored shops are found in city and large town centres. In addition to a set of different areas selling a wide variety of products (a standard description of a departmental store is 'a collection of different shops under one roof') shoppers may relax in a coffee bar, eat at a restaurant, or book a flight to Majorca. All the purchases can be made on credit cards, especially ones issued by the store. Each department is run as an individual cost/profit centre; and parts of a floor are rented out to sellers of specialist products. Special promotions for the store as a whole, or for individual products, take place – for example, cosmetics and electrical goods. Selfridges, Harrods, Debenhams, Lewis's and Bentalls are typical examples. The major drawback at the moment is that many of these stores are located in areas which were ideal 50 years ago but which now have little access to immediate, free, or cheap off-street parking; and which also have very high rates and other charges.

5 **Supermarkets**. The supermarket – selling keenly-priced food and basic household items – came into its own with the abolition of resale price maintenance in 1956. Technically, to be called a 'supermarket' a store must occupy an area of over 2000 square feet, and have at least three check-outs, but many much smaller outlets, with a self-service provision and stock easily accessible to shoppers on open shelves, give themselves this title. Some concentrate on an uncluttered and ultra-clean image (Waitrose); others on aggressive pricing strategies (Tesco, ASDA); but all benefit from the basic idea of freedom for the shopper to chose goods at leisure, and the economies of scale that bulk purchasing brings.

6 **Superstores**. Originally a French idea, a superstore is now officially described as being over 25 000 square feet in area,

and with 10 to 20 check-outs. These are now found on the outskirts of large urban areas. They have vast, free parking lots, and a very wide range of goods. Like supermarkets, they concentrate on low-cost, high-volume trade (but with limited services to customers) and immediate payment, normally cash or cheques. Where they differ is in the range of goods – including such items as gardening tools and mowers; books; records; kitchen equipment - and even in having a filling station to sell you petrol before you go home.

7 **Hypermarkets**. These are the most recent development. They must be over 50 000 square feet, and with 15 or more check-outs. A larger version of the superstore, these can lease space to sellers of specialist products. Hypermarkets are found on the outskirts of large areas of population, and have very substantial parking facilities.

8 **Discount stores**. The abolition of resale price maintenance has allowed retailers to charge whatever price they chose to fix. Some retailers have moved into the discount market, providing the minimum of customer services, and product display. The stores are usually located outside town centres, in districts where it is less expensive to buy, lease, or rent property; and in exchange for low prices they give little in the way of delivery or after-sales services. The main attraction is the low prices offered – only possible because of the low overheads, and the minimal services offered. Comet Warehouses and MFI are typical outlets.

9 **Mail order**. A variety of firms are involved in mail order. They include:
 a *Catalogue houses.* Most of you will have seen the catalogues produced by Freemans, Gratten, Littlewoods, and Kays, for example. Originally intended for people who could not get to town stores, they are now used by customers from every part of the country. In this type of operation, mail order houses make arrangements with manufacturers to supply a wide range of household products, clothing, and leisure equipment. The items are then featured (lavishly photographed in colour) in catalogues, which are sent to past customers and those replying to extensive and continual magazine advertisements. Goods can be ordered 'on approval', with 'free' credit terms offered (though the goods featured can often be bought more cheaply in the High Street), with payments spread over many months.

b *Mail order houses*. Another sector of the same market, which offers (via the Sunday supplements and other magazines) individual items or small ranges of items. Waxed coats and jackets, clocks, glassware, jewellery, medallions, and digital watches are advertised by such outlets as The Curiousity Shop, Hartington House, Scotcade, and Kaleidoscope. (Many have retail outlets as well.)

c *Small specialist firms*. These advertise in the 'small ads' sections of week end newspapers – often under the heading *Week-End Opportunities* in Saturday or Sunday newspapers. Typical products offered are fishermen's sweaters, items of furniture, computer software, shirts, and curtains. At the other extreme, firms may take full-page advertisements in specialist magazines devoted to sports or hobbies, such as the *Cricketer, Railway Modeller, Amateur Photographer*, or *Practical Computing*. Often the same products are offered by different outlets, each vying to attract customers with discounts, free gifts, credit terms, or speedy delivery.

d *Book Clubs*. Several book clubs regularly advertise nationally, but W H Smiths were a market leader in offering a whole army of apparently separate clubs which are in fact all run from the Swindon operation. (Subsequently, this package of clubs was sold to overseas buyers.) The choice of subjects includes railways, history , gardening, fiction. Others (eg *The Literary Guild*) concentrate upon a narrower market. Similarly, record clubs offer discs and tapes by post.

10 **Franchising**. A franchise is a legal arrangement between *franchisors* and *franchisees* in which the franchisor provides initial and continuing services (for which he is paid), and has an obligation to maintain an ongoing interest in the business of the franchisee. The franchisee operates under the banner or name of the franchisor, eg McDonalds. Typically the franchisor has dreamed up an idea (weight watching); invented a process (making a type of hamburger, or cooking chicken a special way), or an item of equipment (motor car), and has had an initial success on his own. He then licences others – the franchisees – to exploit the idea or process etc within a defined geographical area.

The franchisee has to make an initial, substantial investment to secure a franchise: McDonalds current charge is over £250 000, plus continuing payments. In return, the franchisee gets advice and guidance in the selection of a site, the modification and fitting out of the chosen premises in the franchisor's 'house-style', and in running the operation. Where appropriate, specialist equipment will be provided on lease. (Training for the franchisee and his staff may also be part of the franchisor's offer, both in the business aspects and in the mechanics of the production process.)

Often there is extra back-up from national advertising, marketing information, and a guaranteed flow of products (or ingredients) to sell.

The franchisee is still the owner of his or her own business, but will have to undertake to provide products or services of a given quality or standard, and be liable to inspection by the franchisor.

Over the past decade franchising has grown in magnitude and scope, from fast foods and car rental into a wide variety of operations. Recent entries to the market have been slimming clubs (the Cambridge Diet), environmentally friendly products (the Body Shop), and steak houses (Berni, via Grand Metropolitan Retailing). (Berni ask about £300 000 for each franchise package, plus a 15 per cent charge on turnover for the franchisor's support.) Sales in franchising operations are estimated at between £2–£3 billion annually now, and are increasing.

(Note there is another version of franchising – the exclusive distribution of a single product or product line, such as Volkswagen cars. Here the franchisee is tied to one make in return for a guarantee of no competition from other dealers within a given mileage. The franchisor here has much less control over the franchisee's business. A related situation exists in the franchises for commercial television: a nominated company has the exclusive rights to transmit programmes over a specific geographical area.)

11 **Miscellaneous non-store retailers**. These include door-to-door sellers (of groceries, brushes, milk, or fish); vending machines (especially useful where refreshments are needed and a 24-hour catering service is not economical), and 'Party-plan' selling. The latter was popularized by Tupperware, but is now used widely by other manufacturers of household items, cosmetics, and a wide range of clothing. The basic method is to use a person's private house as a venue, and involves the 'hostess' inviting a number of friends to a party (usually during the daytime), at which a sales person from the company concerned displays or demonstrates goods for inspection and purchase.

Activity 2

One or both of the following tasks can be attempted, in groups or singly, as preferred.

1 Visit a local shopping centre. Make a note of all the retail outlets, and classify them under the headings discussed above. Evaluate the resulting 'mix'. In particular, ascertain which types of outlet are found in the 'prime' shopping areas (ie where most people congregate), and which are found in the 'quieter' places.

2 Examine several consecutive (recent) issues of a local weekly paper. List all the retail outlets advertising, and classify them under the headings discussed above. Which types of outlet use large 'display' adverts, and which rely upon smaller 'display' or 'classified' headings?

Choosing the channel

In this section you will be introduced to some commonly used channels in product distribution. Some guidance is given in making choices, based on the comments on the various channels.

1 Producer →→→ final customer direct

The most direct and least complicated. Used for distributing:

a Industrial consumable products. Raw materials for industrial use (eg, coal for power stations): products bulky in volume, and large in relation to value; products sold in large quantities to a small number of outlets.

b Industrial durable products. Items with a large technical content; specially made to order; or large pieces of plant or machinery.

c Consumer consumable products. 'Buyer collects' ('pick your own' produce, farm shops, etc.); party plan (where seller delivers or brings); door-to-door (bread, milk), mail order.

d Consumer durables. Where producer has own retail outlets (Wesley-Barrell furniture, Pilkington Glass ('Glass Age' Store, Sevenoaks), Boots, Laura Ashley. Producer bears all the costs of delivery and point of sale selling, but has complete control over marketing; and is in direct touch with customers.

2 *Producer → → → retailer → → → final consumer*

a Industrial consumables. Rarely used, except for odd purchases: stationery, etc.

b Industrial durables. Very rarely used.

c Consumer consumables. Widely used where retailer is large (eg supermarket chain), and orders fill whole lorry loads going to one drop point. (Even when the items in question are of low value, but sold in very large quantities, it makes sense to deal direct.) Franchise operations.

d Consumer durables. Widely used for electrical goods – TV sets, washing machines, microwaves, etc – especially where retailer is an Electricity Board or a recognized large retail chain or discount store. Unit distribution costs are relatively low.

3 *Producer →→→ wholesaler →→→ retailer →→→ final customer*

a Industrial consumables, durables. very rarely found.

b Consumer consumables. Widely used for small, rapid turnover items, sold to a large number of small and geographically dispersed outlets, eg tobacco, sweets, newspapers, etc. (Changes are, however, taking place in the distribution of national dailies.)

A traditional, 'prevailing' method, going back well over 100 years, used especially where the producer is only small- or medium-sized, or relatively new to a market.

4 *Producer →→→ voluntary chain wholesaler →→→ retailer →→→ final customer*

You will have noted earlier that small, independent retailers use this method to overcome some of the problems of competition from larger groups.

5 *Producer →→→ agent →→→ retailer →→→ final customer*

Where producers wish to deal with only one outlet in a large area, they use a *manufacturer's agent*, who will deal with wholesalers calling on small retail outlets. Much less common in recent years.

6 Producer →→→ industrial distributor →→→ final customer

Used widely for industrial consumables. The distributor is a kind of merchant wholesaler. (Builders' merchants are good examples; small builders buy basic building materials, tools, and equipment from these merchants/distributors.)

Some guidelines in choosing a product's distribution channel

1 **Always** have the final customers (and their needs) in mind. The best choice takes account of customers' buying habits; where they are located, and how many of them there are.

2 **Consider** the nature of the product: what is its unit value; is speed essential in delivery? Can it easily pass through a sequence of owners? Has it a high technical value?

3 **Take into account** the order size (quantity and physical volume): the larger the order, the more likely the route will be direct.

4 **Review** your own resources. Are you able and can you afford to hold large stocks of finished items? Can you serve all your customers all of the time, or will you need the help of others?

5 **Evaluate** the costs and economic advantages and disadvantages of using different channels.

6 **Calculate** how much control you want over the way the product is finally presented and sold. Do you want intensive distribution – a very large number of outlets; selective distribution – a much more limited number of outlets; or exclusive distribution – to a few select outlets or franchises?

7 **Pay attention** to the 'customary' or 'prevailing' methods of distribution (if they already exist).

Choosing a channel

By now you will have realized that some general conclusions can be drawn from this review: the greater the number of outlets, and/or the greater the degree of dispersal of the outlets, the more attractive the use of middlemen becomes. Conversely, the more specialized and/or technical the product, the fewer the customers, the more attractive direct delivery is.

| Activity 3 | Discuss in groups what channels might be chosen (and why) by the producers/importers/owners in the following situations: |

1 An importer of high quality fishing rods intended for the dedicated amateur.
2 A manufacturer of industrial heaters presently using a sales force to sell direct to industry, and now intending to add a 'patio barbecue' set to its product lines.
3 A married couple who wish to set up a business making and selling expensive, heavy-duty knitwear (sweaters etc.) for both sexes.
4 A farmer growing peas and runner beans on a very large scale.
5 A builder of a small estate of 25 detached 4-bedroom houses.
6 The owner of a single detached 4-bedroom house.
7 A manufacturer of domestic double glazing equipment.
8 An importer of expensive ladies' perfume.

Groups should then compare answers, and prepared to defend their choices.

The distribution of services

A similar pattern emerges when you look at the distribution of services, though the *reasons* for the choice of particular channels may sometimes be different. Three important channels are:

1 Service provider →→→ final customer direct

The most common of all. The provider and user 'go together': solicitors or accountants and their clients; plumbers and householders; banks and their customers; doctors and patients; portrait painters and their subjects; undertakers and the bereaved – all these offer what are called 'personal services'.

2 Service provider →→→ agent →→→ final customer

Also a well-used channel when specialist advice, help, or information is needed (or is useful) to achieve something: buying life assurance from an insurance agent; booking a foreign holiday. For industrial or commercial customers, advertising agents, stockbrokers, and employment agencies provide similar specialist help or advice.

3 Service provider →→→ *retailer* →→→ *final customer*

Used where a retailer offers a service (eg film developing) to customers, but contracts a service provider to do the job for him.

<table>
<tr>
<td>

Activity 4

</td>
<td>

1 In groups consider what distribution channels could be chosen by service providers to sell the following:
a Endowment insurance policies.
b Hotels in seaside towns with empty rooms available for letting.
c Unbooked theatre seats.
d Car hire.
e Package holidays abroad.
f Factory security services.
2 By research find out the precise role played by the following in the distribution of services:
a Insurance broker.
b Travel agent.
c Tour operator.
d Employment agency.
e Finance house.
f Independent tutorial college (for 'A' levels, GCSE, etc.).

</td>
</tr>
</table>

Multi-channel distribution

Some producers do not stick to one single method of distribution (perhaps you spotted this when working on the last two activities). For instance, when:

1 Different products demand different channels. A cosmetic manufacturer might have an 'exclusive' range of products marketed through specialized 'high fashion' outlets, but with a cheaper range for the general market sold by High Street chemists.

2 The same product is sold to some customers in large enough quantities to justify only those customers 'missing out' a middleman. A manufacturer of lawn mowers could sell direct to large retailers (department stores, super/hypermarkets) but at the same time also sell to wholesalers supplying ironmongers, hardware shops, and small garden centres.

Deciding to use multi-channels can be a hard choice. as there is always the chance that that middlemen may object to the retail trade being supplied direct, and threaten to pull out of existing arrangements.

The costs of distribution

You have probably already learned something about the costs of running a business. If so, you will no doubt remember that in calculating the cost of an item, a manufacturer takes into account the costs of **raw materials, labour costs**, and **manufacturing expenses**. Extra costs are then added, traditionally called **overheads**. Normally overheads consist of such costs as **heating, lighting, rent**, and **rates** – the **factory overheads**. In addition you may have met the **non-manufacturing overheads**, including **staff salaries, administration**, and of course the costs of **distribution**.

In more detail, distribution costs break down into the following:

1 *Transportation costs, seller to buyer.* (Note: where goods pass along the distribution chain via middleman, cost are incurred *each time* goods are sold on.) The favourite channel in Britain for physical movement has largely switched from the railways to road transport. In some cases bulk deliveries of coal by the 'merry-go-round' system as an example, rail is still reasonably cost-effective.

2 *Administration and handling costs.* These include costs of storage, internal materials handling, packing and loading, after-sales service, complaints handling.

3 *Selling Costs.* Commission paid to sales people or agents; advertising and promotion.

4 *Wholesalers' costs.* Wholesalers incur all the costs mentioned above, but in addition must take into account the cost of goods purchased from producers.

5 *Retailers' costs.* The costs of the premises occupied are increasing as rents, leases, rates, and freehold property prices continue to rise, especially in the south, south-east, and parts of eastern England. Goods need to be presented or stocked in windows and on shelves and other fittings – all costing money. Staff wages and commissions, local advertising, costs of in-store promotion – all add to the final bill.

It should now be quite clear that the distribution process adds to or increases the final cost of products or services. Indeed distribution costs can become the single largest element in the final cost. Naturally, this expenditure is passed on to final customer, by being included in the price he or she pays for the product/service. However it can be seen that the benefits of the product being in the 'right place at the right time' do **add value** to the item. Thus purchasers will need to balance the benefits gained with the costs incurred in distribution.

Distribution trends

Forecasting the future is always difficult, but several trends in distribution seem to have been established recently; and others look likely to occur. The more important are:

1 Multiples and supermarket chains are becoming the dominant force and form in retailing, taking on both the wholesaling and retailing functions. This is to the detriment of smaller retailers.

2 These large organizations prefer suppliers to deliver direct to central warehouses (eg Tesco; Sainbury). Daily replenishment from the centre cuts down the individual store stockholdings and leads to generally smaller and more frequent deliveries. This gives the retail manager more control of day-to-day demands, ensures goods are fresh when delivered in store, and allows staff to handle inputs on a regular, controlled basis. (Some stores are looking at buying 'ex-works': collecting goods to achieve 100 per cent control of distribution. Where profit margins are as low as 5 per cent on some lines, the distribution operation will need to be under close supervision.)

3 Many in the retail trade see a situation in the early 1990s when all store orders are generated automatically, by EPOS (electronic point-of-sale equipment reading 'bar-codes' on products, not just to price them for individual sales, but to trigger off a reordering procedure). **Administration costs** will thus be reduced, and the salesperson's role will be less of an order-taker, more of a delivery-facilitator.

4 Independents continue to lose ground. Disadvantaged by being small, which leads to smaller turnover, lower discounts, and less variety, their strength has been that they can open flexibly (Sundays, Bank Holidays etc.). Now supermarkets and superstores are opening for longer and longer hours, and many have ample parking. Many also indulge (often illegally at present) in Sunday trading.

5 An increase in 'one stop shopping outlets', where a very wide variety of goods are found in one area or precinct.

6 A gradual increase in 'armchair shopping' via computer networks. (This, interestingly, could lead to an eventual reversal of the present practice of customers 'going to the store'. Stores could deliver the 'monthly shop' ordered electronically to the customer's house or premises. Some feasibility work has been done by retail chains on this idea.)

Activity 5	Divide into groups and attempt one or more of the following tasks:

    1 Choose a local firm (particularly one where contacts exist with the college, and/or where class members work full- or part-time), and, by contact, interview, or other research, establish:

       a its distribution requirements as a customer of other organizations,

       b how it distributes its own products or services.

    Prepare a report on your findings, contrasting any differences between *a* and *b*

    2 Assume the role of the transport manager of a large, high-class department store in the nearest city or town to your college. You are asked by the management to work out the best method of transporting the following items to the store, and to provide an estimate of the costs incurred, your firm arranging and paying for the carriage involved:

       a Six items of jewellery each worth £5000 to be collected from the manufacturers near Paris.

       b A consignment of 60 washing machines arriving in Felixstowe from the Continent.

       c 100 copies (required urgently) of a dress which was a sensation at a fashion show put on by a London dress-making firm three days ago.

       d A protype version of a new Formula One racing car (which is to form part of an in-store promotion) made by a firm in Didcot, Oxfordshire.

Summary of skills

The intention of the study in this unit is not only to learn facts about marketing, but also to develop skills which will be of use in the business world. This section at the end of each block indicates the skill areas covered by each activity.

Skills

Skill	*Activity in which skill is developed*
a Numeracy	5
b Learning and studying	1, 4, 5
c Identifying and tackling problems	1, 3, 5
d Information gathering	2, 4, 5
e Communicating	All activities
f Working with others	All activities

Block 9
Marketing and Non-commercial Organizations

Introduction

So far you have been looking mainly at the role of marketing within essentially profit-making organizations in the private sector, providing products or services; or non-profit-making organizations which *do* however engage in some significant commercial, profit-making activities. These activities (eg leisure facilities provided by local councils; short courses for industry run by colleges) can be profit-making in themselves, or help to reduce an overall deficit.

There is a third category of organization – the **non-commercial organization** (NCO), which can be said to have virtually no profit-making activities, and whose income is wholly (or for the most part) derived from funding, grants, or donations from central or local government, the business community, trusts and charities, and the general public.

However, these organizations also undertake marketing-related activities.

You will, then, be examining such organizations and the services they provide. (NCOs are mostly providers of **services** as opposed to **products** except, of course, when they for example clothe the needy or feed the starving.) Some consideration of the problems found in NCOs, and the sort of marketing activities used to attempt to overcome these problems, will be necessary.

It is obviously impossible to review the problems of every kind of NCO: for the purposes of this block you will be looking at *representative* organizations in some depth – a local authority's social services department, the National Trust in respect of one particular marketing solution to a problem it faced in the mid-1980s, and a registered charity giving a local service. Additionally, reference will to be made to sundry other organizations to illustrate points made.

The kind of problems you will be studying are those of *establishing need; matching service to identified need; promotion of services offered*; and the sometimes conflicting, sometimes complementary, elements of *compulsion* and *choice* in the provision of NCO services. *Pricing and charging* for such services is a complex matter, but one requiring analysis.

The non-commercial organization

There are different interpretations of what is meant by *a non-commercial* (sometimes called a *non-business*) *organization*. In my view, an NCO can be either **publicly** owned (like the Home Office, many schools, museums, or hospitals), or quite **private** (again, some schools, museums, or hospitals). There may indeed be some which have elements of both public and private

ownership or funding (like many universities). What is common to all of them is that they are essentially *non-profit making*.

This does not imply that a church cannot qualify as an NCO if it runs the odd disco to swell the funds, nor again a local playground which sells a few cakes in a local market place on a Saturday. If we find the great proportion of incomes from subscriptions, collections, or a grant from, say, a local council, and any surpluses earned are all ploughed back into the organization's work, then clearly it is an NCO. Political parties, CND, the Boys' Brigade, the Red Cross, your college, the police, the Citizens Advice Bureaux, Cancer Research, the Salvation Army – all of these are NCOs.

| *Activity 1* | 1 In small groups decide (giving your reasons) whether the following qualify as NCOs: |

1 In small groups decide (giving your reasons) whether the following qualify as NCOs:
   * Oxfam (which issues mail order catalogues for Christmas goods).
   * A stately home open to the public.
   * MIND.
   * British Rail.
   * The Labour Party.
   * Your local Fire Brigade.
   * The National Trust.
2 In the same groups make a list of at least six other NCOs known to you. Groups can then compare their findings.

A local social services department: a case study

You may not be aware of the functions and duties of a typical social services department. These are set out below for a specific department covering one division of a county in the Thames Valley, under three major headings (all of which are varieties of *caring*).

Residential care
Children's homes
Homes for elderly people
Homes/hostels for people with a mental handicap/illness
Residential nurseries

Day care
Childminders, playgroups, and day nurseries

Intermediate treatment
Day centres for elderly people/younger physically
   handicapped
Adult training centres
Family centres

Care in the home/community
Provision of daily living equipment
Adaptations to households for
   disabled/elderly/handicapped people
Home help/home care
Issuing of disabled driver/passenger car badges
Social work counselling, help, and advice
Registration of handicapped people

Local authority
social services
department
functions and duties
1987–8

Future plans at that time included a *family centre* (for families
and children under 5 years at risk, with specific programmes
for parents and children – teaching the importance of play,
for example); activities for children at home; and
fostering/residential care for those unable to be at home.

The **budget allocation** 1987/88 was:

	£
Residential and day care establishments — running costs,	
fuel, provisions, furniture, equipment etc.	315 087
Children's community support budget	34 000
Special case budget	22 500
Office equipment	4 000
Home care service equipment	800
Foster parent advertising	750
Books and publications	550

General and specific objectives included:

1 To help individuals to be able to make choices.
2 To uphold the right of individuals to be independent.
3 To ensure the positive, constructive, and planned use of
   residential care.
4 To put emphasis on preventative measures to avoid
   unnecessary use of residential care.
5 To encourage individuals to exercise their rights to
   benefit from care in the community in which they live.
6 To provide opportunities for handicapped people to get
   involved with the community in which they live.
7 To seek to maintain, and enhance, the quality of life of
   the elderly.

Establishing needs

You have many times during this course looked at definitions of marketing: all centre round first establishing customers' needs, then satisfying those needs. This authority like many others has a problem in establishing current needs, never mind forecasting future ones, for reasons beyond its control. Such reasons include:

1 *Hidden needs*. Some people in need of help (from Social Services) prefer not to ask for it. Some are frightened that the stability of the family will be threatened by, for example, a wife complaining about her husband's attitude to the children (and/or to her). Such needs may never surface, or remain hidden until a crisis is reached. Some people are simply too proud to ask for help.
2 *Diguised needs*. Others with complicated problems may only reveal part of the story, especially if family violence is involved.
3 *Needs revealed to other agencies*. Agencies such as a Citizens Advice Bureaux (see Block 12 for more details on the work of this organization) may be approached for help rather than the Social Services. Obviously cross-referral systems exist, but some overlap is inevitable.
4 *Needs emerge 'out of the blue'*. A problem can emerge in a family over a weekend. Even those concerned may not have appreciated the seriousness of the situation as it deteriorated.
5 *Difficulties in establishing the total situation*. Some people find it difficult to explain their problems and troubles: essential bits of information may be unknown to the department. (Obviously attempts are made to overcame these difficulties, and besides both full- and part-time conventional social workers, this department engaged a community-based worker).
6 *Ignorance of the help available*. Some potential customers (often called *clients*) are totally unaware of the services they can call upon.

Matching services to needs

Once needs have been identified there are further difficulties in matching the service available to those needs. Money constraints may prevent sufficient qualified staff to be on hand to cope with all the work load all of the time. In addition, social work seems to have a low 'status-rating', particularly after the many criticism levelled against social workers by the media in the last decade. Recruitment is in consequence more difficult.

Another dimension of the same problem is the shortage of foster home placements for children who have to live apart from their families. To try and alleviate the situation, this department appointed a fostering and specialist adoption worker.

Excess demand

As demand increases (and it will as the client-base slowly becomes more aware) and more need is revealed, there comes a limit as to what can be done with the resources available. One way to cope is to 'ration' the response, that is to differentiate between the needs of different people, dealing first with those in greatest need. (In a slightly different context a local authority housing department allocates 'points' to applicants for council rented accommodation. If only one property is available in a particular locality, and three applicant families are considered, the family with the greatest need – usually the highest number of points – will be offered it.)

As you will see from the 'Volunteer Link-up' case study, another way out is to persuade a voluntary agency to do the job. In the case of council tenants needing home adaptations to cope with old age or disability, the council concerned is requested to foot the bill.

Promotion of social services

The Social Service department is, to quote one of its officers, 'not a very saleable product'. Whilst it can advertise for staff, foster parents, or home helps, it is difficult for it to promote its services. Those who do not have an immediate need for a social worker or a place for a handicapped relative are hardly likely to file a leaflet or a brochure to await the time a problem does emerge. What can be done is to ensure that all other related agencies – doctors, lawyers, voluntary organizations, police, etc. – who may need to refer cases have all the necessary information on the social services available.

Pricing and charging. The services are normally free.

Activity 2	As a group, organize an in-depth investigation into one of the following:

1 a local hospital.
2 a local charity.
3 your local Citizens Advice Bureau.

4 one of the service-giving departments of your local district or city council.

5 a local non-commercial organization of your choice.

Look at the organization chosen under the headings used in the Social Services department above. What are the similarities and differences between the case study organization and the one you have chosen?

Enterprise Neptune (National Trust): a case study:

This case study relates to the mid-1980s project by the National Trust (NT) to acquire and preserve a stretch of coastline in the Poole region. The background was BP's wish to prospect for (and, if appropriate, to extract) oil in two areas, one of which was Studland Point. The situation raised the typical marketing dilemma: was the application a *threat* or an *opportunity*? The NT saw it as the latter.

Enterprise Neptune was an idea born 20 years previously (the target being to ensure that as far as possible the coastline was preserved for public use by acquisition) but not as yet fully developed. The 'oil issue' was an emotive one, and could be used to get national attention.

Promotion of Enterprise Neptune

The National Trust, being a public body, could only take a stance when it was itself directly involved in an issue. Enterprise Neptune was such an involvement. However NT realized it needed to shake off its rather élitist image and appeal to the widest spectrum of the population, in order to raise sufficient money and be successful in opposing the exploratory drilling operation.

In fact BP did give way over Studland, so the problem became how to raise the purchase price. An obvious strategy was to place large (but expensive) advertisements in the newspapers. Instead the NT chose to invite professional writers to do the job as part of their normal work.

A wide selection of journalists (including freelance ones), contributing to Sunday colour supplements, *Country Life*, *Woman's Own*, *Family Circle*, and other magazines were taken on a trip to see both land in private ownership (with caravan sites and similar developments), and some 2000 acres of NT property in which, for example, a medieval landscape or small fields had been preserved. The latter demonstrated what good site management could do to keep the countryside looking unspoilt.

Stops were made, and the journalists encouraged to walk about the NT holdings. The guides stressed that the operations were profitable as well as being sites of outstanding natural beauty. Illustrated literature was distributed.

The outcome

The campaign was a complete success. The articles in the (very different) publications stimulated considerable interest. Money poured in. The NT, within four months, added eight miles of coastline to its property portfolio.

Lessons learned

The major lesson learned was that for this kind of campaign, harnessing the goodwill of the press was essential. Secondly, that including illustrations in publicity material was valuable. Thirdly, that the old adage in selling of 'get the prospect to see, handle, touch, taste the product' applies in conservation, just as much as in selling cheese or good quality cloth.

| *Activity 3* | In small groups discuss: |

In small groups discuss:
1 Why the 'obvious' choice of extensive national newspaper advertising was not adopted.
2 Why the journalists were invited to view the properties in a group, rather than being taken round individually.
3 Any additional ingredients you would have included in the campaign, if you had been responsible for planning it.

Volunteer Link-up (West Oxon): a case study

Volunteer Link-up (West Oxon), or VLU, acts as a link in the local community between those who seek voluntary help and volunteers able and willing to provide it. Founded in 1983, this registered charity's clients include local authorities, other charities, and individuals needing assistance. Here is a selection of requests received:

1　*Support for the statutory services*

Social services:
>Transport for children's homes; visiting relatives.
>Support for disadvantaged teenagers.
>Toy library.
>Gardening/decorating/repairs.

Area health authority:
>Transport of patients to health centres, hospitals.
>Support for patients with depression, strokes etc.
>Hospital visiting.
>Outings; horse riding for mentally handicapped.

Probation service:
>Transport for prison visiting.
>Help with young offenders.
>Finding tasks for people serving community service orders.

District council;
>Gardening (for elderly council tenants).
>Home maintenance (also for elderly council tenants).
>Distributing firewood to elderly tenants.
>Social activities for people in sheltered housing.

2　*Regular assistance to other voluntary organizations*

Clients include Age Concern, Cruse, Save the Children Fund, OXFAM, RNIB. These and local charities are represented on the Management Committee.

VLU volunteers helping teach horseriding to mentally handicapped children

3 *Assistance to individuals*

By far the most important role is *befriending*, that is being prepared to spend time and effort in visiting the lonely and housebound.

Matching service to need

In 1987, 400 new requests for voluntary help were received; and provisional figures for 1988 were 500. Some requests may require a single visit; others mean a continuing series of calls. All require careful matching of the volunteers' skills to the particular needs of an applicant.

Each volunteer is carefully interviewed to establish his/her skills, interests, and capabilities. All applicants complete a questionnaire; references are required, and are taken up. All accepted volunteers are put on a register. All applications for help are then carefully matched against the appropriate volunteer(s).

Excess demand

Whilst the 200+ list of volunteers can cope with most requests, occasionally some have to be refused. Increases in demand could become difficult to meet in future, and priorities may have to be introduced.

Promotion of VLU

The local weekly newspaper often prints articles and other news from VLU under its distinctive logo. Potential clients can find out from these stories how to contact the office. Requests for volunteers also appear in the same medium. Satisfied individual clients tend to tell their friends.

Until 1989, funding was from central and local government sources. The need for alternative funding, to maintain and increase the services, calls for considerable and carefully-planned fund-raising, and well-publicized promotional efforts to be made within the local community. (In 1987–8 the cost of providing the service was £7852.

Charging for services

All the services provided by VLU are free to the recipients, even though modest travelling expenses are payable to volunteers. However donations from satisfied clients are received and accepted from time to time.

| Activity 4 | In small groups assume you are involved in the management of a charity similar to VLU. Consider the following problems, and come up with possible solutions: |

1 The possibility of recruiting highly unsuitable volunteers (eg those with a past criminal record, especially relating to theft from houses, or violence).

2 Encouraging people with minimum skills and/or little confidence to participate in voluntary activities and ensuring the work is done satisfactorily.

3 The possibility that government funding will cease next year, while demand is increasing from the statutory services (consider where you might be able to obtain the necessary money, and how you would approach these potential sources).

Choice in the provision and receipt of services

There are in fact very few services which people are totally compelled to use without choice: being sent to prison is one. Some would argue that education is another, but in fact, whilst the state demands that children from 5 to 16 years old be *educated*, there is no compulsion to use any specific service provider. Children may be sent to local authority or state-run schools, and even here there is often some element of choice, the decision not totally dictated by catchment areas. A second choice is the private (sometimes called the *public!*) sector. A third is a steadily growing one where parents educate their children at home.

(There will always of course be those in the lowest income groups for whom choice is, and will continue to be, very restricted.)

Pricing and charging for non-commercial services

As you have seen, there are non-commercial organizations which normally do not charge for their services, the whole of the operating costs being borne from income derived from sources external to the organization. There are, however, organizations which do charge, sometimes in a complex way.

An interesting example is a local college of further education. Full-time students aged 19 or under at the start of a college year attend free; part-time ones over the age of 19 attending recognized courses are charged in accordance with the 'level' of the course (so-called 'advanced' courses being charged at a higher rate than non-advanced ones), and the number of timetabled hours. The actual prices charged are laid down centrally by the authority. Thus the college (as at 1989) does not control the price element of the marketing mix, a fact you may already have discovered if you have investigated as an assignment your college's marketing effort. What is clear is that all these prices are subsidized by the county council from its general income.

On the other hand, where a college is involved in preparing and running courses for local industry, these courses have to be 'self-financing', that is, the prices charged must at least cover the costs of putting them on. The usual situation is that a profit element (which may be wholly or in part retained as revenue by the college) is added to the full costs.

One of the difficulties of public regulation of prices is that political, social, or environmental considerations may be given greater emphases than economic ones.

| *Activity 5* | In groups, consider the kinds of considerations which seem to operate in the following instances, other than cost-covering/profit-making ones:
1 Prescription charges.
2 Parking charges in city/town centres.
3 The community charge (poll tax).
4 A local council which makes no charge for pest control visits to private houses.
5 A rise in the price of road fund licences for private cars. |

Summary of skills

The intention of the study in this unit is not only to learn facts about marketing but also to develop skills which will be of use in the business world. This section at the end of each block indicates the skill areas covered by each activity.

Skills

Skill	*Activities in which skill is developed*
Learning and studying	2, 5
Identifying and tackling problems	2, 4
Information gathering	1, 2, 5
Communicating	All activities
Working with others	All activities

Block 10
The Marketing Planning Process

Introduction

You have now reached the stage when you can stand back from the detailed work you have done and start looking at marketing as an integrated process. So, instead of focusing attention on an individual marketing activity such as marketing research, advertising, or distribution, in this block you will be involved in seeing how these, and other similar activities, can be united into an overall marketing plan; which, in turn, is part of the organization's total plan, the **corporate plan**.

From this plan are derived corporate objectives and strategies, including marketing ones.

After considering the overall corporate plan and how it is put together, you will be introduced in some detail to the process of **marketing planning**, including how much plans are prepared and used. (This part of the block will also look at the vexed question of resources allocation.) You will also need to revise and refine the role of the marketing function within the organization.

Next you will need to consider how the ways in which the **management style** of top managers (the way in which they manage) affects the corporate plan, and in particular, their organizations' approaches to marketing, including the marketing planning process. Finally, you will learn how ideas and skills acquired elsewhere in the course about the management of change can be applied to an organization's marketing effort.

An introduction to the planning process

The kinds of planning processes you are going to look at in this block are complex and involve many stages. However, when you examine them carefully, you will notice that there is a simple underlying structure, similar to that shown below.

> ## Stages in a planning process
>
> (A logically organized set of activities designed to produce a series of objectives and the development of strategies and plans to fulfill these objectives)
>
> Stage 1:   review   'Where are we now?'
> Stage 2:   formulation of objectives   'Where do we want to go?'
> Stage 3:   formulation of strategies   'How shall we get there?'
> Stage 4:   formulation of plans/programmes 'What do we have to do to get there?' (ie how shall we organize our resources?)

A simple view of the planning process

Whether you are dealing with a small firm at the beginning of its life, a medium-size service provider with a history of ten years of growth, or a giant public sector organization with 100 years of service to the community behind it, the same questions can be asked.

The first question: '*Where are we now*?' is really inviting us to take stock of our current position in some detail. It implies supplementary questions like 'What markets are we supplying now?'; 'What are our present resources (eg premises, cash, plant/equipment, workforce and its skills and knowledge)?', and 'What are the good and bad points about those resources (our *strengths and weaknesses*)?'; and 'What markets (or segments of markets) can we go for, bearing in mind our current resources?'

Stage 2, '*Where do we want to go*?', makes us look at our objectives in the short, medium, and long term. Of course, what we discover from our review – particularly our strengths and weaknesses – will help to point the way. A small firm's objectives will probably be those of the owners or partners who run it; whilst the larger enterprises should really be following objectives which are in the best interests of all the shareholders, not just of those running the organization. These objectives could be financial (profit objectives); sales (in terms of goods sold, services offered); increases in our share of existing markets, or indeed entering new markets where appropriate, with a specific target of sales or market share in view. All these objectives should be business-like and obtainable.

'*How shall we get there*?', Stage 3, invites us to look at ways and means of attaining our objectives. If we are looking at products or services for example, we shall need to consider what the marketing mix should be for each. Indeed each separate product/service will need to have its own strategy worked out.

Finally, '*What do we do to get there?*', requires us to make specific plans or set out programmes of activity so that the agreed strategy can be successfully followed. For example, if a strategy were to deliver direct to customers, the question arises how do we do this? By our own transport (do we need to buy more vehicles, and if so, what kinds)? By carrier (which one)? By the GPO (which service)? Delivery frequency, size of loads, times of delivery – all these and many other points will need to be settled and arrangements made which both match the customers' wants and are cost-effective.

| Activity 1 | Pottem Ltd is a small company in the Cotswolds. It grows and prepares plants for bedding out in the spring and summer months, and indoor plants for tables and window ledges. Tony Blossom is the managing director, and his wife Mary and daughter Joan are the other directors. |

Pottem has been in business now for 26 years, and the firm owns a nice house with five acres of land attached. (Two acres are presently leased to a local farmer for sheep grazing.) Three full-time staff help to run the place, with part-time help as needed.

Tony did not do well at school, and left at 16 to work on a farm. However he found working with plants more attractive than with animals, and soon took a job as a labourer with a local horticulturalist. By the time he was 23 he was in charge of an acre of greenhouses growing a wide variety of produce, including lettuces, tomatoes, and vegetables, some for immediate consumption and some for bedding out.

While still living at home, he started to get interested in growing flowers, and began to win cups and prizes at flower shows. He quickly got the reputation of being able to grow excellent specimens. Mary, then his girl-friend, helped Tony with the floral arrangements; and while she finished her 'A' level biology at college, worked part-time for a florist preparing wedding bouquets and funeral wreaths. Before marrying Tony, and until Joan was born, Mary worked at an agricultural research station, investigating pests and pesticides.

Soon after Joan was a year old, Tony and Mary set up a business together wholesaling bedding plants to garden centres. They made a poor start as they only knew a few local centres, but over the years they have built up a network of customers. They enjoyed a reputation for quality plants which increasingly they are growing themselves. Their six long greenhouses are of current design, with the latest heating, lighting, and watering systems. Besides their own car, the firm only runs a transit-type van as many of the customers like to come to view, choose, and take away their orders.

Sales have fallen slightly over the last 18 months, as some of the garden centres' managers have changed, and Tony has been so busy supervising the work (now Joan is away at university reading horticulture) that he hasn't had time to visit the new managers.

Six months' ago a large DIY supermarket opened half a mile away, and Tony was approached last week by their buyer with a view to him supplying the store with pot and bedding plants, and some vegetable lines. Tony estimated that if he accepted, 60% of his total output would go to this one outlet. Further, he would have to divert capacity to vegetables. There was also talk of supplying cut flowers. 'Do a good job for us, Tony, and you could be supplying the whole group in two years!' he was told.

Tony has called a board meeting today (to include Joan) to discuss the situation.

In groups of three or four assume you are the board of Pottem Ltd.
1 Carry out a review of Pottem as at today, including its strengths and weaknesses.
2 Discuss the pros and cons of taking up the DIY store's offer. If you decide not to accept, how else will you tackle the problem of falling sales?
3 Consequent on any decisions taken in 2, discuss and prepare a list of objectives in the short/medium/long term.
4 Discuss and prepare a list of strategies appropriate for attaining the objectives.
5 Outline the plans and the resources you would need to be able to organize the business to attain the objectives.

At every stage of this activity, make a note of any *extra* information you feel you should have/would find useful to have, in order to make sound decisions.

Constructing the corporate plan

By the term **corporate plan**, we mean a plan similar in outline to the kind of plan you have just considered, but drawn up for a larger organization, large enough to have separate financial, marketing, production, personnel functions, for example.

At first sight the corporate planning process seems complex and difficult to follow. The diagram below attempts to simplify matters; and when you begin to examine it carefully, you will see it very much resembles the process you have just been looking at. There are some differences: the organization is larger; the process has been split up into separate compartments, one per function, finally amalgamating into the complete plan. A conflict resolution stage has been added, and so on.

Stage 1: establishing financial objectives ahead

The initial activity is one of setting long-term goals, expressed in financial terminology: examples are turnover targets, pre-tax profit levels, returns on capital invested in the organization. (For a non-profit making organization, the target incomes and revenues needed to carry on its activities would be established.)

A distant planning horizon is normally chosen: the average is 5 years ahead. Some organizations may have tentative objectives 10, 20, even 25 years into the future, but forecasting that far ahead is a very speculative business.

Stage 2: the 'management audit'

You are probably now aware that in business the word **audit** is generally used to mean a review or evaluation of some function or activity. Very often, it is applied to the finance and accounting operations but we can use it to cover other activities as well. You will see in the diagram above, under the main 'management' heading, that the following are covered: marketing and distribution; production; the financial operation; and the personnel function. (Some marketing writers treat *marketing* and *distribution* as separate and equal functions when dealing with this topic. As we have seen, distribution is part of marketing, and they can be discussed together.)

Such an evaluation should be a regular (annual) activity in all organizations; not just a way of dealing *ad hoc* with a crisis, or sudden change of fortune. As with any appraisal, it is best done as objectively as possible.

The construction of a corporate plan Some extra steps have been included here, not shown in the last diagram as they would have over-complicated it.

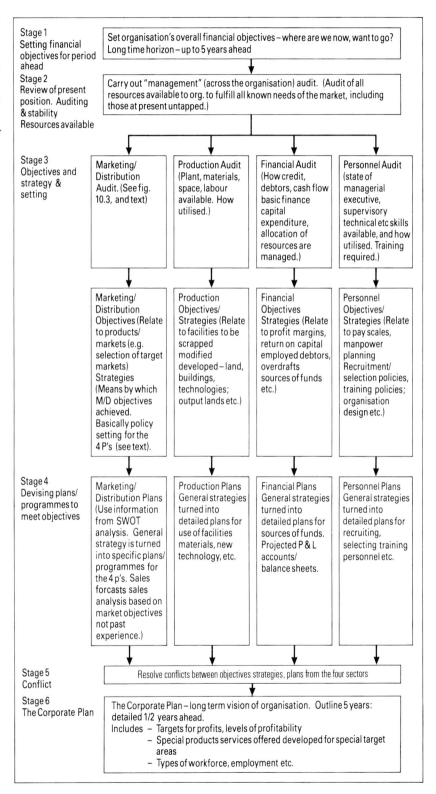

Stage 1 Setting financial objectives for period ahead	Set organisation's overall financial objectives – where are we now, want to go? Long time horizon – up to 5 years ahead			
Stage 2 Review of present position. Auditing & stability Resources available	Carry out "management" (across the organisation) audit. (Audit of all resources available to org. to fulfill all known needs of the market, including those at present untapped.)			
Stage 3 Objectives and strategy & setting	Marketing/ Distribution Audit. (See fig. 10.3, and text)	Production Audit (Plant, materials, space, labour available. How utilised.)	Financial Audit (How credit, debtors, cash flow basic finance capital expenditure, allocation of resources are managed.)	Personnel Audit (state of managerial executive, supervisory technical etc skills available, and how utilised. Training required.)
	Marketing/ Distribution Objectives (Relate to products/ markets (e.g. selection of target markets) Strategies (Means by which M/D objectives achieved. Basically policy setting for the 4 P's (see text).	Production Objectives/ Strategies (Relate to facilities to be scrapped modified developed – land, buildings, technologies; output lands etc.)	Financial Objectives Strategies (Relate to profit margins, return on capital employed debtors, overdrafts sources of funds etc.)	Personnel Objectives/ Strategies (Relate to pay scales, manpower planning Recruitment/ selection policies, training policies; organisation design etc.)
Stage 4 Devising plans/ programmes to meet objectives	Marketing/ Distribution Plans (Use information from SWOT analysis. General strategy is turned into specific plans/ programmes for the 4 p's. Sales forcasts sales analysis based on market objectives not past experience.)	Production Plans General strategies turned into detailed plans for use of facilities materials, new technology, etc.	Financial Plans General strategies turned into detailed plans for sources of funds. Projected P & L accounts/ balance sheets.	Personnel Plans General strategies turned into detailed plans for recruiting, selecting training personnel etc.
Stage 5 Conflict	Resolve conflicts between objectives strategies, plans from the four sectors			
Stage 6 The Corporate Plan	The Corporate Plan – long term vision of organisation. Outline 5 years: detailed 1/2 years ahead. Includes – Targets for profits, levels of profitability – Special products services offered developed for special target areas – Types of workforce, employment etc.			

The diagram does include, to enable you to have an overview of the whole process, some detail of the items/activities reviewed in non-marketing areas. For example, the financial audit would cover such items as resource allocation – how does the money get shared out between departments (by past practice, by giving most to those who shout the loudest, or to those whose need is greatest?), and who decides, and what evidence is prepared on which decisions are made?

A more detailed analysis of the marketing aspects is made in the next section.

Stage 3: objective and strategy setting

This is not an easy task to accomplish in a large organization. It combines both formulation of strategies and formulation of objectives.
Again some indication of the areas covered in the non-marketing functions are given. Under personnel we might decide an *objective* might be to give all staff in commercial and administrative jobs keyboard training to a given standard. The *strategy* might be to arrange for a local college to do the training on a three-day block-release basis.

The marketing functions are dealt with in the next section.

Stage 4: devising plans or programmes to meet objectives

In this stage, the strategies are turned into firm and detailed plans for one year, and less detailed ones for future years. The equivalent stage in the 'planning process' was also the fourth (*formulation of plans, programmes*).

Carrying on with the example above, the planning of the keyboard programme would entail such detailed matters as who would have overall responsibility for the training being arranged; plus timing, costing, venues, syllabuses, evaluation of the training, and so on.

Stage 5: resolving conflicts

One of the problems of having different departments setting their own objectives is, no matter how much liaison there is between functions, there is always the possibility that the objectives chosen by different functions may conflict.

Sales policy may be very customer orientated, with a major objective of maximizing orders, and achieving a specific turnover figure. Sales may want to introduce new lines to meet identified needs, and to deliver when, where, and in whatever quantities requested by customers – all laudable targets in themselves. On the other hand production may not have the capacity, equipment, or expertise to cope with new lines; and one of their objectives may be to lower production costs by concentrating on long runs, without interruptions for small special orders. Capital may not be available for any new capacity needed, unless some other project (eg a marketing campaign or training programme) is deferred or abandoned.

You will be looking later in this block at the role of the chief executive (and other top management) in marketing planning. He or she is the person who has no particular departmental responsibility and can best decide between the conflicting demands, choose what is practicable, and arrive, with those concerned, at a workable compromise.

Stage 6: the corporate plan

The integrated plans and programmes are then embodied in the **corporate plan**, a long-term vision of the future of the organization. It will contain a summary of what it is intended to achieve financial objectives, strategies, and plans; products and markets; the make up of the workforce; and other matters such as the *image* of the organization), detailed forecasts for 1 or 2 year(s) ahead and on outline for up to 5 years.

Activity 2	In groups discuss, and record your conclusions for reporting back to the whole class, the following: 1 Does an organization need to plan ahead at all? (Surely you can *never* completely forecast the future, thus any plan is only a good guess at best?) 2 Suppose you agree that planning should be done, why look ahead five years? Surely circumstances may change dramatically in that time: should one, or at most two, years ahead be enough? 3 Are conflicts over objectives, strategies, plans, and programmes between functions good for or harmful to organizations?

The marketing planning process in more detail

Now you are in a position to look more closely at the **marketing planning** element of the corporate plan. The diagram illustrates the process, this time using a 9-stage approach.

The full
marketing plan
process

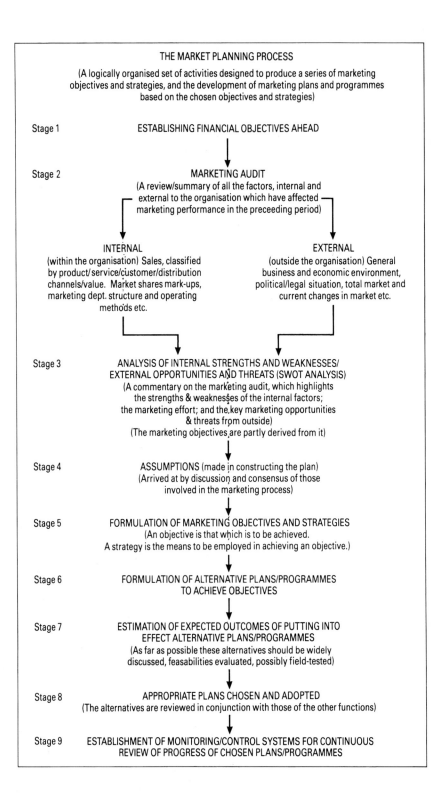

THE MARKET PLANNING PROCESS

(A logically organised set of activities designed to produce a series of marketing
objectives and strategies, and the development of marketing plans and programmes
based on the chosen objectives and strategies)

Stage 1   ESTABLISHING FINANCIAL OBJECTIVES AHEAD

Stage 2   MARKETING AUDIT
                 (A review/summary of all the factors, internal and
                 external to the organisation which have affected
                 marketing performance in the preceeding period)

INTERNAL   EXTERNAL
(within the organisation) Sales, classified   (outside the organisation) General
by product/service/customer/distribution   business and economic environment,
channels/value. Market shares mark-ups,   political/legal situation, total market and
marketing dept. structure and operating   current changes in market etc.
methods etc.

Stage 3   ANALYSIS OF INTERNAL STRENGTHS AND WEAKNESSES/
                 EXTERNAL OPPORTUNITIES AND THREATS (SWOT ANALYSIS)
                 (A commentary on the marketing audit, which highlights
                 the strengths & weaknesses of the internal factors;
                 the marketing effort; and the key marketing opportunities
                 & threats from outside)
                 (The marketing objectives are partly derived from it)

Stage 4   ASSUMPTIONS (made in constructing the plan)
                 (Arrived at by discussion and consensus of those
                 involved in the marketing process)

Stage 5   FORMULATION OF MARKETING OBJECTIVES AND STRATEGIES
                 (An objective is that which is to be achieved.
                 A strategy is the means to be employed in achieving an objective.)

Stage 6   FORMULATION OF ALTERNATIVE PLANS/PROGRAMMES
                 TO ACHIEVE OBJECTIVES

Stage 7   ESTIMATION OF EXPECTED OUTCOMES OF PUTTING INTO
                 EFFECT ALTERNATIVE PLANS/PROGRAMMES
                 (As far as possible these alternatives should be widely
                 discussed, feasabilities evaluated, possibly field-tested)

Stage 8   APPROPRIATE PLANS CHOSEN AND ADOPTED
                 (The alternatives are reviewed in conjunction with those of the other functions)

Stage 9   ESTABLISHMENT OF MONITORING/CONTROL SYSTEMS FOR CONTINUOUS
                 REVIEW OF PROGRESS OF CHOSEN PLANS/PROGRAMMES

Stage 1: establishing financial objectives ahead

This was fully covered in the previous section.

Stage 2: the marketing audit

This is a review of all those factors, both internal and external, which have affected the organization's marketing performance in the preceeding period – usually one year. The review includes the previous objectives, strategies, plans and any assumptions upon which the objectives, etc, were based. (See also Stage 4, below.) In addition the plans, programmes, the way in which they were carried out, and the degree to which they were successful, will need careful scrutiny.

The **internal audit** is ideally both intensive and extensive. It covers not only sales, categorized under many headings, but also market shares for each product/service; the profitability of each line; every one of the elements of the '4 Ps' (which you met in earlier blocks); and the way in which the marketing/ sales operation is run and monitored, including the degree of efficiency of marketing research and intelligence gathering, and the manner in which the information obtained is put to use.

A careful study is made of marketing budgets: how they are drawn up, and how well they take into account the need for capital resources and revenue expenditure as indicated by the agreed objectives.

The **external audit**, on the other hand, will gather as much information as possible about the organization's environment. Some of this will be available from published material (government statistics on employment, trends, output, balance of payments etc: CBI forward forecasts on industrial trends, for example). Some information may have to be gained from market research into the total market for the products/services offered: its size, its growth or contraction; technical developments, trends, the number of competitors; individual market shares for major competitors, the marketing mixes they use, their strengths and weaknesses.

Stage 3: analysis of the organization's strengths and weaknesses: opportunities and threats (from outside) – SWOT analysis

This is a key part of the marketing planning process. The marketing plan will normally not include all the details of the audit, but it *would* include the SWOT analysis. (The term

SWOT analysis, is derived from the initial letters of strengths, weaknesses, opportunities, threats.)

The accent will be on **key factors**, those strengths (eg excellent quality products), and weaknesses (eg delays in delivery, or lack of brochures/catalogues or good point-of-sale material) which mark out or distinguish the organization from its competitors. The whole point of this analysis is to produce a precise, clear, and relatively short account of where the organization is now; how it sees itself in the market-place as against its competitors; what shortcomings need to be overcome, what opportunities can be turned to advantage; where it can do better than the competition; and what is required for all these things to be achieved.

It has even been suggested that this idea should be taken further in organizations: individual managers should carry out departmental SWOTs. The final SWOT will then be a balanced overview of the whole organization.

| *Activity 3* | Individually, or in groups if more appropriate, carry out a SWOT analysis on an organization known to you. |

Examples could be the college you attend; the organization which employs you; a club of which you are a regular member; or a church, charity, or youth group you are involved with.

(Note: the notion of 'competition' can still apply in virtually all of these organizations; it will be other groups with similar objectives or any other group which could attract members away.)

Stage 4: making assumptions

Everyone has to make assumptions about the world. Think about the ones you make every day: that the car will start straight away in the morning, or that the bus will pick you up as usual. All your plans for the future contain assumptions. If you book a package holiday abroad, you assume there will be an aeroplane seat for you, a courier to meet you on landing, and a hotel bedroom ready.

Organizations' plans also contain assumptions, but they should be specific and reasonable ones. Usually they are concerned with the external environment: assumptions about the political future (eg a government continuing in office or possible changes in industrial policies); about the economic future (eg inflation levels or the strength of sterling); about competition (new products coming on to the market or changes in market prices, particularly in commodities like oil), and so on.

Assumptions can of course, turn out to be wrong; it may, therefore be necessary to have alternative plans available to cover the different possible future conditions brought about by changes in the external environment.

Stage 5: formulation of marketing objectives and strategies

Where a long-term plan (say 3–5 years ahead) is being developed, the long-term objectives and strategies will be shown in outline; but it will also be necessary to set out next year's (one-year) plan in full detail. Everything appearing here will need to take the SWOT analysis into account.

Stage 6: formulation of plans/programmes to achieve the objectives

These, of course, are based on the strategies, noting (from Stage 5 above) that alternative sets of plans/programmes may have to be prepared to meet possible changes in the external environment. All these plans should be thoroughly tested out (as far as it is possible to do so in, for examples, test markets) and widely discussed by those given the task of putting them into action.

Stage 7: estimation of expected outcomes of adopting alternative plans/programmes

A careful assessment is needed to establish and evaluate the possible outcomes of the plans or programmes adopted. This is especially important where plans could have 'knock-on' effects on the rest of the organization. For example plan to put in attractive incentive or bonus scheme for the sales staff in the showroom, related to orders taken, and you may have to cope with a request from the order office staff to enjoy the benefits of a similar scheme.

Stage 8: appropriate plans chosen and adopted

The detailed plans for products/services; product/service mixes; campaigns, launch-dates, timings; sales target allocations to representatives; and the consequent costs and budgets, etc., are now ready for adoption.

But, although you may have tried to ensure that the objectives and strategies of other departments do not conflict with your own, a final check is still necessary to make sure that the

marketing plans harmonize with the plans of the other
functions – finance, production, etc.

*Stage 9: establishment of monitoring/control systems for review of
progress of plans/programmes*

Once targets are agreed, and plans made, it is essential to check
that the plans are 'on target' from time to time. Such reviews
should be ongoing – just like the continuous assessments you
have had throughout the course, to ensure that you are meeting
course objectives.

Activity 4	Individually, or in groups if more appropriate, take the organization you chose in Activity 3, and *either*

1 prepare marketing plans or programmes for it based on
   the information you have already; *or*
2 If you do not have enough information, work out
   precisely what information you would need to make such
   plans.

Resources allocation

Resources in organizations are often thought of totally in terms
of money, but you need to consider people, time, and space as
well. In a badly planned concern, each function, each
department, and each section will compete for resources. How
much they will get often depends upon how much power or
influence each possesses.

You will clearly see that if corporate planning is practised,
budgets (and by implication all other kinds of resources) are
allocated to perform those tasks agreed by management. When
resources are lacking for any reason, then what is available is
allocated to those plans or programmes generally agreed to be
the most important to the survival and growth of the
organization. Thus resource allocation in a planning-orientated
concern is less likely to be arbitrary and haphazard, and is more
likely to be controlled, consistent, and appropriate.
There will certainly be a much better chance that the planned
use of resources will produce more profit than the unplanned one.

The role of the marketing function

Activity 5

In groups discuss the role of the marketing function, particularly in the light of what you have learned from this block. Is it:

a peripheral (inessential, marginal, minor) to the rest of the organization?
b of equal value as any other function to the organization?
c an essential, key function?
d the most important function of all?

Each group should appoint a chairperson to report back its findings to the whole class. All four views should be considered in turn, and the reasons for acceptance or rejection worked out.

Management styles and marketing

You have probably already looked at **management styles** in the unit *People and Organizations*. Writers on this topic use several different types of classification, though many of them are really variations on a similar theme: at one end there is the **autocrat** (task-centred, relies on power, keeps information, rarely delegates; communication is all one-way – downwards; fears and threats are constant weapons); and at the other is the **consultative/participative manager** – or even more extreme – the **democrat/abdicator** (who consults, delegates, and perhaps even let the group make its own decisions, on, for example, majority votes). There are, of course, types that fall between these extremes.

A somewhat different version contrasts managers with a primary concern for production/results (**task-centred**), and those with a primary concern for the staff (**people-orientated**).

However the best model with which to try and answer the question: 'How are organizations' approaches to marketing affected by their management styles?' is W Reddin's *3D Theory of Managerial Effectiveness*. This suggests that both higher and lower levels of effectiveness exist for four basic styles.

Reddin's basic styles
These are:
1 **Related.** This kind of manager likes to relate to other people: to communicate with, and persuade them.

2 **Separate**. An individual who has lost heart and motivation; who doesn't get involved if at all possible.
3 **Dedicated**. A person totally committed to the organization, and task-centred.
4 **Integrated**. A more 'rounded' manager, who is both task- and people-centred, who aims at getting a committed workforce and a highly productive team.

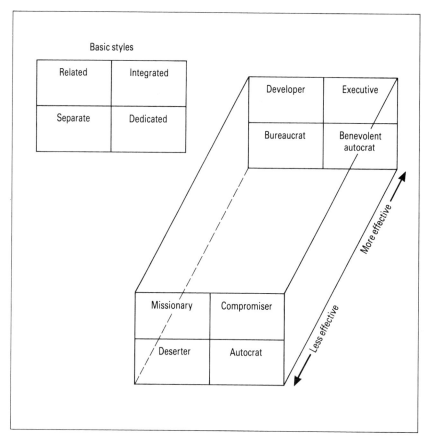

3D model of managerial effectiveness

The 'lower-level' **missionary** gets enthusiastic about new ideas, tries to sell them to others (though might later tire of a project and go on to something else). The 'higher-level **developer**, however, likes to teach, train, and assist others in assimilating and putting new ideas into practice.

The **deserter** is an employee who has become totally disillusioned with the organization, and does as little as possible. The **bureaucrat** sticks to the rules, is impartial, stays remote from the action; and in the worst version, believes that the further one is from the less pleasant sides of the business – dealing with customers, coping with production problems – the better.

The **autocrat** has already been mentioned; the **benevolent** version does delegate a little, but with close policy control; he or she likes to have a finger in every pie, thinks more in terms of reward than punishment, and is keen on unswerving loyalty to the organization.

The final pair consists first of the **compromiser**: someone who likes harmony, and will attempt to defuse conflict; a 'fixer' or go-between. The higher level version is the **executive** who has a balanced 'management mix'; he or she exercises authority when occasion demands, but also who consults and involves, delegates and motivates.

Activity 6	Individually, or in groups (as appropriate), select a manager, supervisor, youth leader, or someone playing a management role at least part of the time, known to you and attempt to classify him or her into one of the eight categories of the '3D Model'. You may find the person chosen has elements from two or even more categories: there is nothing unusual in such a finding. (You might decide it would be better to look at the theory in more detail in a management text-book first.)

What types of manager does the marketing function need?

Peter Drucker, a well-known writer on management, once said that organizations had only two essential activities: innovation and marketing. Others have echoed this simple statement. The implication is (provided the statement is true – and I think it is) that if a company wants to be thriving and profitable over a long period of time, it must exist in a culture which supports both innovation and the marketing concept – the serving and servicing of customers' needs.

Consider the diagram below. It suggests that there are two distinct ways for an organization to make more money (or gain more money to spend on its objectives, in the case of a charity for example). One is to run the concern more efficiently (ie to increase productivity). Most concerns have some areas where in the short term costs can be reduced; but once the 'fat' has been removed, further cost-cutting can start to become counter-productive (eg machines are replaced less often, staff salaries are held down, the advertising budget is pruned).

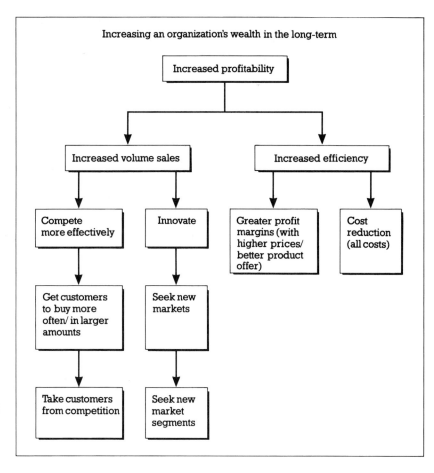

Ways of increasing an organization's wealth in the long term

Increasing prices to make more profit is less easy: only by offering more in the terms of the mix of a product or service can sales be maintained while the price is raised. A sporting or hobby magazine which contains action photographs may couple an increased cover price with more pages, and more photographs in colour. (Of course the extra value/benefits being offered will probably add to the total cost, but if the changes are carefully planned the end result will be more revenue.)

The other routes to greater profitability depend upon selling more of what you have to offer. Getting customers to buy more can be achieved by keeping or even improving upon high quality standards; improving distribution; or doing better than the competition, and taking customers from them. More vital still is the need to innovate: to look for new markets for existing products (or even design new products for existing and potential markets). Accurately predicting changes in fashion (in, say, clothes, music or videos) means that you can have a product ready as soon as the new demand arises.

Innovation is hard work, time consuming, and needs managers right from the top downwards who:
1 Believe in the marketing concept.
2 Understand the role of the marketing function in obtaining profitable business for the organization.
3 Understand the need for and support the marketing planning process.
4 Encourage co-operation between all functions in the organization.
5 Realize that the customer, not the chief executive, is the most important person, and that a firm should develop around existing and future customers.

Research done by the Cranfield School of Management seems to indicate, regrettably, that too few chief executives fit this sort of bill.

| Activity 7 | Individually, or in groups (as appropriate), consider what particular management style (or combination of styles) a chief or senior executive of an organization should have to make a proper contribution to both the marketing planning process, and the continuing well-being of the concern. |

The management of change

This is another topic you will probably have already dealt with, but in the context of planning, introducing, and managing changes in work patterns, technology, and work methods *inside the organization*. In such a context, the people the management will want to take into account primarily are the *work force*.

You will remember some of the points managers should bear in mind when introducing change:
1 Give maximum warning of change.
2 Explain the reasons for change.
3 Involve workers/work groups at all stages.
4 Brief and explain.
5 Ensure benefits and rewards accruing from the change are understood.
6 Offer and provide training.
7 Consider individuals as well as groups.

Where marketing planning is taken seriously, it can be seen that the final plans could involve changing fundamentally the direction and nature of the concern. It follows that the proper management of any consequent change is highly relevant. The plans themselves are 'change agents'.

All the above considerations apply equally to the marketing/sales/distribution staff when new products are launched, new services offered, or new promotion campaigns prepared. But there is a new element to consider – *the customer*.

Customers (both the final purchaser and any middlemen) need to be prepared for change too: discontinuation of one product, substitution by another; changes in delivery arrangements, discount structures, or sizes of container; changes in appearance (eg the *Guardian* re-launch), and increases in complexity of hi-tech products) – all these need action of a very similar kind to that in the list above.

Forthcoming promotions will need to be announced to retailers; training may be offered to firms buying new computer systems or programs (which will affect individual workers); students of 'open learning' may be helped to get used to a new way of studying.

| *Activity 8* |

In groups assume you are members of the Board of Elite Furniture Ltd, a Yorkshire firm which has been selling high-class furniture to AB class customers through department stores in the South of England for 50 years. From some research you have commissioned, it seems that there are many existing and potential customers within a 30 mile radius who would now have to travel a long way south to buy their suites.

You decide upon setting up a shop within the factory, and propose as a start to open up the factory to customers on Saturdays, when the place is normally closed.

Discuss the steps you would take to introduce the change to:
1 the staff of the factory;
2 the customers.

Barriers to marketing planning

Unfortunately, not all organizations practise marketing planning and control. Even those who *do* have some formal planning system may not use it to the best advantage. Senior management (including the chief executive) may not really be marketing-orientated; and may be more attracted to cost-cutting as a way of increasing profits than to innovation and aggressive marketing.

A rigid, bureaucratic, hierarchical structure does not help either; it promotes conflicts between functions, and rivalry over resource allocation. Innovation is minimized by splitting people up into separate, specialist, activities. It is not surprising in environments like these to find resentment and opposition to the whole process.

A third factor is a lack of understanding by managers of what marketing is about. Those who don't know, vote no! The pay and fringe benefits of many executives depend partly on the present week's or months' performances, so they tend to be absorbed in the 'here and now', and not in the future, which is the concern of marketing planning.

Summary of skills

The intention of the study in this unit is not only to learn facts about marketing but also to develop skills which will be of use in the business world, This section at the end of each block indicates the skill areas covered by each activity.

Skills

Skill	*Activity in which skill is developed*
a Learning and studying	1, 3, 4, 5, 6
b Communicating	All activities
c Identifying and tackling problems	1, 2, 3, 4, 8
d Information gathering	3, 4, 6, 7
e Working with others	All activities

Block 11
Financial Implications of Marketing Activities

Introduction

In the previous ten blocks you have learned many things about marketing. You are now asked to consider its financial implications.

In Block 10, *The Marketing Planning Process*, you looked in some detail at marketing planning. Once this process is complete, a set of marketing objectives, strategies, plans, and programmes will have been drawn up. Now, in this block, you will consider more closely the **marketing budget** arising from the activities proposed to achieve the targets.

You will also be identifying which elements of organizational expenditure come under the heading of **marketing costs**.

Pricing and pricing strategies are of vital importance to an organization's profitability, and you will need to look at alternative pricing practices.

Finally you will plan a range of marketing activities and calculate their financial implications.

Budgets, budgeting, and budgetary control

You will have realized by now, especially if you have covered the material in the previous block, that an organization has a better chance of surviving and prospering if it has clear objectives, appropriate strategies, and well-developed plans. But these, important as they are, are not enough. Also needed is some **monitoring and control system** with which to measure progress towards achieving the objectives, and to highlight differences (or variations) from the predetermined objectives.

If such differences do occur then the system should have some built-in procedure for getting back 'on track' as far as is possible.

The use of budgets, and a budgetary control system, is such a control system.

A **budget** is a statement (approved by management) set out in financial, or sometimes in volume, terms of what is planned or expected to happen during a forthcoming, precisely identified, period of time. A **financial budget**, more specifically, is a set of forecasts of costs and revenues, based partly on existing data. Thus a budget is part of a planning system. **Budgeting** is the process of drawing up budgets.

Budgetary control is the use of budgets in helping to ensure that the responsibilities and tasks carried out by individual managers relate to the objectives, strategies, plans, and programmes as laid down. This process is essentially one of continuous monitoring, comparison, and appraisal of actual results against those originally budgeted. The intended outcomes of the process are either the fulfilment of the objectives, strategies, and plans; or the provision of a basis for revision. (Note that budgets themselves need not necessarily be unalterable; the objectives, strategies, and plans could be changed, and consequently the budgets too, if they are shown to be unrealistic.)

The corporate budget and marketing implications

The **corporate** or **master budget** collates all the information on expected income and expenditure in the period under review. Whilst the detail of such a budget is more properly dealt with under finance or accounting studies, one part of it is a responsibility of the marketing function. The budgeted income figure is virtually all going to be made up from the expected sales revenue (which is itself part of the marketing budget).

Whilst the final figure must be a management decision, a great deal of work is required to assemble as much information as possible to assist the process of arriving at the target income figure.

As you saw in Block 4, *Making Sense of Researched Data*, data used in forecasting demand is derived from three distinct sources:

1 that available internally,
2 that supplied from marketing/sales,
3 that available externally.

Internal information includes:
* existing, firm, orders on the books to be delivered during the budget period.
* records of past sales (analysed to reveal trends up or down).
* knowledge of progress in the development of new products, and their expected launch dates.

Marketing/sales information includes:
* information derived from market and marketing research on future sales of existing and new products.
* details of advertising and promotion campaigns, and their expected impact on sales.
* home and export sales staff (and/or their agents) providing their estimates of sales to be achieved for each product in each market or market segment.
* any information on competitors, their plans, products, and estimated sales.

External information includes some of the assumptions about the economy, tax changes, and possible government intervention in the economy, that you looked at in Block 10, *The Marketing Planning Process*.

A considerable amount of care is essential in assessing the relative value of all this information. For example, you could ask: Was the research reliable enough to produce realistic figures? Were sales staff over-optimistic, or deliberately underestimating sales, to allow targets based on their estimates to be attained without much effort? In addition it must be admitted that forecasting revenue does pose problems since a quirk of fate, a change of fashion, or a new competitive product on the market may make nonsense of carefully laid plans.

Ultimately the corporate budget should reflect the whole of the marketing planning process that you looked at in the previous block; and not be based just on the assumptions of some members of the sales force, nor be a stab in the dark by senior management. Compiling it should not merely be a game of numbers. Projected volume sales will then be translated into potential revenue income, remembering to take into account sales at less than list price, early payment incentives, and so on.

The marketing budget

The marketing budget covers both sales revenue (revenue expectations), and the estimated costs of generating that income. The first has already been considered, and some of the associated problems mentioned; the second has problems too.

When organizations were won over to the idea of budgeting, a tendency soon developed of working out expected revenue, deducting the desired profit figure, and leaving the rest to be shared out between the various functions. The result was that each function (including marketing/sales) was awarded what became a fixed amount of money, never mind what actually happened afterwards.

Imagine a real marketing opportunity presenting itself, for example in August, when all the budget has been allocated. Your company's products have been associated with an unexpected British success in the international sporting field; it is the considered opinion of the marketing team, and your advisers, that full-page adverts in the daily papers could capitalize on the publicity and lead to a much greater turnover. Then comes the message: 'You're already overspent your budget; there's nothing left for such expenditure! Anyway, it's far too risky'.

This kind of situation can occur in a rigid, annual, static budgeting system; as can its reverse, often found at the end of a budget year: 'We must find *something* quickly to spend that £15 000 left in the budget on, or it will be taken away from us next year!'
An organization with a more flexible system, which can accomodate unscheduled expenditure is, when you think about it, much more marketing orientated.

Zero base budgeting

One way of getting over this kind of difficulty is not to dole out a sum, fixed or 'elastic', to the marketing function; but to operate a **zero based** system. This type of system requires that every item of expenditure has to be shown to be in accordance with corporate/marketing objectives, strategies, or plans. If an agreed strategy to launch a new cheese is a series of 'in store' tastings, with demonstrators offering shoppers small portions of the cheese on biscuits, then all the expenditure for arranging the tasting nationally, promotion agency fees, etc., must be seen to be derived from an approved plan.

If changes have to be made to the detail (eg the promotion is so successful in gaining acceptance for the new cheese that it makes sense to run it for another fortnight), then these can be justified on the grounds that they are still in line with an original objective and derived strategy; and are indeed achieving more than the original expected outcome. (You have come across this idea before when considering communications' budgets in Blocks 6 and 7, only there it was called the *task method*.)

Activity 1	Full-time students, in groups, refer back to Activity 7 of Block 4, *Marketing Sense of Researched Data*, and carry out research into the following: 1 How the college's marketing budget is established. Is it a fixed amount (and if so, how was it arrived at)? If it is a variable amount from year to year, on what basis is it calculated? 2 Under which particular headings is it analysed? Part-time students may prefer to look at their own organizations, budgets, or budgets of other organizations known to them.

Marketing costs

It is difficult to give a tight, precise, definition of a marketing cost. The main reason is that cases can be made out for particular costs (eg packing goods for delivery, or the actual transportation costs to the customer) to be classified under marketing ones, or under some other heading (say *production* in the packing example; *distribution* in the second one).

(Many organizations in fact treat *all distribution* costs as being in a separate category. I would call them marketing costs).

However, as a guide, you can treat all costs (as applied to products) incurred after finished goods leave the storage area, or factory floor, as being marketing ones; plus those concerned with:

* *promotion* – advertising, PR, point-of-sale material, and other marketing communications expenditure;

* *price* – special discounts, introductory special prices, sales and agents' commissions, royalty payments to authors, bad debts, invoices remaining unpaid after the expiry of the agreed credit period, free replacement of goods under complaint: anything reducing potential gross income in fact.
* free services, including 'hot-lines' for puzzled users of newly purchased computers and programs;
* after-sales service;
* wages and salaries and expenses of all marketing/sales staff not covered in *commissions* above;
* information costs, including marketing research; statistics collecting and analysis done internally;
* administration of goods returned/under complaint.

(This list cannot claim to be exhaustive.)

When looking at *services*, the guide-line would be to treat as marketing costs all those costs arising after the service has been provided; plus, again, any of those mentioned above.

Activity 2	Either singly, or in groups, consider the following lists of costs incurred recently by Shambles Ltd, cosmetic manufacturers whose newest product is an anti-sunburn cream, Sunglow Suncreme. Please help the accountant to identify and single out the marketing costs.

	£
Carboard boxes (outers) for Sunglow bottles	7200
Prizes donated to town carnival	277
Postage charges (one month)	3200
Catalogues and price lists of cosmetic ranges	4544
Press reception to launch Sunglow	1376
AGM expenses and reception for shareholders; also attended by the national press	871
Labels to go on Sunglow bottles	500
New carpets for the board room	2316
New carpets for the showroom	1976
Landscaping/maintenance of factory surroundings	5276
Tour guides' fees to women's clubs' visits	670
Press advert for sales office manager	200
Press advert for telephonist/receptionist	100
Royalty payment for name Sunglow	250
Mail shot to wholesalers (contracted out)	1000

Pricing for profit

Before you tackle this section, you would be well advised to re-read earlier comments on this topic in Block 2, *More about*

Marketing, (pages 38–9), as one part of the 4Ps; and a somewhat more detailed examination in Block 5, *How Purchases are Made*, (pages 90–93) relating pricing to purchasing behaviour. The points previously made will not all be exhaustively re-examined here.

What is a price?

Standard economic theory tells us that **utility**, **value**, and **price** are related ideas. **Utility** is that aspect of a product or service that makes it able to satisfy needs or wants. The **value** that is put on a product of service is a quantitative measure of its worth (which may often reflect the degree of its utility to users of the product/service; or the assumed degree of utility in the minds of the suppliers!). The **price** of a product/service is the value expressed in pounds and pence, dollars and cents, etc. Following this argument, you might say that the price of an item is the value put on its utility (real or assumed), expressed in money terms.

What you *can* say is that a price of an item or service is that amount of money needed to acquire it.

Whilst in general conversation you may frequently use the word *price* particularly when buying products, note that there are many other words used to convey the same idea. Some of them are set out below. The one thing which stands out is that all of the items on the list refer to *services*.

Other names for price	
What you pay	**What you get**
Admission charge	Entry to cinema, theatre, sporting event
Commission	(Usually) sales of goods, services, made on your behalf
Fare	Train, taxi, bus journey
Fee	Services of a professional adviser
Interest	Use of someone else's money
Poll tax (or Community charge)	Availability of local goverment services
Rent	Use of living accomodation, office or car, video, etc. for a specific period of time
Retainer	Ability to call on someone's services for a specific period
Subscription	Membership of club, trade union, delivery of magazine
Tuition fees	Education, training

Activity 3	Singly or in groups (as appropriate), list as many other names for price as you can, and the circumstances in

which they are used. Then compare notes. Are all your answers still to do with services?

Factors affecting price

Some of the more important factors and constraints to be taken into account when making pricing decisions are:

1 *Objectives.* Pricing objectives are derived from, and should be consistent with, corporate objectives, short- and long- term. Very often they are not expressed in a formal way by organizations, but can be inferred from the policies adopted.

Typical objectives affecting pricing are:

> * To increase overall profitability
> * To maintain or improve market share
> * To increase market share (by a quantified amount)
> * To meet, overcome, or prevent competition (*discourage newcomers to the market*)
> * To achieve a (quantified) return on net sales made
> * To maximise profits in the short-term (*especially for a product with a limited life, or one being launched to cream-off the market*)
> * To maximise profits in the long-term
> * To ensure all prices cover the total average cost per item
> * To ensure no price exceeds that charged by nearest competitor (*We are never knowingly undersold – ie where competitors offer very similar products*)
> * To ensure all prices yield at least 5%, 7½%, 10% etc, on investment

2 *Organization's Market Profile.* If the company/concern is a prestigious one, and its products of high quality, then higher prices will be expected by customers; if its range is at the bottom end of the market, then they will expect low price levels.

3 *Competitors.* Although firms often try hard to develop and offer products or services which are 'different' from those offered by others, the fact remains that most products, and a great many services, do have competition. The closer two firms marketing and product mix are, the more likely the dominant firm will be the one with the lowest price. (*The moral once again is to be as different as possible.*)

Potential competitors have to be taken into account as well. If you price high when launching a new product, you may be inviting someone else to move in at a lower price. (As soon as the *Filofax* was marketed widely, many copies emerged – some of which were plastic and very cheap (£3–£4), others of which were medium-priced, such as the 'Personal Organizers' by WH Smith, in the £15 range.

4 *Need to have differential pricing.* This is where products (but more often services) are offered at different prices to different market segments. For example, a railway region may have a complex product mix to cater for the early morning commuters into a large city. Demand is high; high fares can therefore be charged. After 9.30 am the railway would be virtually unused if prices were left unchanged. To get more overall revenue, 'off-peak' fares which may be as much as 30–40 per cent less then the full fares, are offered to travellers.

A seat in the stalls costs more than a bench in the 'Gods'; a room with a view is more expensive than one facing an inner, blank wall. A telephone call after 6 p m is cheaper, to encourage the social, as opposed to the business, call. The reasoning behind all this is not difficult to see.

5 *Legal constraints.* The number of legal constraints on prices is not at the present very great. For a short period, when prices and incomes policies were in their heyday (about 1967) the prices of industrial products were frozen, in the hope of beating inflation. Such polices were eventually abandoned.

Before 1956 manufacturers were able to fix and enforce the final retail selling prices of their products; but subsequent acts of Parliament (the latest being the *Resale Prices Act* 1977) have allowed the ultimate seller to fix the prices paid by consumers. However, where books (and also newspapers and magazines) are concerned, the Restrictive Practices Court ruled that 'net book' agreements – designed to enforce retail price maintenance – were acceptable. It was felt that to remove these types of agreement was not in the public interest, as small bookshops and many minor publishers issuing small-run volumes would quickly go out of business. (In late 1988 this 'net book' agreement system came under threat; and some books were issued without bearing the retail selling price. Newspapers, however, still kept to the 'cover price'.)

One area of concern in 1988 was the price of money, or **credit**. Rates quoted in a survey by Birmingham consumer protection officers revealed charges from 100 per cent to 5000 per cent on short-term loans. The Director-General of

Fair Trading in his annual report cited one case of 18 billion per cent! The Moneylenders Act laid down a maximum of 48 per cent per annum, but it was replaced in 1974 by the Consumer Credit Act. Section 139 of that act allows a court to look into a credit deal if it is 'extortionate'. Regrettably the word was not defined, and perhaps there is a case for legislation here.

6 *Customer/consumer attitudes.* In virtually every market, customers/consumers have a sense of what the prices should be. Go to a big event where ice-creams are £2, or cups of tea £1 each. Many may refuse to pay; those that do pay, may complain: 'It's a rip-off!' If the prices were even higher, few (if any) sales would result. Thus in pricing there is an upper 'too high' limit. (There may be a 'too low' limit as well: a 5p cup of tea may be considered suspect.)

Price, then, relates to 'value for money' in the minds of purchasers. This has implications, too, when prices are changed, up or down: customers might think
* the quality of the product has changed;
* the product is about to be phased out (if there's a price cut);
* the supplier is in difficulties, is selling up, etc.

7 *Costs.* The detailed processes of costing belong more properly to the financial and accounting (and even to some extent to the economics) aspects of your studies, but some points are relevant here.

First, a decision has to be taken on the pricing objective appropriate to a product. On the face of it, the selling price of a product should at least be in excess of the total average cost per item. However, the average cost contains an element of the organization's fixed costs – which do not vary whatever quantity of goods are produced.

Suppose, however, you have arranged the costing of existing items to recover all your fixed costs, and now decide to bring a new product into production.It can be argued that the average total **variable and setting up costs** are the only ones which need be considered: provided the price fixed is above this level, either a **contribution** is being made to the fixed overheads, thus lightening the load elsewhere; or (seen another way), everything in excess of the total variable (or 'marginal cost') is profit.

The net results would be a lower selling price for that item, possibly thereby substantial sales, if demand is elastic; and an overall increase in profitability.

Secondly, even if all the fixed overheads are not yet covered by a particular selling price, you may want to penetrate a market with a new product; and by pricing down for a while, create a high demand. You hope eventually to move into profit as the total average costs fall due to economies of scale. Alternatively, the initial low price is only temporary (the 'introductory offer'); and a higher price substituted after an interval.

8 *Position in the product life cycle.* This needs careful thought. The following comments are generalizations, but do represent what often happens. At the beginning of a product's life, a firm can set low prices (as mentioned above) to penetrate, and get a good share of, the market. On the other hand (as was done with the ball-pen just after the Second World War) the initial price can be set very high to make large profits quickly ('creaming-off').

In the growth stage, unit costs decrease, and price can remain stable and yield good profits. But into maturity the market becomes more difficult: a saturation point is arrived at, and competition is usually encountered. Profits decline and the ability to combat competition with price-cutting is restricted. With decline come falling sales and further reduced profit margins. Even then it may be necessary to reduce the price to keep sales (unless some other strategy such as re-vamping the product is adopted).

9 *Geographical distance.* The price of some products may vary according to the geographical distance between producer and consumer; the differential price reflecting the different transport costs.

10 *Channels of distribution.* The choice of selling products through middlemen involves allowing the following discounts:
* Trade discounts to compensate middlemen for holding stocks in bulk, selling on, etc. As a result the recommended retail selling price will have to be higher to leave a good net price for producer.
* Quantity discounts (independent from the trade ones). Incentives for purchasing in very large quantities at a time.
* Promotional discounts (where middlemen or retailers are themselves involved in product promotion).
* Cash discounts for prompt payment.

| *Activity 4* | 1 | Topcrafts Ltd manufacture a wide range of middle-of-the-road personal jewellery, including men's gold watches. They find there is a demand for 9 carat gold watches, and they design one with an automatic date change, sweep seconds hand, and a real leather strap. The total average cost of making a first 'run' of 2000 is £72.50 each. Topcrafts find the competition are selling a basic watch in the £140 to £155 RRP range. |

To try and make the product 'different', however, Topcrafts decide to offer the watch 'personalized'; that is, engraved with the customer's own short message (20 letters maximum), and two names (10 letters maximum each). The cost of doing this extra work is allowed for in the £72.50.

Topcrafts negotiate a deal with Horology Marketing (a 'catalogue' house) who require a 50 per cent discount on the final RRP, plus an extra 5 per cent for reserving the whole 2000. Individual watches would be engraved as and when called for.

Topcrafts have the following pricing objectives:
* To maximize market share
* To maximize profits in the long term
* To ensure all prices charged cover total average costs per item

Decide upon a suitable RRP, taking into account the objectives, the market, and the other factors you have already considered.

2 Qwikprophits have been in the clothing business for over 100 years. Earlier today Charles Twist, the sales manager, reviewed the stocks of the Snappy stonewashed men's shirt range. Unfortunately the shirt's styling was becoming a little 'dated'. Worse, a competitor, Swiftgains, had just brought out a double-breasted version with two pockets and the latest collar design, selling to the trade for £8.50 each.

Charles found there were 9500 Snappys in stock. The total average cost was £8.97 each; and the marginal cost (ie total variable costs) £4.98.
'The company say we must never sell below full average cost', he tells you. 'But if I don't move these shirts soon, £50 000 of stock will be left on our hands, and I'll be in real trouble.'

'Swiftgains have just offered £5 each for them. Can you advise me what to do?'
Decide what advice to give Charles Twist.

Common pricing strategies

To complete the survey of pricing, there follows a list of the strategies in common use – many of which have already been mentioned:

1 Creaming off.
2 Giving away trading stamps.
3 Giving discounts.
4 Cost-plus pricing. This involves calculating the average unit cost of the product and adding a desired profit – usually by adding a specific percentage, say $33\frac{1}{3}$ per cent, 50 per cent, $66\frac{2}{3}$ percent, or 100 per cent, to get a selling price. Very widely used in business, but is it scientific, marketing-based, and does it take competition into account? The answers must all be no! However, it is extremely useful where a job has to be done, and not all the work can be foreseen, such as a car repair; or where the customer asks for extra work to be done while a contract is in progress.
5 Promotional allowances.
6 Geographical/zone delivery pricing.
7 Loss leader pricing. Many shops cut the price of one or more items – 'this week's bargain offers!' – to entice customers into the premises. The items are normally ones well-known and bought often, like sugar or soup. The prices quoted could be below the cost of buying them in originally. The idea behind this strategy is that people will visit the shop to take advantage of the special offer, but will buy much more once they get inside. The shop will then end up with an increased turnover, and greater profit overall.
8 Price lining. This involves the seller – usually a wholesaler/retailer – restricting the numbers of different prices charged to say five or six, possibly even less. Before the Second World War, the Woolworths chain stores proclaimed under their shops' name-boards '3d & 6d Store'; the implication being that all the goods in the store cost either 3d or 6d each.

Today's version is the dress-shop with 'All frocks on this rack £19.99'; and several other racks with a similar message, but higher or lower prices. The customer can go in with a price level in mind and can go straight to the goods in the preferred price area. Buying decisions are easier to make; it is also easier for the assistants to charge up purchases.

9 Odd pricing (sometimes called psychological pricing – see Block 5, *How Purchases are Made*). Houses are listed for sale at £99 950 rather than £100 000; 3-piece suites at £399 (not £400), and so on. It is believed that such prices appear lower than they are.

10 Temporary reductions. To clear out old stock, or give a particular line a 'push'.

11 Prestige pricing. Pricing a product well above the competition, to emphasise its (alleged) quality or, superiority.

12 Diversionary pricing. This takes several forms, the basic idea being to quote a low, basic, price for goods, or a service; but when the customer comes to purchase he or she finds they have to buy extras (eg batteries, plugs, or adaptors) to make it work; or they find that vegetables are extra to the dish, that coffee after the meal is not included). In some cases (offset pricing), the extras are very highly priced.

13 Guaranteed-by-results pricing. Here the seller promises to charge the customer when and only when the desired outcome is achieved. American lawyers have used this idea for decades – 'no result, no fee'. Estate agents only take their commission on a sale when that sale is complete. Customers are made to feel they 'cannot lose'.

14 Negotiated pricing. Here the seller and buyer negotiate the final price; they 'bargain', as we say. Large industrial contracts, fees for consultancy services, or salary levels are often arrived at this way.

Activity 5	1 In small groups consider the following products or services, and suggest appropriate pricing strategies for each. You may find you will want to recommend a combination of strategies, or have both short- and long- term ones. *a* Very short runs (no more than 100) of replicas of dresses designed by a team who supply clothes to both Royalty and pop-stars.

b A new preparation which appears to stimulate the regrowth of hair on previously bald male heads.

c A once unique one-coat white paint (ie requiring no undercoat; can be put on over existing paint of any colour or on bare untreated wood) which is now facing competition from two other suppliers. You started with a price 25 per cent above normal gloss white prices for all sizes of tin. The competition has launched just above normal prices. (Your margin on cost to wholesalers is 33⅓ per cent at the moment; your paint costs you just 5 per cent more than normal white gloss to make.)

d A local catering service offering dishes or complete meals delivered hot to peoples' homes within one hour of the order.

e A builder working to an agreed estimate for a house extension who is asked by the house owner 'while you are here' to modify a fireplace.

2 In groups of five or six, assume you are setting up a firm, BTEC Enterprises Ltd, to employ students in their spare(!) time. You plan to make and sell polished wooden plaques of different shapes (some quite random) bearing house names, and appropriate symbols, scrolls, etc. The artwork is burnt into the wood with equipment already available in your college, and all the other tools needed are also to hand without charge.

You need to price the work to yield a profit for BTEC student funds to subsidize a travel and tourism visit to Malta; and to pay for work carried out.

You have the following information only (*you* research into the competition):

a The manual work involved is done by a maximum of three of you. Shaping the wood, polishing, and burning in the letters takes on average three hours per plaque. Workers are paid £1.50 per hour.

b A maximum of nine hours per worker per week is available for the work.

c The fourth team member is a sales rep, who visits the homes of those interested to get orders; and is paid £1.50 per order taken.

d The fifth member is the accountant who does the books; and receives £5 per week for doing this.

e The sixth person deals with all enquiries in the first

place, organizes and monitors the production, and chairs board meetings. Salary: £6 per week.

f Enquiries are generated by a leaflet costing £1 per 1000 and inserted in a local 'free paper' at £9 per 1000. 8000 leaflets are actually distributed, with return slips for the request of more details.

g The estimated response rate of people replying is 5 per cent; and it is estimated that the sales rep will convert 60 per cent of those called on to firm orders.

h The whole project is to be completed in the period September – June.

i Enough wood for 100 plaques is available from scrap. The rest must be bought in the open market; as will the staining and varnish.

Fix a price per plaque (unfitted) from this information and any extra research you do into the market. You will be expected to justify the basis on which you set your price.

Summary of skills

The intention of the study in this unit is not only to learn facts about marketing but also to develop skills which will be of use in the business world. This section at the end of each block indicates the skill areas covered by each activity.

Skill

Skills	*Activities in which skill is developed*
a Numeracy	4, 5
b Learning and studying	1, 5
c Communicating	All activities
d Identifying and tackling problems	1, 2, 4, 5
e Information gathering	1, 3, 5
f Working with others	All activities

Block 12
Constraints on Marketing

Introduction

In this block you will be identifying legal, social and moral (ethical) constraints imposed upon businesses, especially those which affect their marketing activities.

Some of these constraints are in a sense self-imposed (eg voluntary codes of practice); others are less voluntary (strongly influenced by local/national pressure groups); and a third group are forced on organizations (consumer legislation).

You will become aware that besides just reacting to such constraints, and making sure of keeping away from trouble or public exposure (a negative response), a more positive marketing approach is to set one's organization the task of making a virtue of the constraints: selling the benefits, for example, of a product's built-in safety factors, purity, restriction on use, or absence of environmental pollution.

The position of the customer

In times long gone the average customer knew a lot more about what he or she was buying than his or her present day counterpart; in most cases the items or food bought were in common use, their qualities well understood, and they were less sophisticated technically.

Even so tricksters, quacks, and swindlers flourished. (Any of you who have read Chaucer's *Canterbury Tales* will remember for example the Pardoner who sold 'pardons' for sins; and the Miller who short-delivered corn to a university college.) The motto for purchasers was *caveat emptor*! 'Let the buyer take care!' (or guard his/her own interests). This was a warning to the buyer to make sure of the suitability or soundness of purchases before they were made. The law of the time was no help: if the buyer wasn't bright or alert or knowledgeable that was his or her hard luck!

Whilst since the Middle Ages the law *has* intervened to try and improve the customer's predicament (eg the Law of Contract, that of Equity, or the 1893 Sale of Goods Act), the customer's position in many ways has actually worsened. Products are now much more technically complex; users are often far removed from producers, and the latter are more difficult to contact. Tricksters, quacks, and swindlers are even more plentiful. It is less and less possible for the average customer to guard his or her interests.

The contract between employer and employee became very one-sided with the Industrial Revolution: a single worker could do little to redress a wrong or sort out a grievance. An inevitable result was the growth of trades unions which attempted to redress the balance.

It is not surprising that eventually the customers began to band together as well. But it was much later – after the Second World War, in fact – when the consumer movement really emerged in an organized fashion. The reason was simply that only then did a large section of the community become relatively well-off and a wide variety of goods and services come within its purchasing range. Too little information was available for decision-making and thus making wise choices became more difficult.

Activity 1	In small groups spend five minutes in trying to establish the following:

1 The best computer program for household accounts,
2 The best washing machine for delicate fabrics,
3 The best available rates for savers (banks/building societies)
4 The best eating establishment in the nearest town in which to hold an 18th birthday party.

Did you find these tasks difficult? Why? How much more research – and of what kind – do you think you would need to do before a really certain answer could be given?

The consumer movement

In both America and the UK, **consumerism** as a recognizable movement emerged in the late 1950s, though a 'Consumers Union' existed in America before the Second

Which?
magazine

World War. (By consumerism is meant the phenomenon of consumers acting to exercise some control over the quality of, and the process of and buying selling, goods and services.) In the UK the Consumers' Association (CA), founded in 1957, had an over-riding objective to begin with to improve and maintain the standards of goods and services on offer. The way in which this objective was translated into action was by providing information.

You will all at least have heard of *Which?*, the CA's monthly magazine. Each issue provides information about goods and services, based on testing – either by independent laboratories, or indeed by CA members themselves (eg, when dealing with topics like faults noted in new cars, or car repairs). Very often the information is comparative; and some indication given to prospective purchaser of **value for money**, as well as possible drawbacks. (For example, *Which?* of November 1986 reviewed typewriters and word processors: some were put in the *worth a look* category; and in some of the product groups a *best buy* was nominated. Twelve electric typewriters, and eleven word processors, were thoroughly compared.) Where **safety** is involved appropriate warning can be given.

This method of educating the customer/consumer has spread to virtually every specialist magazine for DIY, other hobbies, or computing. (The latter not only review computers, but lots of software too. Programs are assessed not only for content, but ease of use, performance, and documentation. Warnings, too, about programs with 'bugs' or unexpected problems or deficiencies are given.)

Activity 2	1 In pairs visit a college or public library. Look through back copies of *Which?*, and choose from the items reviewed a product or service with which one of you at least is very familiar (eg a hair-dryer, stereo cassette recorder, etc. See if you agree with the comments and recommendations made. Prepare a short report on the product comparing your findings with those of *Which?*. 2 Find out what publications are associated with *Which?*, either as supplements to the main magazine, or as separate issues. 3 Find one special interest magazine and look at the way products or services are covered. Compare similarities and differences from the *Which?* approach.

Other aspects of consumerism

So far you have only looked at what might be called comment on, review of or discontent with private sector products or services, and efforts to remedy such dissatisfactions. Two other aspects of consumerism merit attention.

Nowadays consumerism has spread to the public sector with a vengeance – often aided or abetted by politicians! Complaints are made, for example, about hospital facilities and waiting lists; delays in letter deliveries; and overcrowded commuter trains. In each case there are official bodies set up to monitor the way the services operate; to take up complaints, and publicize the results.

Activity 2	In small groups find out what you can about the official 'watchdog' organizations which (separately) monitor the three areas just mentioned – the hospitals' sector of the health service, the GPO, and BR. What powers do they have: how effective are they?

Finally, there is an area that you have already met in earlier blocks: *concern for the environment*. People may object to plans to build houses in the open countryside; or they may wish to restrict the hours a firm works, the noise or smell it makes, or the amount of traffic it generates, say, on a country road. The consumerist here is not dealing with the selling/buying process itself, but with the consequences for other people (or even for animals) affected by that process.

The role of consumer pressure groups

A pressure group can be defined as a group of people who by skill and/or determination, set out to influence the way decisions are made. In the marketing context, pressure groups – particularly consumer ones – have had considerable influence right from the start. You will not be surprised to learn that many members of these groups are 'activists', that is to say they are prepared to *act upon* their views and attitudes about the world. This is in strong contrast to the population at large who may well be critical of the products they buy, the services they receive, or the advertisements they read, but do little or nothing about it. Thus consumer pressure groups can be said to play a vital role in conveying to industry and commerce popular concerns (though others could, and do, argue that such groups only represent themselves).

Some groups aim to cover a great many different products, services, and industries (eg, the CA); others are very specific (a group of regular commuters acting as watchdogs on the timing, frequency, and comfort of trains on a given route).

The different purposes of pressure groups leads them to having different approaches: there are the **educators,** whose aim is to inform consumers and make them more aware of problems and current issues; the **protectionists** who are concerned to push 'health and safety' aspects (even to the extent of trying to stop people acquiring habits which in the long-term could be harmful to them); and the **change agents** who want to influence politicians, and gain a greater voice in both local and national government decisions about consumer affairs.

Activity 4	In small groups consider the following questions:

1 Do you think the public need to be educated in consumer affairs, and do people want information every time they buy a packet of soap powder?

2 Do people need protecting against themselves? Surely in a free society we can be left to make our own minds up about, for example, cigarette smoking? (Remember many people who smoke do not develop lung cancer.)
3 Is there a need for consumer views to bear on political decisions, which surely have to made in the best interests of the nation as a whole, and not just those of the consumers?

Consumer concerns

In the middle of the 1970s research was done in the UK (by *Monitor*), and three areas of consumer concern were identified in the population, which it seems are still there:

1 *Consumer cynicism.* There was a general feeling that if not kept up to the mark, business would let the quality of goods and services offered decline.

2 *Over-exaggerated claims.* There was criticism that exaggerated claims in advertising could persuade people to buy products and services which they didn't really need, and which might even be harmful to them. More recently this criticism has been applied to drugs, even ones obtainable only on prescription.

3 *Concern about the environment.* Already mentioned in the previous section. (Major concerns in this area at the moment include the greenhouse effect, food additives, depletion of the ozone layer, and the over-use of pesticides.)

The Kennedy 'Consumer Bill of Rights'

In 1962 the late US President John Kennedy announced to Congress what he considered were the rights of every consumer, namely:

A right to safety – that is, a right to be protected from goods or services which could be hazardous or dangerous to health or life.

A right to be informed – that is, a right to be protected against deceptive or dishonest advertising, and misleading or insufficient information about products or services (including operating instructions) and a right to all the facts needed to make an informed choice.

A right to choose – a right to have access, where possible to a variety of competitive goods and services. Where a monopoly exists, to be assured of getting a proper quality of goods or services at fair prices.

A right to be heard – an assurance that consumer interests would be taken fully into account by government when formulating policy; and that fair and speedy treatment by its administrative tribunals would be received.

Whilst this statement of intent was not an Act of Congress, its influence has been considerable. For example, we in the UK now have a Minister for Consumer Affairs. It is politically fashionable to be in favour of consumerism.

Responses to consumer concerns

There have been three kinds of significant response to consumer concerns: the first, already discussed in some detail, has come from consumers themselves, the second from industry and commerce, and the third from government.

Industry and commerce

As far back as the 1960s the food and advertising industries realized that customer complaints made government intervention inevitable sooner or later. In an effort to forestall such intervention they hit upon the idea of producing sets of voluntary regulations, which were essentially models of good practice in their industry.

One of the effects of the 1973 Fair Trading Act was the setting up of the Office of Fair Trading (OFT). One of its responsibilities was to encourage trade associations to prepare and issue Codes of Practice, 'for guidance in safeguarding and promoting the interests of consumers'. The first to do so included those involved with the package holidays industry, dry cleaning, and footwear.

The Motor Agents' Association code, for example, set out to cover transactions involving new and second-hand vehicles, parts, and accessories, and the supply of petrol and oil. A very important aspect of this code was a detailed complaints procedure, with, as a last resort, independent arbitration. In fact a suitable system for handling complaints is a requirement of all OFT-sponsored codes.

<table>
<tr><td>*Activity 5*</td><td>Individually, or in small groups, research into *one* code of practice. (Most libraries should have at least one copy of, or a book including, the *British Code of Advertising Practice*, for example.) Besides making notes about the topics covered, try to find out how many complaints are received annually from members of the public by the body administrating the code, and how many are upheld.</td></tr>
</table>

Enforcement of voluntary codes. Even though a code may be voluntary, to be of any use it must be enforceable. After all, it could be argued, these associations depend upon their members' subscriptions to keep in business; and they might therefore be loathe to discipline or expel member firms.

However, if the trade association goes out of its way to set itself up in the eyes of consumers as an organization which ensures consumers get a fair deal, then a firm which lost its membership would probably lose a considerable amount of business as well. Tour operators, for example, would look very critically at agreements they had with any member of the Association of British Travel Agents (ABTA) who was expelled from that body.

Other difficulties with the voluntary code idea are first that not every industry has one and second, that not every firm in an industry which does have a code is a member of the appropriate trade association.

Marketing bodies' codes of practice. Members of several marketing bodies are also asked to subscribe to voluntary codes of practice as individuals. Examples are the Chartered Institute of Marketing (1973), and a joint code for members of the Market Research Society and the Industrial Marketing Research Association. You may already have looked at the *British Code of Advertising Practice* (see Activity 5., above). The latest version dates from 1985. The *British Code of Sales Promotion* deals with premium offers; vouchers, coupons, and samples; prizes and competitions, amongst other items. The *British Code of Advertising Practice* (see Activity 5 above). codes, but has one of its own as well – covering, for example, telephone selling.

Consumer law

Consumer law is a subject in its own right, and it is not possible to cover every Act in detail here. Much of earlier legislation grew out of business practice (eg the 1893 Sale of Goods Act), and the law of contract, which many of you are studying now. The last quarter-century has seen a great deal of consumer legislation – most of which was influenced by the consumer movement, but some, more recently, by the government's policy of increasing competition where possible.

As opposed to voluntary codes, Acts of Parliament can and do have sanctions and penalties for non-compliance which can be exacted on all guilty offenders.

The more important Acts which affect marketing (directly or indirectly) are listed below with a very brief indication of significant provisions. You are recommended to check with the text of any Act if in doubt.

1 *Food and Drugs Act 1955 (as amended)*. This regulates terms used in food advertising and labelling.

2 *Trade Description Act 1968 (1972 Act now repealed)*. It is an offence to sell or supply any goods of which false descriptions are given. A garment described as 'pure wool' must be just that. Applies also to services: a hotel claiming to offer various facilities must indeed have them available for guests to use.

3 *Unsolicited Goods and Services Act 1971*. It is offence for a supplier to demand payment for goods or services not ordered by the recipient.

4 *Fair Trading Act 1973*. This established the Office of Fair Trading, and its Director General. The main task of the OFT is to review trade practices which may unfavourably affect the economic interests of consumers (in the UK), and to collect information on trading practices which seem to be unfair to consumers. Additionally, it encourages the preparation and publication of trade codes of practice relating to consumers; and under Part III it has power to take action against traders in the courts.

5 *Prices Act 1974*. This, along with subsequent orders, only permits terms like 'Sale Price!', 'Bargain Offer!', 'Genuine Reductions!' to be used for bona fide price reductions. Where terms like 'normal price' are used as comparisons, there must be evidence that the item advertised at a reduced price has been on sale for a continuous period of 28 days within the preceding six months at the 'normal price' quoted.

6 *Consumer Credit Act 1974*. The Director General of the

OFT was made responsible for the enforcement of its provisions: that suppliers of credit – banks, finance houses, retailers with arrangements with lenders – be licensed; that there be 'cooling off' periods for credit agreements signed away from trade premises; that goods on HP are 'protected' after the debtor has paid at least one third of the purchase price; and that there are remedies for credit card holders if goods purchased do not come up to expectation, especially if the supplier goes out of business. Further, all advertisements for credit must state both the cash and credit prices, and the rates of interest to be charged.

7 *Consumer Transactions (Restrictions on Statements) Order 1976.* It is an offence to set out guarantees or other conditions of sale in such way that customers might be lead to believe that their statutory rights had been lessened or cancelled.

8 *Unfair Contract Terms Act 1977.* This applies more to service-giving organizations. Prior to this Act firms could rely on 'exclusion clauses' which limited traders' liability for loss, damage, or injury resulting from the service (or sometimes goods). Now traders cannot limit nor contract out of liability for death or personal injury arising from negligence or breach of duty. Also banned are clauses in contracts for the supply of services and goods together, where such clauses seek to exclude or diminish liability for the goods failing to meet the description applied to them, being of lesser quality, or not being fit for their intended purpose.

9 *Competition Act 1979.* This Act empowered the OFT Director General to investigate anti-competitive practices in both the public and private sectors; that is practices which restrict, pervert, or prevent competition in the manufacture, supply, or purchase of goods and services. The D G can refer cases to the Monopolies and Mergers Commission.

10 *Consumer Protection Act 1987.* This consolidates various Acts, but adds new points. Where any damage is caused wholly or in part by a defect in a product, the producer – or anyone purporting to be the producer – of the product, or an importer of it, shall be liable for the damage, subject to some technical qualifications in section 2(3). An offence may be committed if a person offers, supplies (or agrees to

supply) exposes, or possesses any consumer goods for sale which are unsafe (there are a few exceptions, including tobacco).The way the goods would be marketed, published safety standards, and the existence of any reasonable possibilities of making the goods safer must all be borne in mind. The Secretary of State has the power to make safety regulations which could list a host of provisions about contents, design, packaging, finish, standards, etc of particular goods.

Additionally, 'a notice to warn' may be served on anyone, requiring that person to pay for and publish a warning about goods he has supplied which the Secretary of State feels are unsafe. A 'prohibition notice' can be served on anyone prohibiting him from supplying, offering, etc any goods which the Secretary of State thinks are unsafe. Subject to certain provisions, an offence may be committed if anyone gives consumers misleading information about the prices at which goods and services are available. The Secretary of State may make appropriate regulations, or draw up a code of practice to cover misleading prices.

Consumer protection organizations (CPOs)

Consumer protection has a political dimension. There is a debate as to who should do it, and who should pay for it. It does seem clear, however, that the government is committed to CP, and the OFT with its wide remit is not the only government agency involved.

At present such ministries as the Agriculture, Fisheries, and Food (remember Chernobyl and the problems with contaminated livestock), Social Security, Transport, etc have as part of their activities an element of consumer protection.

There are government sponsored bodies which include:

Office of Fair Trading (OFT). Already mentioned above. Its basic aim is to encourage competition between firms which is fair to each of them, and also fair to the consumer.

Consumer Protection Advisory Committee (CPAC). This deals with trade practices referred to it by the OFT or the Secretary of State for Trade and Industry. (Practices examined cover terms and conditions of sale; prices; advertising, labelling, and promotion of goods and services; and methods of salesmanship,)

National Consumer Council (NCC). This is an agency financed by government grant. It presents the consumer viewpoint to industry and central and local government. It does not deal with individual consumer complaints.

Other public sector organizations include:

County Councils: **Trading Standards/Consumer Protection Departments.** Once known as Weights and Measures Departments, these are the local enforcement agencies for many of the acts and statutory instruments (SIs) relating to consumer protection. Additionally they deal directly with complaints from members of the public, and give consumer advice. Some councils run consumer advice centres sited near busy shopping centres.

District Councils: **Environmental Health Departments.** These are the local enforcement agencies for offences against particular acts and SIs relating to shop hygiene, Sunday trading, food and drink unfit for sale, nasty smells coming from businesses, and the like. They deal directly with complaints under these headings made by members of the public.

Independent and voluntary organizations include:

Citizens Advice Bureaux (CABs). Whilst these bureaux deal with a wide variety of enquiries on housing, debt, social security, and other matters, they also accept consumer enquiries and complaints. Besides giving advice, CABs are prepared to take up complaints with shops and suppliers. Each CAB is self governing, and relies on grants from local councils and other benefactors.

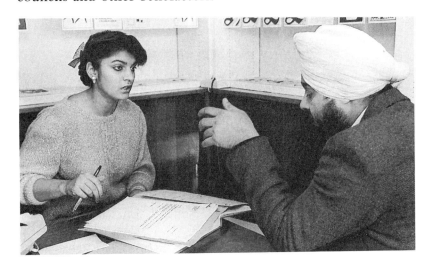

Consumers' Association (CA). Mentioned earlier. Funded by members' subscriptions. Publishers of *Which?*

Miscellaneous help available for consumers. The list includes your MP, local councillors, newspapers, TV stations, local law centres, and local consumer groups. Also the professional bodies regulating the medical, legal, and similar occupations.

Activity 6	In small groups research which avenues of complaint are available, and which seem on balance to be the best to try first, in the following situations.

1 A solicitor fails to turn up to represent you in the local magistrates' court.
2 You bought a hair dryer from an electrical shop in a nearby town recently. The dryer overheated after 10 minutes' use, and the plastic melted. The shop says it's your fault, and it is not their policy to give refunds.
3 The post is not being delivered to your street until noon each day; and mail you are expecting seems to have gone astray.
4 Your family have a bereavement. The funeral directors quote a price of £350 for the funeral, but you find extra charges for notices in the papers (which you did not ask for), and for 'waiting time' while the service was being conducted.
5 Your car is serviced in a local garage which proudly proclaims it is a member of the Motor Agents' Association. You receive a schedule of work done, but find contrary to this statement no oil change has been carried out, and the brakes have not been re-adjusted. Furthermore, work you did not ask for (clutch replacement) was done.

Morality and marketing

In a country which has been moving further and further away from the idea of a socialist state towards one where free enterprise is highly valued, and where fewer rather than more controls on business activity are preferred, there are bound to be critics. Some may feel that the profit-makers are exploiting both workers and consumers; others deplore what they see as the development of a materialistic and selfish society.

It is not surprising that such critics highlight deficiencies (and bad and of course illegal) practices. The consumer is painted as defenceless; helpless, and vulnerable against the tricks and ploys of the clever marketeer.

Marketing itself has been attacked on the grounds that it creates wants which were not there previously; and, moreover, wants for items which people don't really need. This is to confuse *needs* with *basic necessities* for survival. People do have quite justifiable needs: to amuse themselves, to attract others, to visit other countries, for example. (Remember Maslow's analysis of needs.)

The fact that marketeers analyse these needs and wants and provide means of satisfying them is not immoral in itself. Problems do arise however when peoples' existing needs are immoral, and satisfaction of those needs is anti-social or dangerous to themselves, or worse, to others. To attempt to market 'crack' or heroin would be unethical as well as illegal.

The most difficult areas are those where the product is not (yet) considered illegal, but is thought by some to be anti-social or dangerous to others, The marketing and advertising of cigarettes, or the provision and selling by British Telecom (BT) of 'chat-lines', for example, fall into this category. (Late in 1988 the Office of Telecommunications (OFTEL), the telecommunications watchdog, requested the Monopolies and Mergers Commission to amend BT's licence to restrict 'questionable' phone-in services. It seems young children have been 'listening-in'; and incidentally incurring their parents quarterly bills of hundreds of pounds.)

Advertising seems to be particularly culpable. Criticism levelled at advertisements include:
1 They make misleading claims (about the product itself, its price or availability; or about the competition).
2 They use sophisticated psychological techniques of persuasion to make sales.
3 They tap into human greed, and other failings (the 'seven deadly sins').
4 They add to the cost of goods (they would be cheaper if less lavishly promoted).
5 Both people with talent and skills, and vast resources, are wasted. They could be used elsewhere in the economy to better advantage.

Activity 7	1 Consider, in groups, the criticisms mentioned above. How far are these valid?
	2 John Sparkes, manager of Ambridge Electrical, was

concerned about falling sales of vacuum cleaners. He discovered that a competitor, Borchester Appliances, was extensively advertising 'good second-hand cleaners' for £39, with a free home demonstration.

However, on investigation, he found the Borchester rep had a very old, down-market model to show customers, who seemed very reluctant to purchase. At this reaction, the rep then produced a brand new machine at £69.99, and gave it a hard sell, usually leaving it on trial at the conclusion of his visit.

John told his area manager who suggested John should try the same idea, but advertise the second-hand model at £29, and offer customers Ambridge's basic new model at £57.99.
John asks your advice. What would you tell him to do?

Making the most of consumerism

You will have realized by now that, on balance, consumerism is with us because it is needed; and that it is here to stay. Firms can adopt two strategies to deal with it. Either they can keep just within the law (ie, make the minimum concession), or they can welcome it.

You started this book by finding out what was meant by the 'marketing concept'. Remember that basically it is to establish customers' needs and wants, and satisfy those needs and wants at a profit. By attending to the concerns and complaints of customers, firms *will* be following the concept. The only addition now required to our original definition is that we must take into account the community at large, and not merely our customers' interests.

There is not conflict between honest marketing and genuine consumerism. In fact consumerism can be profitable. Organizations can adopt it in the following ways, which can only improve their standing with their customers:
1 By supplying as much information as possible to customers and potential customers about what is offered; drawing specific attention to hazards, safety aspects, the right way to use or operate the products; giving clear details of what is being supplied.
2 By ensuring that all advertising is 'truthful, honest, and decent'.

3 By taking great care over the advertising and promotion of 'sensitive products' (e.g. alcoholic drinks, cigarettes, drugs/medicines, children's toys – and nuclear power).

4 By belonging where possible to a reputable trade association; and being familiar with/abiding by any voluntary code of practice.

5 By having all orders ready/delivered on time.

6 By studying carefully, and acting upon, complaints received (and offering proper recompense where appropriate). A complaint well handled can create goodwill.

7 By offering prompt and technically adequate after-sales service.

8 By offering the kinds of goods the consumer movement approves of: 'organically grown', 'free range', 'lead free', 'flame proof'.

9 By training staff to look after customers.

Activity 8	In groups of five or six assume you are the board of *either* a manufacturing company *or* a large independent electrical retailer. You have decided to adopt a philosophy of generating long-term profits by being 'pro-consumer'. You will not just be satisfying the needs and wants of the customers, but also adopting the best possible trade practices, and making that fact known to the world.

1 Design an illustrated set of rules and guidelines for staff which embody this concept.

2 Decide how you would inform the public about your new policy.

Summary of skills

The intention of the study in this unit is not only to learn facts about marketing but also to develop skills which will be of use in the business world. This section at the end of each blocks indicates the skill areas covered by each activity.

Skill

Skills	*Activities in which skill is developed*
Learning and studying	1, 2, 3, 5, 6
Identifying and tackling problems	1, 4, 6, 7, 8
Design and visual discrimination	8
Information gathering	1, 2, 3, 5, 6, 7
Communicating	All activities
Working with others	all activities

Appendix 1

The European Community and 1992

We are fast approaching 1992, a year of great significance for all citizens of the European Community; and especially for marketeers. This topic does not form a part of the BTEC National Level syllabus, but does merit a mention in a book of this kind. Accordingly, you will find a brief description of the background to the impending changes; and details of the legislative changes and their marketing implications.

You will want to know about the sort of jobs available, and the main personal qualities that count. There is also some advice on marketing-related qualifications, and where you can find further information.

A Europe without frontiers?

The original Treaty of Rome (1957) visualized that the prosperity of the European Community (EC) would depend on there being one single undivided market with a free movement of peole, goods, and services, including capital. Despite the passage of over 30 years many barriers remain, for example controls at frontiers on the entry and exit of people and goods; different technical specifications for goods; different standards of health and safety (including environmental health); and differences in taxation. Furthermore, when economic downturns have occured, EC members have not taken a joint, European, approach to mitigate the effects, but rather have concentrated on defending and protecting their own national markets. What is abundantly clear is that we still have a series of separate markets, all trying to compete not only with the USA and Japan but with each other. At last the decision has been taken to attempt to create within the EC as single economic system.

The question to be answered is will the Single European Market (SEM) really be achieved by 1992?

The Commission's white paper of 1985

This paper (ECWP), published in June 1985, recognized that the Community was still an 'uncommon' market; and that the member states had many economic problems in common. The ECWP aimed to be totally comprehensive, and to create an integrated economic fabric. There would be no exceptions. All barriers to trade would have to be lifted. Without the removal of all barriers, there could be no truly free, common, market.

As an example, frontier controls would go. The existence of *just one reason* for maintaining frontier controls would mean that they would remain; and this one reason would frustrate the whole intention. The ECWP looked at the consequencies of the removal of each barrier; and set out the action required to ensure a co-ordinated implementation of the necessary changes.

The timetable

The timeable for discussing, adopting, and implementing the changes required runs from 1985 to 1992. The aim was to complete drafting all the detailed proposals by the end of 1988, leaving 1989–92 for adopting and implementation. By the end of 1988, about 90% of the programme had been prepared, and 45% adopted by the Commission.

The Single European Act came into force on 1 July 1987. Amongst its sections is one which modifies the original Treaty of Rome requirement for all decisions of the Commission to be unanimous, which stipulation meant that any decision-taking was slowed to the pace of the most reluctant member country. Now there is a **qualified majority** requirement for decisions relating to the establishment and functioning of the new internal market. It is hoped that this change alone will stimulate quicker decision-making.

Policy areas and the SEM

1 *Economic smoothing.* It was felt that the new SEM could make the successful countries (or regions) even more attractive for firms and capital to move to. The 'Golden Triangle' of South East England, Holland/Northern France, and the Ruhr could increase its dominance of the EC. The Commission's policy is to work towards narrowing the gap between the richer and poorer regions to safeguard the EC's economic cohesion. It will be necessary to provide Community funds to assist the development of poorer regions.

2 *Competition.* The Treaty of Rome provided for rules to ensure that competition in the EC was fair. The rules sought to prevent firms from abusing their power by, for example, price-fixing, by agreements to share markets between a small group, or by restricting production. In future these rules will be applied rigorously.

3 *Community Law.* There must be a greater respect for, and application of, Community Law. After appropriate discussion and eventual consensus on every change, some 300 items of Community legislation will be agreed. Then every item will have to be passed by the legislative body of each member state! Then law enforcement procedures will need to be tightened, at a national level.

Removing the physical barriers

People

The proposal is for the practice of internal frontier controls on people to check passports/ID cards for immigration purposes and for customs' duties/VAT payments to cease in 1992. (The provisions to deal with criminals, drug traffic, non-EC nationals, etc. are beyond our scope here.) The appropriate excise duties and VAT will have been paid already (see *Removing the Fiscal Barriers*, below).

Goods

The vast amount of paperwork to be processed every time a lorry-load of goods crosses an EC frontier, plus physical checks on the load, creates frustration, causes delays, and increases costs. (The possible impact of such procedures on the Channel Tunnel traffic hardly bears thinking about.) All these border checks are, however, to be abolished in 1992. The aim is to carry out checks away from the frontiers; 70 different forms used have already been reduced to one only.

Free market conditions are to be restored for steel production and sales across EC frontiers. Statistics currently collected at frontiers on trade in goods and services will need to be collected in other ways (not specified). It is envisaged that animal and plant health checks at frontiers will be replaced by the mutual recognition of each member's controls and inspections prior to departure. (The long-term objective is to raise all animal/plant health standards to the same, high, levels.)

Transport

Member states traditionally have fixed and enforced separate national requirements upon hauliers and their vehicles. Often the number of journeys each vehicle can make in other countries is limited. The aim is to adopt common safety standards, and equivalent checking and enforcement methods, and the complete removal of journey 'quotas'. There will then be no need to check vehicles specifically at frontiers.

Removing the technical barriers

Removing frontier controls does not, in itself, create a common market. Technical barriers exist as hidden obstacles. Ostensibly created as safety standards and consumer safeguards, they function as national protections against competitive products from elsewhere in the EC. (The ECWP cities the fact that British chocolate was denied access to some EC countries simply because the latter had a different definition of chocolate.)

The effect of such production standards makes selling to other EC countries more difficult and costly, and protects a country's internal industries.

In some limited cases (eg the *Cassis de Dijon* case), the European Court of Justice has confirmed the basic principle of the free movement of goods within the EC, but more will need to be done. Consumers must be given the widest possible choice of goods from the whole range being produced within the EC, yet at the same time, products will have to meet standards appropriate to them.

To attain these objectives, safety standards and the like will have to be 'harmonized', as the ECWP puts it. (Previous attempts to do this have foundered not least because of the view of the man in the street – and of business, too – 'it's a load of interfering Brussels' bureaucracy'.) Community 'harmonizing' legislation will cover regulations applicable to production and marketing in the form of general levels or standards: working out the detailed rules will be the job of the European bodies responsible for standards.

National rules in EC countries outside these essential requirements will not be included in Community legislation, but will be recognized automatically throughout the EC – though here again, these will not be allowed to keep out foreign goods meeting *their own* national standards.

Food Law
The Commission's way of tackling the truly enormous volume of food regulations within the EC is to ask for legislation that requires food providers to guarantee their foods can be eaten safety, and, on the labels, to fully inform the customer of what their foods contain (eg, including additives and preservatives). Otherwise food can be freely sold throughout the EC.

As with goods other than food, national rules can be maintained on matters not relating to health and safety; but EC members will have to allow into their territories products from other EC countries, prepared in accordance with the other countries' rules. Thus chocolate from Britain will be able to be sold everywhere in the EC.

The free movement of people
An EC citizen may still be hampered at present under various regulations and practices as to what he or she can do once in another EC country.

1 *Education barriers.* Different approaches to, and methods of, education in EC countries have meant a reluctance on the part of one country to recognize others' qualifications. Specific proposals have been put forward to allow the mutual recognition (provided the student had attained certain basic qualifications) of higher education diplomas.

2 *Professional qualifications and training.* Very often professional people have found it difficult to practise in an EC country other than their own. (One area where real progress *has* been made is with doctors, nurses, dentists, vets, etc.) The Commission has applied the *Cassis de Dijon* ruling and concluded that if an individual is thought fit and able to practise a profession in one EC country, then in principle he or she is fit to practise it in another. The idea has been proposed that there should be a single system of mutual recognition of the higher qualifications leading to an 'entitlement to practise'.

3 *Vocational Training Qualifications.* The Council was working in 1989 on a scheme for the mutual acceptance of vocational training qualifications for apprentices, with the introduction of a European 'vocational training card' – to act as proof the holder of the card had reached a standard generally acceptable in the Community.

The free movement of capital
The objective is the complete freedom of movement for all forms of capital: cash, bank transfers, etc, investments, current and deposit accounts, and loans and credits. (These will be subject, however, to control on short-term movements in the case of monetary or exchange-rate emergencies.)

Public Procurement. The objective is to ensure the public sectors of all member countries go to tender for works and supplies on a much wider scale than that at present. (Only 2% of public authorities' needs are currently (1989) met by companies from a Member State other than their own.)

A common market for services

The ECWP equates goods and services: as with goods, services should operate throughout the EC without restriction.

Harmonization, again, is to be achieved by 'mutual recognition', and there will be common rules.

1 *Financial services.* The approach here is to confine 'harmonization' to the safeguarding of 'financial security and prudential practice', plus 'mutual recognition'. Accordingly, the Commission's plan of action includes the setting of basic standards for protecting investors and policy-holders. Once established, the way is open for providers of financial services situated in one EC country to offer those services to all.

Commercial concerns will be able to raise credit Community wide. Thus a much wider choice of such services will be on hand.

2 *Transport.* Comprehensive proposals have been made to deregulate all forms of transport. Particularly with air transport, there are world-wide agreements which reduce competition; in Europe itself, governments have fixed fares with little scope for competition have been taken, though not all of the proposals have been adopted.

3 *New hi-tech services.* These are mostly connected with information technology. There is a chance here for the Community to lay down standards right from the start of new developments.

4 *Broadcasting services.* These are increasing in availability at an unprecedented rate. Television satellites and cable networks mean individual nation-state audiences are becoming a thing of the past: soon all programmes will be seen in all countries. It is felt that no single EC country can provide either the programmes or the technical equipment that will be required. Unless joint EC action is taken, outside competition from the USA or the Far East will meet these needs.

Accordingly, a directive is proposed to ensure the free circulation of programmes; and to give a boost to EC countries' production and transmission capacity. One implication of this will be the need to co-ordinate laws on advertising, sponsorship, and the protection of the young.

(*Exclusively* national broadcasts may stay within EC countries' own rules.)

Common standard for transmission and reception will be vital and essential.

Removing legal and administrative barriers

As cross-border economic activity increases, a legal framework enabling companies to operate in all EC countries becomes more and more essential. There is a proposal for a form of company (a European Company Structure, or an ECS), which could be set up in any member country. Harmonization of accounting laws would reduce some administrative headaches. Further proposals cover EC-wide rules on company taxation, cross-border mergers, and patents, trade marks, and copying. Special provision is to be made for the legal protection of computer software. (Semiconductor chips are already covered.) A recent proposal concerns the position of biotechnical inventions.

Removing fiscal barriers

A 'frontierless' EC will need to cope with the problems of levying and collecting taxes such as VAT and excise duties. For some years, VAT has been the common 'turnover tax' of the EC, but a glance at the current rates charged by the member states shows a marked variation and inconsistency. A major difficulty would arise in a 'frontierless' EC if those rates remained as they are: people would just buy in low-taxed countries, and transport the goods off for 'off the record' resale. Serious trade imbalances would result.

In accordance with an existing provision (dating back to 1967), sales and purchases across borders would take place as if they were in a single EC country. Further, it will be necessary to reduce the inconsistencies between countries in levels and incidence of VAT and other taxes to such an extent that 'smuggling' goods across borders would cease to be worth while. (Standard rates of VAT will be fixed within a band 14 per cent to 20 per cent; with a reduced rate of 4 per cent to 9 per cent. Main excise duties will be adjusted so that, when VAT is added, the final price of a good will not differ much between countries. We will thus have here *approximation* rather than *harmonization*.)

The attainment of a SEM

At the beginning of this survey of the proposals the question was asked: 'Will the SEM really be achieved by 1992?' Despite the confident tone throughout the ECWP, there are some reasons for being unconvinced.

1 Why, if most of the ideas being considered were already in the original Treaty of Rome, were they not implemented long ago? Perhaps the answer is that EC members didn't want them to be! Some countries still have protectionist economies. Will they really want to change?

2 Some problems seem to be incapable of solution. The Agricultural Policy is still contentious. Governments tacitly favour their own local suppliers when buying goods. The air fares question mentioned above is going to be a difficult one to resolve. Despite EC pressure to reduce prices, the British motor trade prices are higher than those in other countries.

3 The introduction of majority voting could lead to 'outvoted' countries proceeding to implement harmonizing legislation slowly, with minimum sanctions for non-observance. In one area, in 1988, the British government made it clear that ' . . we shall insist on our right to determine zero rating (in VAT).'

4 The better-off countries will be asked to contribute towards the increased competitiveness of the less-developed ones. Will they really want to?

5 The opportunities for delay, backsliding, and loss of enthusiasm are infinite.

6 Exports (and imports) can be greatly affected by exchange-rate movements. Resultant disruptions of trade can be much larger-scale than those caused by protectionism.

7 Will countries with high standards (eg, of safety) be prepared to settle for consensus lower ones, especially where there are strong internal consumer pressure groups?

8 Some matters of UK public policy would be profoundly affected. Excise duty changes would entail reducing the price of cigarettes by about 12p per packet, resulting in an estimated increase of 4 per cent in consumption. One of the reasons for high excise duty here is to discourage smokers. A 20 per cent reduction in alcohol duties would cost the Exchequer £2.3 billion a year, and would lead to an undoubted rise in alcoholism.

9 Will all frontier-barriers, in fact, be removed? There is the vexed question, for example, of terrorists and drug-traffickers. Mrs Thatcher (in Bruges in September 1988) appeared to be opposed to the abolition of frontiers.

10 The London market could be under threat as the pre-eminent financial centre in Europe. One of the reasons for its success is that it has operated in a much freer environment than that in other countries: this has encouraged a considerable inflow of business. Deregulation of competing centres would reduce the City's advantage. The key issue for the government is, should it champion the cause of the City, or

encourage (in the spirit of the new order) other EC financial centres to compete directly?

11 The implications of the reunification of Germany may add further complications to what is already a complex situation. The new Germany could be a minor superpower and could upset the balance of the EC.

Whilst it seems unlikely that all the target 'harmonizations' will be achieved by 1992, it does seem clear that many significant changes will have taken place by then.

Implications for marketeers

Assuming most, if not all, of the proposed changes do take place eventually, the implications for marketeers seem to be as follows:

The UK as a whole

1 The government will no longer be able to step in to 'rescue' firms which have had a temporary downturn, but which could be rescued eventually with good management. If the SEM becomes a reality, then neither support by 'instant nationalization', nor by specific contracts (eg, ships for the navy allotted to a shipyard to keep a workforce employed) will be permitted.

2 A much fiercer wind of competition will blow within Europe. One study (the Cecchini Report) asserts that where losses in domestic markets occur, they will be more than offset by greater export opportunities. If this is true, then many more UK firms will have to start exporting to stay in business. The one big fear is that some UK companies will lose ground to imports from other EC countries, and be unable or unwilling to make up the shortfall in turnover by exporting. (Hot on the heels of '1992' will be '1993', the expected completion date of the Channel Tunnel, which will further facilitate a flood of imports.)

3 The possibility exists that some EC members will still have some kinds of protection for their industries in 1992, especially if these can be made to take obscure forms. The worst position for the UK would be if we removed protection totally (ie 'played the game'), but others did not. The European Court *could* be asked to rule, but it is not renowned for speedy judgements. Specific UK industries could suffer for a long period before receiving any redress.

4 A report by DRI Europe Inc. (an American forecasting organization), quoted in the *Financial Times* of 21 April 1988 and based on computer modelling, predicts the winners from '1992' will be small member states such as Denmark, Greece, and Holland. Greece, Spain, and Portugal being on the outer fringes of the EC, geographically, will have most to gain from the abolition of border controls as their goods have to cross more frontiers on the way to their customers than do those, for example, of France or Germany.

5 Even if the EC reforms do succeed, the 'new common market' will not be as free as, for example, those of Japan or the USA. Differences in national tasts and habits will die hard; and the objective of offering standardized goods over all the EC will be difficult to achieve. Consumers will prefer their own regional products: the market will still be divided.

Summary

After 1992 there will be more business opportunities for UK firms. Unless they make a conscious effort to exploit the situation, competitors from within the EC will fill the gaps. A *totally* open market by 1992 is unrealistic.

Appendix 2

Careers in Marketing

Now you have read this book and taken a course in marketing (calling for some active participation in developing relevant skills), you may want to explore the possibility of a career in a branch of marketing.

Getting in

There are many different routes to a marketing career. Many successful BTEC students start in sales departments. Sales experience is particularly useful as the potential marketeer gets to meet and learns to handle customers – finds out how they 'tick'. Other prefer the more 'glamourous' image of advertising as a beginning, moving on eventually to PR, for example. Yet others decide to go into marketing research companies. A rather different approach is to join a bank, insurance company, hotel chain, or even local government in the main stream of business as counter clerk, cashier, assistant manager, and so on, and to transfer to marketing later. In fact some firms prefer to offer management trainees a wide general experience in an organization to start with, allowing them to choose a department upon the successful completion of the training period.

The best kinds of job to go for in your chosen field are those which offer release to follow part-time courses at colleges or polytechnics, as well as appropriate on-the-job training.

Further qualification first

Some of you may decide that you would do better to obtain further qualifications in addition to the BTEC National Award. Both BTEC and SCOTVEC programmes at institutes of higher education may offer courses with options in subjects such as marketing, marketing with languages, exporting, or retailing. For Higher National Awards, students are normally expected to have at least passed a National Award, but some provisional acceptances may stipulate the number of subjects required at merit or distinction level.

Degrees in business studies are offered by both universities and institutes of higher education or polytechnics. Some of these have marketing options, for example, marketing with engineering, or textile marketing. The more attractive of these are 'sandwich' courses; that is, part of the time (possibly as much as one year) is spent working in a larger organization. Not only can you get paid this way, but the extended work experience is a useful addition to your CV when applying for a job.

Later qualifications

The Institute of Marketing offers bothe a part-time Diploma (a three year course) or a Certificate (a two year course). A BTEC National Award in Business and Finance secure entry to the Certificate course. To start the Diploma you will need either a Certificate (in Marketing), a BTEC Higher Award, or a relevant degree.

The CAM (Communications, Advertising, and Marketing) Foundation similarly runs a two-year Certificate, and a three-year Diploma, with (naturally) an advertising bias.

Typical jobs to aim for

There are, as you have probably realized, marketing jobs in different sectors of industry and commerce. The product or service is different in each, so is the 'marketing mix', and the marketing strategy.

With FMCGs (Fast Moving Consumer Goods, like baked beans or soap powders), the products are made in large quantities and sold on a continuous basis to wholesalers or large retailers, for immediate consumption. Consumer durables, in contrast, are products which last longer, are bought less often, and can be major purchases (eg, three-piece-suites, cars, or washing machines). Industrial marketing is basically selling products to industrial firms. Sometimes they can be quite small (spares for machines), but they tend to be substantial products (pumps, machine tools, or forklift trucks).

Service marketing is an expanding field: typical ' products' are company pension scheme, personal insurances, or building society savings schemes. Finally, exporting marketing is concerned with the many problems involved in selling abroad, for both products and services.

Marketing Manager

Do you remember Mark Crayford from Block 1, *Introducing Marketing*? If you check back you will find he covered a wide variety of work – marketing research, sales promotion, managing the sales force, liaising with production. In addition, pricing policy, trade fairs, exhibitions, and taking part in the general management of the organization fall to the Marketing Manager's lot.

BTEC National, and better still, BTEC Higher Awards and/or the Diploma in Marketing, are all useful entry qualifications to such a post; but some experience at trainee or assistant level would normally also be required, plus evidence of being able to innovate, and be ahead of events. A 'feel' for the market, the ability to understand and use statistics, and a broad knowledge of the business world are a considerable advantage in this kind of job.

Market Research Executive

While there are going to be differences between the ways in which agencies or firms operate, the kinds of activities you have already looked at in this book will cover most situation. Working for agencies will involve questionnaire preparation, data collection, and the analysis and interpretation of collected data. Working for organizations which produce goods or offer services will involve the commissioning of research, and monitoring of results.

There are in excess of 200 good MR agencies, and opportunities also exist in larger companies, central and local government, and quangos such as the Office of Population Surveys. It is mainly young graduates in business studies who are selected for training, but suitable qualified and experienced staff can be promoted within a department.

Possession of a diploma from the Market Research Society (MRS), which can be studied through evening classes, is an advantage.

It is an essential requirement for market research executives to be confident people, and to be able to make their findings known to top management clearly and concisely, in either reports or verbal presentations. Good analytical skills are needed for the interpretation of statistics.

Advertising careers

There are many specialist jobs in advertising. Organizations which advertise may have some staff liaising with agencies, and some doing more mundane jobs such as preparing leaflets of promotional material for exhibitions (and working on exhibition stands), or writing the text of instruction manuals. People in such jobs may get promotion through flair and effort and some move on to agencies in due course. The media have many staff working in areas such as tele-sales for advertising space, and the checking of advertisements at the proofing stage. Advertising agencies, as you saw in Blocks 6 and 7, *Marketing Communications and Direct Marketing* have different departments with specialist staff.

The **account executive,** you will remember, liaises with clients over individuals advertisements or complete campaigns. A good executive will need to be a skilled negotiator, firm yet diplomatic with both clients and agency staff, with considerable imagination, commitment, and staying power. A formidable combination. **media planners** assist by preparing costs, and a detailed plan showing the media used. Again, a good diplomatic manner is important for dealing with clients. **Media buyers** purchase time and/or space for advertising, and spend much of their time negotiating the best spots at the keenest rates. Strict attention to detail and the ability to keep within budgets are essential personal characteristics. Normally these positions are filled by graduate entry, but some may get a job on the strength of a CAM Certificate or Diploma.

In addition, anyone working in advertising should have **adaptability** (the ability to keep several jobs going at the same time); **commitment** (working late when the job requires it); **stamina** (in a very stressful environment); **ability to work with others** (team work with the client and within the agency); and **ability to keep information confidential** (clients will divulge highly sensitive information which you must keep secret).

Sales careers

Sales representative

Another demanding job. A good knowledge of the goods or services offered (training in this is usually given), the ability to get on with people, and selling skills are required. Meeting customers, getting to know them as individuals, and negotiating with them successfully are all part of the job. A clean driving licence, complete honesty, a smart and well-groomed appearance, and the ability to carry on after a setback are essentials. (Customers can be unwelcoming and rude.) Entry is by interview, and a BTEC National Award in business studies is very useful. Technical product selling jobs may be restricted to those with an appropriate degree or BTEC Higher qualifications.

Sales manager

The person responsible for translating the sales objectives into action. Setting targets, watching progress, keeping to budgets, are all part of the job. A major responsibility is engaging, monitoring, motivating, and controlling the sales representatives. Work is done when it is needed – in the evenings, at week ends, or during holidays. All sales managers will initially have had experience as reps. Whilst some employers will look for highly qualified staff, others are prepared to engage people on the basis of a good record of sales achievement and evidence of management potential.

Retail manager

Do you remember all the retail outlets you looked at in the block on distribution? Everyone of them (other than a small family business) will have a manager to take charge of a department in the store, or indeed, of the whole store. The manager will try to increase profits, which usually means increasing sales. Targets may be set (by, for example, the head office), and will have to be met. Attention must be given to well laid-out display. Administrative work in booking sales (recording cash, cheques, and credit card transactions and controlling stock) is followed by duties related to the security, maintenance, and hygiene of the building and its contents. Finally the manager will (normally) take part in the interviewing , selection, training, and welfare of the staff.

Retail managers are normally 'on view' to the public. Thus they need to be well turned out, pleasant, and helpful even at the end of a trying day; they must be adaptable and able to make decision on the spot.

Entry requirements vary widely. Many graduates, (in business studies for example), are recruited by the larger firms, but others will take on those who seem to be promising material and train them to the required standard. Trainee managers may well spend time in several departments, and receive supervisory training (possibly the NEBSM Certificate in Supervisory Management). A range of BTEC awards is offered by the College for the Distributive Trades. The work is physically demanding: you have to lend a hand from time to time with stock, and a lot of standing and walking about is involved. The utmost honesty is called for, as large amounts of cash may be under a manager's charge.

Summary

The important message is to get all the information you can on your chosen career, and on any further qualifications required, from your course tutor, librarian, or careers service. Also note that the more highly qualified you are, the better the chances of getting a job of your choice. Finally, you need to appreciate that all marketing-related jobs call for communication and numeracy skills; the ability to work with others; to identify and tackle problems; to gather information; and, in some cases design and visual discrimination skills – all to be found in the BTEC Skills Statement.

Index